Tourist's Experience

JAAKKO SUVANTOLA

Ashgate

Published by
Ashgate Publishing Limited
Gower House
Croft Road
Aldershot
Hampshire GU11 3HR
England

Ashgate Publishing Company
131 Main Street
Burlington, VT 05401-5600 USA

Ashgate website: http://www.ashgate.com

British Library Cataloguing in Publication Data
Suvantola, Jaakko
    Tourist's experience of place. - (New directions in tourism
    analysis)
    1.Travel - Social aspects 2.Tourists - Attitudes
    3.Intercultural communication
    I.Title
    304.2'3

Library of Congress Control Number: 2001097263

ISBN 0 7546 1830 7

Printed and bound by
Antony Rowe Ltd, Chippenham, Wiltshire

Contents

List of Figures and Tables

List of Figures and Tables

Preface

As an impressionable 22 year old I travelled around the world with a friend of mine. The early anthropologists like Malinowski and Mead, who travelled and stayed in the South Pacific, inspired us. We decided to spend a few months in Fiji and Samoa, to gain insight to the local culture, which was supposed to be well preserved. In the end we realised that we had learned a lot about life, people, and ourselves, but little about the people among whom we had spent those months. Since that trip I have been interested in how our experience of the Other takes place. Why did we learn so little about the Other people?

This work is an attempt to uncover some of the processes involved. It was submitted and accepted (after a round of revision) for the degree of PhD at the University of Adelaide in December 1997.

My endeavour to carry out this work would not have been possible without the funds provided by the Australian Government's Overseas Postgraduate Research Scholarship, and the University of Adelaide Scholarship. I was also greatly helped by the travel grant the University of Adelaide offered me.

I am indebted to my supervisor Peter Smailes, who guided me with patience. Apart from his considerable academic support, he also demonstrated genuine compassion in the moments of desperation. I am also grateful to Prof. Ian John and Dr. Petri Hottola for their useful comments and advice. Pertti Saarelainen did a great job of getting the layout in shape. Prof. Markku Tykkyläinen, the head of our geography department here in Joensuu encouraged me to publish the book. The people who participated in my study gave me a lot to think about, and I warmly thank them for their co-operation. Of course, all shortcomings are my own.

I also want to thank my travel companion and friend from childhood, Marko Juntunen, who passed his enthusiasm to me. The biggest personal thanks I owe to my wife Leila, who has always cheered me in my pursuits. Finally, I want to acknowledge the impact of my parents Riitta and Vilho Suvantola, who always cultivated learning in me.

Joensuu, 28 May 2001   Jaakko Suvantola

ix

1 Introduction

In the academic study of tourism, the experience of tourists themselves has often had a small role. Even when it has been the object of the study, the focus has customarily been on marketing. However, the importance of travel experience can go far beyond mere consumption. As a geographer, I am particularly interested in travel experience as a change of place. In travel we are forced to pay attention to a new place. The experience there can reveal something about our relationship with places, and also about ourselves. What does it mean in the life of a tourist to experience a place?

Geography's contribution to the study of tourism has traditionally involved mainly environmental, regional, spatial, and evolutionary considerations (Mitchell and Murphy, 1991). The environmental considerations include for example the impact of tourism in the natural environment (Butler, 2000; Baldwin, 2000). Development of the orientation is the emergence of the study of eco-tourism from the end of the 80s (Draper and Kariel, 1990; Farrell and Runyan, 1991; Cater, 1993; Fennell, 1999). The regional orientation has appeared mainly as interest in tourism as a means of economic development (Hall, 1992; Milne, 1992; McCarthy, 1994; Walpole and Goodwin, 2000). The spatial orientation deals with spatial gravity models (Mansfeld, 1990; Meyer-Arendt, 1990) and the spatial perception of tourists. The latter has much in common with cognitive mapping, which features especially prominently in studies on the borderline of geography and psychology (Pearce, 1988; Walmsley and Jenkins, 1992). Finally, the evolutionary orientation emphasises the meanings of processes by which tourism trends and developments change through time, thus dealing with history of tourism developments (Demars, 1990; Hoffmann, 1992), their socio-cultural impacts (Toops, 1992; Hobbs, 1992), and evolutionary models such as the resort life-cycle (Butler, 1980; Cooper and Jackson, 1989; Gordon and Goodall, 2000; Johnston, 2001). Most recently, additional themes have come into focus: travel as consumption/production (Ateljevic, 2000) and travel and gender (Hottola, 1999; Pritchard and Morgan, 2000). From the traditional orientations, the behaviourist quest for explaining the development of tourists' cognition of the destination comes closest to understanding of the tourist's experience. However, the experience involves much more than just spatial cognition. The later themes of consumption and gender are more relevant in the context of personal experience. These must be taken into account in any attempt to understand a personal experience of travel.

Many themes of humanistic geography are clearly relevant in this context. In humanistic geography most interest has been placed on studying the experiences that take place in our familiar home environment, but for some reason the tourism experience has been neglected, or presented only as an illustrative component (as in Tuan, 1974, 1977; Seamon, 1979, 1985; Buttimer, 1980; Godkin, 1980; Paasi, 1984; Karjalainen, 1986a and b). The best-known exception to this is Relph's (1976) study of 'Place and Placelessness' in which tourism is seen as one of the unauthentic attitudes in creating and experiencing places. Another smaller scale attempt to see tourism from the perspective of humanistic geography is Duncan's 'The Social Construction of Unreality; An Interactionist Approach to the Tourist's Cognition of Environment' (1978). Like Relph, Duncan sees tourism as an inauthentic way of seeing a new place. While Duncan's article had a humanistic tone, it had elements that anticipated post-structuralism.

Tourist's experience has been studied in other social sciences more than in geography. However, it is hard, and unfruitful, to subdivide the essentially multi-disciplinary tourism research into distinct disciplines; most of the themes overlap anyway. The focus of the study of the tourist's experience was initially on criticism of its perceived spuriousness (Boorstin, 1972 [orig. 1961]; Turner and Ash, 1975). Although this kind of critique persists, a quest for tourism with high moral (ecological, cultural, economic) standards has emerged (Krippendorf, 1987; D'Amore, 1993), as well as a view of tourism as a meaningful recreational experience, in which spuriousness or authenticity is largely irrelevant (Jokinen and Veijola, 1990; Urry, 1991). Also the symbolic structures, which characterise tourist experiences, have aroused interest (Barthes, 1972; MacCannell, 1976; Culler, 1981; Dann, 1996). Some of this semiotic interest concentrates specifically on the pictorial symbolism inherent in tourist experience (Barthes, 1977; Sontag, 1977; Uzzell, 1984; Urbain, 1989). In anthropology, the focus of study was at first on the effects of tourism in the host culture (Smith, 1977), but later there has been increasing interest in studying the tourist's point of view. Initially these studies derived from Turner's ideas of travel being structurally similar to a rite of passage (Turner, 1973, 1974, 1978; Turner and Turner, 1978; Gottlieb, 1982; Graburn, 1983; Murray, 1990). During the 1990s the emphasis has shifted from this analogy towards analysing tourism as one kind of a cultural discourse of the world (Bruner, 1991; Bruner and Kirshenblatt-Gimblett,

1994; van den Berghe, 1994, Harkin, 1995). The discourse has been considered as part of the production and consumption of tourism destinations and attractions (Pretes 1995; Halewood and Hannam, 2001). An important similar post-structural perspective is the one of gender (Desmond, 1999; Johnston, 2001). Within psychology there are several important topics pursued. One is the analysis of tourists' motivations (Dann, 1977, 1981; Crompton, 1979; Pearce, 1988). Further central topics are destination evaluation and satisfaction (Echtner and Ritchie, 1991; Ross, 1993; Vittersø et.al., 2000) and the study of attitudes (Milman and Reichel and Pizam, 1990; Pizam and Jafari and Milman, 1991; Anastasopoulos, 1992).

The starting point for this study is that the dialogue between this kind of primarily qualitative tourism research and social and cultural geography has been 'virtually unexplored' (Squire, 1994, p. 3). It still is; the dialogue has never been explicated in much detail. I am particularly convinced about the relevance of many of the concepts of humanistic geography to the qualitative research of tourist experience. In the words of Squire (1994, p. 4):

> Place experiences are integral to what tourism is about and such concerns have been central to sociological research on tourism. Surprisingly, they have received less attention from [humanistic] geographers, even though similar issues formed a large part of the humanistic agenda.

During the 1980s the humanistic agenda in geography has largely been replaced by post-structural interest in structures of power and meaning. The perspective of tourist's experience has been dealt within the framework of consumption and representation. In this work I shall retrieve some of the concepts used in humanistic geography and apply them in this more recent post-structural conceptual environment. From the present perspective, the problem with humanistic approach has been that it has paid too little attention to the structures within which personal meanings develop. In this work I intend to treat the topic of tourist's experience of place in such a way that the concern with structures of meaning precede the analysis of personal meanings. It is thus possible to complement the insights gained from one approach with the ones of the other. I use this approach in order to add the perspective of humanistic geography to the qualitative traditions in cross-disciplinary tourism research and integrate the two. The experience of place is pivotal in providing the basis for such integration. I also try to uncover processes, both structural and psychological, that make the experience of a tourist. This aim involves post-structural analysis of the discourse of tourism and phenomenological analysis of the tourist's experience within that discourse.

The analysis is based on my own experiences that I have complemented with interviews and analysis of travel brochures (which are thus part of my own experiences). Following humanistic traditions, personal experience is thus the experiential ground on which the ideas and understanding achieved is laid. Interviews of the others provide a plane on which my own personal experiences can be reflected. Thus it becomes possible to compare my experiences with the experiences of the others and chart the ground for generalisations. It is meaningless to separate between the ideas gained from my own experiences and the ones gained from the experiences of others. Using humanistic approach means that the research of others would provide little, if the researcher did not have personal understanding of the subject. The very subjectivity of the researcher is the prerequisite for a success of a humanistic study. In this study I am going to be shamelessly subjective, to the point that is bound to attract criticism. I firmly believe that understanding of the experience of one can add to understanding of the experience of another.

2 Humanistic Geography Revisited

Post-humanistic Geography?

It is somewhat old fashioned to go back to the concepts and methodologies of humanistic geography. There is thus a need to do the time warp through some more contemporary ideas. I find it useful to approach humanistic thinking through post-structuralism and its concern with discourse and representation.

Discourse and the Other

In geography the concept of discourse has been discussed especially in the context of landscape (Barnes and Duncan, 1992; Smith, 1992; Daniels, 1992; McGreevy, 1992; Daniels and Cosgrove, 1993b; Raivo, 1997). Landscapes are interpreted as texts, which have taken shape in a certain discursional environment. This means that a landscape represents something; it is a story. Using this point of departure, McGreevy (1992) writes about the landscape of Niagara as a metaphor for death. In a similar vein, Pocock (1992) analyses how the landscape in which the English author Catherine Cookson lived, is nowadays interpreted as an inspiration to her stories by a tourist operator. What a landscape, or a place, represents, involves thus the adoption of a certain discourse from which the particular representation arises. Naturally, the kind of discourse adopted depends on what is already known. Thus, for example, world elsewhere becomes interpreted through what is here (Relph, 1976, p. 53). From this the post-structural concept of the Other is just a few steps away.

    The concept of Other has been used as a counter-category of Self, as in the work of Deleuze (1994 (orig. 1968), pp. 260-261). According to Deleuze, the Other is a structure of being that makes it possible for us to distinguish ourselves from the world outside (Ibid., pp. 281-282). The concept, however, has received a more concrete meaning in post-structural writings. Drawing from Foucault post-structuralists, post-colonialists and feminists alike have adopted the term to mean a social group and its culture that differs from one's own. Foucault provided a ground for conceptualising discourse and the power structures involved in the operation of the discourse (Said, 1979, p. 3; McDowell, 1995, p. 289). Post-structuralists and feminists consider the construction of the Other a demonstration of these processes. McDowell (Ibid.) mentions Said's critique of Orientalism, rewriting the history of colonial India, and feminist struggle against exclusion of women in representation of Western culture as examples of the use of Foucault's ideas in revealing the construction of the Other. The concept of the Other thus means a domain on which we project our socially formed ideas about peoples and cultures we aren't familiar with.

Single discourses are standpoints from which social groups perceive the world according to their intentions. Barnes and Duncan (1992, p. 8) write that because of the coexistence of different and often competing discourses, each discourse is defined largely by its relationship to other discourses. 'Our' discourse is contrasted to 'Their' discourse; familiar 'Us' is contrasted to the unfamiliar 'Other'. The discourse that is familiar to Us and characterises the values, intentions and ontological organisation of the group, is experienced as comprehensible, homely, and convenient. In contrast, another discourse of another group is regarded as the opposite because its internal logic is based on different social contexts, or simply because it matters so little to Us. This unfamiliarity, incomprehensibility and indifference gives raise to the typification of the Other by using terms and contexts which are familiar within one's own discourse. Both the discourse of the Other and the Other itself become labelled with these typifications. Daniels and Cosgrove (1993a, p. 6) write that 'the typification of the other as an abstraction, a collective social fact, is a denial of the complexity of other cultures'. The concept of the Other is most explicit in the context of cultures; the distinction between 'Us' and 'the Other' is tangible.

In a typified definition, the power to define the Other arises from the centrality of 'Our' discourse to the life of the in-group. Cultural practices and values which arise from particular ontological beliefs and which govern the daily environment are internalised so that they self evidently are regarded as the most natural way to look at the world. Ethnocentrism is one actualisation of this natural tendency to rate the Other discourse according to the yardstick of one's own. The obvious result is the confirmation of the superiority of one's own discourse. Since there is little comprehension of the Other, it has to be typified using concepts that are available in one's own discourse, which gives the illusion that it is possible to govern the Other from within this familiar framework. Duncan (1993, p. 39) writes:

...difference in the site of the Other is 'recuperated' by appropriating it into a categorical framework that is familiar and useful within the site from which the recuperation emanates. ... By analysing these [discursional] relations of power, we can more clearly see how interests play a constitutive role in vision and representation.

This power to define the Other favours strong groups. Not only do they define the Others; if powerful enough, they can also use the definitions to create circumstances in which those Others have to act. Examples of this are the creation of the Orient in Western art, literature and science (Said, 1978; Hourani, 1991; Vehkavaara, 1994), and the Western discourse of Africa (Mudimbe, 1988; Löytty, 1994). Militaristic and economic hegemony of the West has made it possible to extend the Western discourse of capitalism in all parts of the world. Therefore the Other of the 'Orient' or 'Africa' have not been asked what role they would like to play within this discourse. The discourse of the Other displays our intention towards it. In European discourse of 'Africa', Europe represents progress, civilization and power, Africa is backward, savage and in the need of supervision. Here the meanings created by the discourse both illustrate and *are* the power of Europe over Africa, Us over the Other.

Post-structuralists pay a lot of attention to the social construction of the Other. Following Said's critique of Orientalism (1978), there has been a great deal of discussion about the power of representation to convey (intended or unintended) messages about the Other and our relationship to it (e.g. Young, 1990; Hourani, 1991; Bruner, 1991; Bruner and Kirshenblatt-Gimblett, 1994; Vehkavaara, 1994). Post-structuralists are eager to point out that science is not immune to the inevitability of representation. Duncan (1993, p. 40) introduces two widely used rhetoric ways to describe the Other. The first is the one of objectivity, much used in science. A scientist with enough theoretical knowledge and field experience, using accepted methods of observation, is deemed to be able to provide an objective and truthful presentation of the Other. The belief in objectivity is based on the accepted field-work methods used. The other rhetoric way to describe the Other is to place it into a different temporal location, most usually in the past. An example of this rhetoric is that while Europe represents today, Africa is still inhabited by peoples whose customs and traditions have remained unchanged through history.

The first of these tropes is closely associated with the scientific ideal of objectivity. According to post-structuralists, uncritical drive to achieve that ideal, trying to present something as it is, only leads to blind appreciation of one's own discourse; it is our discourse which is capable of describing the Other objectively. Thus our discourse is the one with power. This display of power is also strongly present in Duncan's second trope. Placing the Other in the past makes it possible to resort to the ideas of cultural evolution (as it was understood a hundred years ago), and interpret Our culture and discourse as superior, contrasted to the cultures and discourses of the Other, which are only remnants from the past. These tropes illustrate the connection between post-structural concern with the social construction of the Other, and concern with power. The former is the origin of the latter. All groups construct the Other and the discourse of it by using the concepts and categories of their own in-group. Whose construct will determine the discourse used in the relations between the groups, is then a matter of (economic and military) power. So far the 'West', and its concepts revolving around market economy, has possessed it.

The question of representation in geography has featured strongly in the study of landscape (Barnes and Duncan, 1992; Duncan and Ley, 1993; Karjalainen, 1993; Knuuttila and Paasi, 1995; Raivo, 1997). The social construction of the Other as such has been tackled mainly from the perspective of relations between ethnic groups (Anderson, 1991; Mitchell, 1993). The power of a majority group to create frameworks, within which the narrative of a minority group takes form, is largely the centre of attention. The study of tourism shares this perspective in the sense that the Western discourse of tourism, which entails the hegemony of capitalism, is analysed as the discourse that produces the representations of the Other places, Other cultures and Other peoples.

Post-structural tourism studies largely follow the footsteps of Barthes and his discussion of texts and myths and landscape as but one myth (Barthes, 1972; 1977). One trait of this Barthesian legacy is semiology applied to the pictorial material present in tourism (Sontag, 1977; Uzzell, 1984; Albers and James, 1988; Urbain, 1989). Of course, the idea of power in the representation of the Other is not limited in pictorial settings at all. The whole discourse of tourism is filled with myths that shape tourism and the impression of the Other it creates. The analysis of such discursional elements (Bruner, 1991; McGreevy, 1992; Bruner and Kirshenblatt-Gimblett, 1994; van den Berghe, 1994; Harkin, 1995) is another important post-structural theme in tourism studies. The third trait is the one in which tourism is discussed as consumption. Tourists and destinations are integrated into tourist production process (Britton, 1991; Waitt and McGuirk, 1994; Richards, 1996; Meethan, 1996). The discourse and the politics of power are thus determined by the production and consumption of tourism.

While following Barthesian footsteps, post-structural tourism studies have also adopted themes from humanists (as in the works of Duncan, 1978; Pocock, 1992) and from structuralists (as in the works of Albers and James, 1983; Britton, 1991; Bruner, 1991; Bruner and Kirshenblatt-Gimblett, 1994). From humanists is derived the perspective of the traveller and from structuralists the concern with unequal power relations. On one hand post-structural study of tourism analyses the relationships between tourists and the discourses within which the tourists experience, on the other hand the relationships between the discourses and the institutional realities from which the discourses arise. Unfortunately, there has been no effort to combine these perspectives in a single work so that personal travel experiences would have been described and analysed against the background of the institutional structures of travel.

Post-Structural Critique of Humanism

In the last two decades humanistic geography has attracted critique from structuralists, post-structuralists and feminists. The main current of structuralist critique is concerned with the sometimes overly individual viewpoint of humanistic geography, which tends to ignore or at least underestimate the larger contexts and structures (typically economic ones) in which the single individual actions and meanings take place (Hottola, 1999, p. 194). Post-structuralists claim that humanistic approach has failed to recognise the politics and power of representation, and feminists use both of these arguments in their contexts.

Much of the structuralist criticism is undoubtedly justified, but it does not change the fact that while structures and conceptual environments do shape experiences and do express certain power relations, experiences still contain personal meanings that cannot be reduced to these. Tourism is indeed a global industry, it is consumption, and it does involve participation into symbolic systems and their interpretation. However, at the same time tourists fulfil their personal dreams and wishes. In this sense, those who criticise humanistic geography for concentrating on too narrow a strip of reality should be careful not to make the same mistake by ignoring the individual.

Humanistic study, and especially its phenomenological method, shares a great deal with post-structuralism through hermeneutics (Eyles, 1988, p. 10). Already phenomenology and structuralism can have quite similar aims in their research. The quest of essential phenomenology (Johnston, 1983, p. 57) to uncover the essences behind subjective experiences resembles a structuralist's reach beneath surface appearances to uncover structures.[1] But if the view that there are no essences to uncover is accepted, the only aim for phenomenological study is the disclosure of the ways in which we experience the world. This becomes closer to the post-structuralist idea that the distinction between surface appearances and structures is not clear-cut. Instead of the opposition between surface and structure we find innumerable layers of meanings. These can be gradually traced down from the surface to what a structuralist would call structures.[2] Doing this can reveal the structures of power. This does not necessarily differ much from the phenomenologist attempt to disclose the elements of our experience; layers of meanings and the constitution of our experiences are often fundamentally tied into each other. In hermeneutic study texts can be seen as layers of meanings (post-structuralism) and also as expressions of lived experiences (phenomenology). Therefore the politics and power of representation can be equally meaningful aspect of enquiry in both humanistic and post-structural study.

The scope for disagreement still remains, though. Although hermeneutics connects post-structural and humanistic study, there is a difference between the aims of the desired hermeneutic understanding of an experience. Post-structuralists aim to understand the experience as a process in which structures, meanings and their relations that guide the experience are interpreted. Instead, humanists are interested in the meanings the individuals concerned give to the results of those interpretations. They do not necessarily pay much attention to the dynamics of what has created the structural frames for the experience. Thus post-structuralists try to understand why something is experienced a certain way, whereas humanists

---

[1] Then, are the essences structures? If all the elements of an experience are disclosed, the essence of that experience is laid bare. This essence is obviously something that underlines all similar experiences and can thus be understood as a structure of those experiences. In this sense there are two kinds of essences, or structures; the ones that are imprinted on what we are and those that are human creations (Johnston, 1983, pp. 88-107). An example of the former could be our need to feel accepted and of the latter the economic stranglehold in which some underdeveloped nations are trapped.

[2] The idea is expressed in Barthes' work about language and myths (Barthes, 1972; a brief discussion will follow in chapter 3.2.).

try to understand what it means to the one who experiences to experience it that way. Post-structuralist critique of humanism largely derives from this difference; humanists are thought to be only interested in one 'end-product' of experience and thus unable to place it in larger contexts.

Phenomenological Method in Humanistic Study

Almost every one of us has been a tourist. Thus the students of these experiences put themselves in a difficult position, because they try to be experts on what almost everybody knows. But there is difference between having gone through an experience and thus knowing it, and understanding the experience; the latter does not always follow from the former. Understanding the experience requires that its components and their meanings are recognised. Of course, an experience is often so complex that this is impossible to do comprehensively, but obviously in research some degree of understanding is better than no understanding at all. To be able to recognise any components of an experience and their meanings means that we have to question things that in a normal, unreflected experience, we do not question. Instead of just experiencing, we have to start asking questions like why do we experience as we do, what is it that we experience, and *what it means to experience*. Understanding of tourist's experience of place may open new ways to apprehend our daily life at home; questioning the unquestioned can be learned.

Post-structuralist contexts are useful tools to answer the questions why we as tourists experience a place a certain way, and what is it that we experience. They make us understand the social construction of the discourse in which we take part in tourism. Common to all these themes is that the experience of tourism seems to be just consumption of some premediated play with symbolic structures. The experience is dealt with limited or no interest in personal individual meanings and values involved in the process. Tourism as consumption is indeed participation in the structures involved, but it is also individually meaningful action in which personal dreams and wishes are lived, or at least reached for. The post-structural approach does not equip us to understand *what it means* in the lives of individuals to experience tourism.

Understanding personal meanings requires that not only the structural frameworks that govern those meanings, but also the intellectual and emotional inner worlds of the individuals must be charted. What something means in a person's life is not merely deductable from the structures in which the events of life take place. In phenomenology our experiences are dissected so that their subjective contents can be recognised.[3] The subjective contents of experiences are the sphere in which the post-structural approach provides less insight than the phenomenological one.

Recognising the subjective elements of experiences and their meaning in a person's life sounds very promising, but unfortunately in practice it is not simple to achieve. The problem is how to successfully enter the subjective personal worlds of others, and how to communicate what was found. It is not possible to *verify* findings in some universally acceptable objective way. Nevertheless, at the philosophical level there have been attempts to create rigid forms of phenomenological method that could at least approach such verifiability (Schutz, 1964; Ihde, 1977). Unfortunately, when those theoretical concepts are brought into the sphere of real lived experiences, their rigidity easily vanishes when confronted with the practical difficulties in grasping the subjectivity of others. Clearly, the task of phenomenology cannot be to provide verifiable results (in the sense of scientific method), but to add viewpoints.

This does not mean that the difficulty of penetrating into the experiences of others has somehow been removed. One solution to overcome the problem is to study one's own subjective world and experiences in it. In this way there is no need to try to re-experience what others have experienced. The problem this time arises from using one's own thoughts to analyse ones own thoughts. In such a setting it is not easy to see everything. Hardly less serious are the problems of how to disclose the processes that are used in the analysis, and how to communicate the results to others. Another deterrent can be that it may be hard to reveal, not to mention analyse, personal experiences that may sometimes attract ridicule or raise some eyebrows. Consequently, reluctance to study one's own experiences is characteristic of human geographers. Relph comments on Tuan's 'Topophilia': '...he draws his material from the diverse observations

---

[3] In 'essential' phenomenology to uncover the subjective aspects of an experience is also supposed to reveal the 'essences', 'truths', of the thing experienced (e.g. Gregory, 1978; Relph, 1981b; Johnston, 1983). The idea is to approach the experience as it is lived, not to evaluate whether it is based on verifiable 'truths'. Eventually, these 'truths' are supposed to be uncovered anyway, once the elements that obscure the truths are disclosed. In this way, a successful phenomenological inquiry achieves two goals at the same time. Not every phenomenologist believes in these essences; I'd emphasise the dissection of experiences as the main project.

of others, but one supposes that he is using these to grasp the character of his own experiences of space and place' (Relph, 1981b, p. 111). Tuan does not claim that he would do so, but nevertheless he obviously does. Relph denies that he himself used his own experiences in his 'Place and Placelessness' but cannot cover up the fact that he did; Osterrieth used Relph's work as an example of how 'the phenomenologist too easily transposes his own subjectivity on other people's experience' (Osterrieth, 1982, p. 65). In this work I am shamelessly going to do the same; my own experiences give me the background from which I approach the experiences of others. It may not be methodologically sound (yet), but it surely enlarges my understanding. At the same time, I hope that I can transmit some of that understanding to the reader.

The difficulties in communicating the processes of this kind of research are also shared by phenomenological inquiry in general. Phenomenological inquiry does not base the justification of its results on the possibility of replicating the study. As that possibility is an important element in the verification process of the scientific method, it is understandable that in the eyes of the positivists the results gained from phenomenological studies are often seen as little more than speculative opinions. They may sound vague and abstract, and as the vocabulary used by phenomenologists is sometimes quite impressionistic, doubts about the operational usefulness of the approach are easily awakened (Osterrieth, 1982, p. 65; Daniels, 1985, p. 148). Phenomenology as an approach in geography is still struggling to get rid of its initial position as mere critique against positivism. This is accentuated by the fact that while phenomenology is a method of understanding, it at the same time is not able to present a 'standard' practical procedure (such as the scientific method) to achieve that understanding. This makes those who do not practice it doubtful of its usefulness. For the same reason those who do practice it may suffer from an inferiority complex and give unnecessary concessions to other approaches (Relph, 1981b, p. 108). All phenomenology can do is to point to reflection which can take diverse forms from reasoning to psychotherapy. Thus phenomenology cannot offer 'straight-forward' guidelines for empirical research. This is the reason why phenomenology is not a good approach for example in problem solving and planning, which both may involve deciding between opposing views. Neither does it add to collective knowledge in a cumulative sense, as does worthwhile positivist research. The justification of phenomenology is elsewhere. Luckily, as time goes by, less and less energy is needed to justify the approach as the increased understanding it has provided justifies itself.

Phenomenology is like an attitude, a way of being, not doing (Relph, 1981b, p. 101). The essential character of that attitude is to reflect on subjective experiences and become conscious of them, thus gaining a richer insight into the nature of one's own existence. In this sense Husserl, the founder of phenomenology, compared it with a religious experience (Ibid.). This inward turned phenomenology can break through the narrative quality of communicated experience to the exclusively subjective area of lived personal experience where feelings and sensations impossible to express in words can receive an illumination of comprehension (compare Lehtinen, 1993, p. 78). Unfortunately, this aspect of phenomenology is not possible to use in an academic inquiry because the latter is always bound to language; there has to be a way to communicate the results and the process of an inquiry to others.

Nevertheless, the phenomenological method is a way to understand and convey subjective experiences insofar as we stick to the aspects of phenomenology that are possible to articulate. At the empirical level there are no unambiguous ways to gain this understanding. While 'striving to achieve understanding' is the common denominator of all phenomenological methods applied to empirical inquiries, this striving can embrace a vast range of different ways in which to conduct a piece of research. These could be described roughly as qualitative; it is of little value in defining the methodology of phenomenology. What is essential, however, is the analogy between the theory itself and the way in which the process of empirical research should be communicated: just as the approach itself attempts to disclose the subjective element in experience, similarly, the communication of how this is done by the researchers should be disclosed by them. Thus others can recognise the process and evaluate it and its findings. In this kind of 'self-reflective writing' (Clifford, 1986, p. 14), the subjective elements in the process of inquiry are disclosed so that it is possible to recognise them and assess their contribution to findings. In phenomenological research this presentational method to at least partially overcome the subjectivity of study is important, no matter what the actual method of doing the research is. This theme is common with post-structuralists, who are concerned with the crisis of representation, i.e. what to do about the inevitable bias and display of power in the representation of what has been researched.

Existentialism

Another humanistic approach, distinguishable from, though closely associated with phenomenology, is existentialism. Together with phenomenology it provides a framework that neatly complements post-structural approach. Existentialism developed from phenomenological ideas and in fact, the kind of existentialism I am going to introduce here is called existential phenomenology. It has its origins in the thinking of Heidegger who rejected the Husserlian idea of 'essences'. He, like Husserl, saw the human being as the creator of his/her own personal world, but instead of believing in 'essences' behind that subjective world he was interested in the 'referential totality' which constitutes it (Karjalainen, 1986a, p. 69). Everything in the subjective world exists only as having reference to other things and to us (Ibid., p. 93). This 'referential totality' of our personal world is thus our own creation because we have to construct the references ourselves before they have any meaning to us. Since our personal world is about meanings, the construction of the 'referential totality' is a necessary consequence of our existence as thinking beings.

The central idea of existentialism and simultaneously the difference between the two approaches has later been summarised by Sartre who declared: 'existence comes before essence' (cited in e.g. Samuels, 1981, p. 115; Johnston, 1983, p. 65; Karjalainen, 1986a, p. 75). This means that there are no essences according to which lives would be directed; we are what we make of ourselves (Karjalainen, 1986a, p. 76). The difference between the approaches can also be expressed by describing phenomenology as a method to understand human beings and their personal worlds, and existentialism as ontology that provides the point of departure for that understanding.

Thus in geography the existential approach could be called spatial ontology of human beings (Samuels, 1978, pp. 25-30). It is interested in our spatial way of being in the world and explores the ways in which that spatiality emerges as the 'referential totality' of an individual personal world. In this work I intend to follow this ontological position as it allows me to analyse travel as an attempt to expand personal worlds. Especially the way in which new experiences are incorporated into the already established 'referential totality' provides an interesting setting for the analysis. This complements post-structural analysis by analysing the relations between the structures of power and the construction of meaning in life.

Structuralists have criticised strongly this kind of existential-phenomenologist portrayal of human being. It accords individuals the freedom to choose what we become, although within the limits of facticities of the world that as such has its foundations apart from us (Samuels, 1981, p. 121). This is seen as undermining the role of society in shaping our reality and us. The structuralist critique claims that in this framework we are allowed too much freedom to act as we wish. The limits of doing so are in practice much stricter than the existential facticities (the fact that we cannot fly, for example). Instead of facticities, the principal limits are imposed upon us by the circumstances that are not of our own choosing (Johnston, 1983, p. 125; Daniels, 1985, p. 151; Lehtinen, 1993, p. 76). These circumstances are created by various structures that govern the spheres of human activity. According to structuralists, the claim that individuals create their own worlds ignores the society's role in the process. Social world has its structures prior to us and thus they create the circumstances in which we act and consequently experience. Our personal worlds are indeed our own creations but we have not created them independently of the circumstances that surround us. While this sounds simple, it does not mean that there is a simple answer to the question of what is the extent of each. This obviously varies between individuals and social groups.

Existentialists admit that our personal world has its foundations in the world apart from us, but emphasise the notion that it is still a creation that emerges from our 'self-full' engagement with the world (Karjalainen, 1986a, p. 87). Some also insist that the social world is a sum of individual personal worlds and thus it cannot be accorded a status of 'autonomous force obeying its own laws and acting upon us as individuals' (Ibid., p. 57). I think that they have got this upside down; surely we experience everything through 'self', but the liberty of making ourselves what we are comes only after we have adopted the intersubjective elements of the social world. We have to learn concepts, a language and other abilities that enable us to interact in the world which we do not inhabit alone. Because we are social beings, we always get socialised into the social group into which we happened to be born (or in which we grew up, if the two differ). Thus the interactionist view that the way in which we construct our personal worlds is itself a social construct makes sense. This is not to say that we are passive receptacles of the socialisation process of our social group. We are that no more than we are totally free creators of our own personal worlds. We 'negotiate' between the determination of our social group and the possibilities to individually create our world (Duncan, 1978, p. 269). According to Entrikin (1992, p. 45), this represents the interaction between 'structural forces of political economy and human agency' and that 'in geography it takes the form of a theoretical balancing act between the role of consciousness in creating meaning and the role of structural forces in shaping consciousness'. The interactionist stance is a reasonable mediator between the existentialist view of free will, and the structuralist emphasis on how individual actions take place within socio-economic structures.

I find it natural to accept the critique of existentialism by structuralists, because I do not see it contradicting the idea of phenomenology. Doing phenomenology involves recognition of subjective elements in our experiences. Seeing the structures that, on their part, shape those elements makes their recognition considerably easier. Thus structuralism brings with it an extension to the practical applications of phenomenology; as the latter can increase our understanding of ourselves through self-reflection, the former facilitates the criticism and possible modification of the structures and circumstances in which our personal worlds have been formed. The implications in education, for example, could be useful in teaching issues like multiculturalism. By encouraging self-reflection, people would be made aware of their biased preconceptions and that should lead to tracing the structures that cause that bias. Once aware of our prejudices and the structures that lead to them we could try to change those structures. Such an *attitude* is useful in tourism also.

I'd like to see post-structuralist concern with the power of discursional structures to set limits on our experiences as another side of the same coin as the existentialist interest to the referential totality. In experience the discursional structures necessarily become a part of the personal referential totality. It is arbitrary not to draw the concepts into the same analysis on the grounds of their theoretical disparity. There are no personal meanings that are important from the perspective of individual's life (the sphere of existential phenomenology) and which haven't been formed within the framework of certain politics of power (the sphere of post-structuralism). Despite the different theoretical underpinnings, I am going to apply terms of humanistic geography in the present conceptual environment dominated by post-structuralism and its concern with representation. In such a pursuit there is scope for difficulties in detaching concepts from their original theoretical surroundings and applying them in another theoretical environment. I would not want to exaggerate these difficulties however; crossing the boundaries and breaking the rules can create something new at best. Of course, there lurks the danger of merely confusing the concepts, ideas, the readers, and oneself. But the lived world is not organised around concepts formulated in research.

I expect that the humanistic approach brings forth fruitful viewpoints to tourist's experience of place once the existence and meaning of the structural and symbolic frameworks are duly acknowledged. The concepts of humanistic geography take us further to the personal meanings of tourist's experience of place than post-structural concepts alone. As a result we can understand the experience of place in tourism as a more or less meaningful part of the life of an individual, not just an act of consumption within certain structures of politics and power.

Existential Space

Spatiality

The ontological necessity of spatiality is a point of departure of the existential approach and as noted above, it stems from the obvious fact that everyone has to be somewhere. In regard to this Heidegger describes our way of being in the world, our existence, using the concept of 'dasein' (Fell, 1979, p. 32). 'Da' ((t)here) is connected with 'sein' (to be). Literally translated it means 'being (t)here', thus revealing the nature of our way of being; it includes the idea of being somewhere. Furthermore, only a being with a human consciousness can have dasein as mode of being; the concept indicates an important part of our ability and need to define ourselves. As far as we know, this distinguishes us from the other animals and non-organic objects which also are bound to be somewhere. We not only are, we 'stand out' (Karjalainen, 1986a, p. 71).

In order to 'stand out', to relate to ourselves and to the world, we must realise the fact that there is ontological distance between us and everything else (Ibid., p. 77). As we 'stand out', we acknowledge the distance and mitigate it by establishing relations (Samuels, 1981, p. 118). Ontological distance is not measurable distance, it is rather a detachment; we can never overcome our ontological distance from the world, it is imprinted in what we are (Heidegger, 1985, p. 232).[4] From this ontological distance between us and everything else arises our spatiality. By establishing relations we pull objects into our personal world, and depending on the intensity of the relationship, they are felt with varying degree of proximity. Ontological distance still remains, but through the relation we have given the object a meaning and therefore brought it into our personal world, where distance is not a geometrically quantifiable property, but an attachment (see Matorè 1966, p. 6; Entrikin 1976, p. 626). Consequently, a friend far away can be closer than a stranger next to us.

---

[4] Here it must be emphasised that all this applies only to Western philosophy. Views of Zen-Buddhism, for example, would be completely opposite.

Many Kinds of Spaces

The spatial character of our being in the world is thus a primary element in our existence (along with our temporality) that forces us to overcome distances by establishing relationships. The result is a web of relations and references, a personal world that constitutes what is called existential space (Matorè, 1966; Relph, 1976, pp. 20-21; Samuels, 1978, 1981). This is the culmination of the basic existential tenet according to which human beings make themselves. By 'standing out' we detach ourselves from other beings and entities and adapt ourselves to the fact that we are thrown in the world. At the same time we define our relation to the world and ourselves. Thus somewhat paradoxically: we have to detach ourselves from the world before we can be immensely involved with it. Existential space is what emerges from this involvement. It is our personal spatio-temporal network to incorporate the relations we have established (Pickles, 1985, p. 34) and in which we define our own place in that network. To put it simply, existential space is our version of the world and of our place in it. As such it has two important characteristics (Samuels, 1978, p. 32): Firstly, it is partial exactly because it is *our* world. It is biased and incomplete as opposed to space as universe that is objective and encompasses everything. Secondly, it is based on the *situations* in which we have given the meanings it contains. These two characteristics are interwoven; while it is our space, existential space has its foundations in the world apart from us. Thus a large part of existential space is intersubjective, because the same world imposes its facticities on everyone and hence the situations in which we find ourselves are to some extent shared also by others. This is emphasised by the society's role in giving us the concepts and meanings that we use in defining our own space; we largely internalise what we have been given in socialisation.

The notion of existential space has a deeply humanistic tone. There are several other ways of approaching space, depending on the perspective adopted. The perspective can be selected within a continuum from abstract thought to direct experience (Relph, 1976, p. 8; see also Tuan, 1979, p. 388). These are the opposite ends of detachment and involvement, objectivity and subjectivity (compare Entrikin, 1991, p. 26). Existential space is the ultimate end of the direct experience of that continuum. Relph (1976, pp. 8-28) distinguishes other types of spaces too: primitive, perceptual, architectural and planning, cognitive, and abstract.[5] However, I see it more useful to follow the organisation used by Couclelis (1992), because it is simpler and more clearly shows the distinction between analytic spaces and space as it is lived.

Couclelis has recognised five different categories of spaces: mathematical, physical, socio-economic, behavioural, and experiental (Couclelis, 1992).[6] Mathematical space is the world of geometry, which has been adopted as a language of expressing absolutely measurable relations in space. Physical space is what encompasses everything there is in the universe. It is usually considered and measured in terms of geometry, but it can also be relative, as suggested by Einstein. Physical space is formalised in the Newtonian notion of absolute space; 'space is a neutral background against which the positions of objects can be pinpointed and their motions described' (Ibid., p. 220). Physical space thus largely equals the common sense concept of space. Socio-economic space is the domain of spatial analysis in which the regional patterns of social and economic phenomena are studied. Behavioural space is an attempt to acknowledge the effects of human perception on how space is actually experienced. The idea is to explore the ways in which the biased and incomplete information we obtain during the course of our everyday life affects our decision-making. While this is the space people experience in contrast to the objectively definable mathematical, physical, and socio-economic space, it is still highly abstract because it has to be expressed in quantifiable terms. People are seen as receiving stimuli and then responding in a certain measurable way. Thus it becomes possible to construct models where certain stimuli produce certain responses. However, this is still the domain of analytic science, far removed from the ways in which we actually live space. Experiental space is the space as it is lived and experienced by us, without these scientific conceptualisations.

In fact, the notion of experiental space is equivalent to existential space. The different terms just reflect the different approaches used in

---

[5] Relph also refers to yet another classification by Hersch: transcendental, practical, social, physical, and mathematical space (Relph, 1976, p. 26).

[6] These categories are by no means exhaustive. Musical space, for example, is not the world of geometry, although it is equally as abstract as mathematical space. Thus it is another kind of abstract space. Then, what about some new kinds of virtual spaces created by computer technology and the 'cyberspace' of the 'information highway'? Where do they fit in these different categories of spaces?

arriving at them. While the term 'existential space' describes the fundamental connection between the act of defining ourselves and our spatial mode of being, 'experiental space' reflects its lived character as opposed to the analytic nature of the other ways to see space. I prefer the notion of existential space because of its close connection to the existential view of what it is to be a human, which I have adopted.

Existential Space and Construction of the Other

There is a serious dilemma here; while existential space is presentational, we should still be able to somehow represent the central features of it. Necessarily the resulting description will be partial, abstracted, and hugely simplified. In geography this partiality of the representation of existential space appears as exaggerated emphasis on its spatial dimension. The language used here is symptomatic to the tendency of conceiving existential space in spatial terms; the term dimension is inherently spatial already. Two meanings of the term spatial thus arise here. The first is the engagement in relations with one's surroundings in the widest possible sense, and the second is the more traditional concern with physical locations. When I write about the spatial dimension of existential space, it entails the latter, narrower sense.

In geography the narrow meaning of the term spatial has been emphasised. This is naturally a consequence of the fact that geography has traditionally been interested in things which have much to do with location. Nevertheless, as our existential space envelops all our relations with the world, to see it only in these narrowly spatial terms can give a fundamentally misleading picture of it. I do not think that enough weight has been placed on expressing its other than primarily spatial aspects. Obviously existential space has also other, less purely spatial dimensions such as temporal, social, political, economic and spiritual dimensions.

There are, however, reasons that warrant concentrating on the specifically spatial dimension of existential space: First, it is so immensely complicated that without structuring it around some sufficiently simple underlying form, it would become very hard to conceptualise it at all. Second, spatiality is not only one kind of experience; it is a dimension of any experience[7] (Nordberg-Schulz, 1971, p. 34). To give some examples from some other than spatial dimensions which illustrate this: I have my *place* in the society (social), the new party fills the *space* between the right and the left (political), the demand has *moved elsewhere* (economic), Jesus is the *way* (spiritual).

An attempt to organise the concept of existential space in spatial framework is made by Nordberg-Schulz (1971). According to him existential space has three elements: centres, paths and domains (Ibid., p. 24). As contrast to the analytic spaces above, existential space is thus not homogeneous; it has centres of diverse importance, connected by paths and surrounded by domains. These elements also appear on several levels within a certain hierarchy. Nordberg-Schulz (Ibid., pp. 27-33) defines five such hierarchic levels of existential space: geography, landscape, urban level, house and thing. Naturally such levels and the idea of a hierarchy are only conceptually evident as the meanings at one level often draw from another. Furthermore, this is only one possible way to express a hierarchy; it should be seen only as an expression of the general idea of how we see existential space spatially as spheres of gradually increasing scale from ourselves to the world and universe (see Buttimer, 1976, p. 284).

Nordberg-Schulz's levels of existential space express its hierarchy in spatial terms. This does not mean however, that the different hierarchic levels would not appear in the other dimensions of existential space too. Nevertheless, using spatial language means that the compatibility of the Nordberg-Schulz's model to other dimensions often leaves a lot to be desired (Table 2.1).

From the perspective of this work, the level of 'geography' is by far the most interesting of Nordberg-Schulz's levels of existential space. The level of 'geography' encompasses a great deal of the motivation to travel. It is the domain on which dreams of being elsewhere are projected. The level of 'geography' in Nordberg-Schulz's terminology refers to the parts of existential space that cannot be observed directly because they are beyond daily domains. Those parts are distant so that the relation to them is mediated through knowledge and impressions, not from experience.

---

[7] Just like time; our existence is organised spatio-temporally. It is easy to give the temporal dimension precedence because the spatial dimension often appears hidden in time. We say, for example, that something is ten minutes away. In everyday language it is thus easy to express spatial dimension in temporal terms. However, it is not as easy to do it another way around, although possible indeed (Paasi, 1984, pp. 13-14; Boorstin, 1972, p. 115). For example: 'When we get there, it is time to...'.

However, they are potentially within the domain of immediate experience; it may be possible to visit them. This level of existential space reflects the spatial organisation of our world view (Paasi, 1984, p. 34), it contains all our knowledge and images of places we haven't been to. As such it naturally gives meanings and a frame of reference to the things we encounter on the more immediate levels of existential space (and *vice versa*). It is worth noticing that 'geography' is so large a level that it can within itself contain various scales. We can think about the earth, the solar system and the universe. The larger the scale, the more of the level is bound to remain outside our immediate experience. Nevertheless, the tiny fractions of the 'geography' experienced in travel, create tourist's impression of large wholes.

Table 2.1   Examples of different levels in some dimensions of existential space

	Spatial	Social	Political	Economic	Spiritual
Geography	Place never visited	People never met	Unknown ideologies	Economy of a distant country	Alien religion
Landscape	Vista from balcony	People from local sport clubs	Political field of own country	Economy of own country	Own religion
Urban	Work place	Work mates	Own party	Company	Own parish
House	Home	Friends	Own opinion	Own economy	Own faith
Thing	Armchair	Self	Vote	Coin	Prayer

The level of 'geography' in our existential space is the sphere of which we do not have first-hand experience. Therefore it is characterised by whatever qualities we for a reason or another happen to invest it with. This is where the context of existential space meets the post-structuralists' concern with social construction of reality. The same way as we organise our existential space into distant level of 'geography' and closer realms, we chart our world by constantly dividing it between the familiarity and the unknown (Spivak, 1988, p. 113; Löytty, 1994, p. 117). In the process we try to control the unknown by constructing the Other on the basis of what is familiar to us (compare Relph, 1976, p. 53). The domain of the Other is thus the level of 'geography'. The concept of the Other illustrates our need to contrast the familiar against everything else (Fabian, 1983; Pratt, 1985; Duncan, 1993; Knuuttila and Paasi, 1995, pp. 55-58). The Other is something that is profoundly alien to us, most often in a socio-cultural sense; there is socio-cultural, and consequently epistemological distance between us and the Other. The distance can only be overcome by intense involvement with it over a considerable period of time. The distance does not have to be a spatial entity. Although the Other resides in the 'geography' level of our existential space, in multi-cultural societies it can be found even in the same neighbourhood, in the form of unfamiliar customs, beliefs, values, etc. In this case, the Other resides within close realms in spatial sense, but can still be distant (i.e. at the level of 'geography') in some other aspects of existential space. In tourist's experience the destination place represents the Other, even to the extent that the *experience of the place is the experience of the Other*.

Elements of Existential Space

The elements of existential space are centres, paths and domains (Nordberg-Schulz, 1971, p. 24). This kind of spatial terminology also has its place in more analytic approaches to space like cognitive mapping and GIS. However, in this work these concepts are not seen as clearly defined entities of the analytic approaches. Here they are metaphoric descriptions of elements through which our involvement with the world is built. Thus the spatial language used to define the elements should not be taken as an implication that existential space would be approached merely as a physically spatial entity. Unlike the *levels* of existential space, its *elements* lend themselves well to analysis on other than the spatial dimensions (compare Tables 2.1 and 2.2). The elements of existential space further organise and conceptualise the tension between the familiar and the level of 'geography', the Other. They help to bridge the gap between the spatial language used and the lived world in which spatiality is just one dimension.

Table 2.2   Examples of centres, paths and domains in various dimensions of existential space

	Spatial	Social	Political	Economic	Spiritual
Centre	Home	Self	Ideal	Income	Soul
Path	Road	Communication	Action	Commerce	Gospel
Domain	Countryside	Social group	Ideology	Market	World

As we create our existential space we need reference points, centres that help us arrange that space. In travel this is clear when new places are encountered. Centres are points where our webs of meanings become especially dense. Some of those points are public; they have meaning beyond personal scale on a societal, maybe even global level. Such reference points are, for example, tourist attractions and cities. These public reference points reflect the intersubjectivity of our existential space. There are also centres filled with private personal meanings that may have little public significance, like the house in which we used to live as a child. Some of the centres have both private and personal meanings attached to them. An example would be a famous tourist attraction where a friend of mine proposed his wife-to-be. Thus the concept of centre describes what we often call places. Relph (1976, p. 21) uses 'place' instead of 'centre' in describing Nordberg-Schulz's organisation of existential space. But a centre does not have to be a place (Table 2.2).

There can be no centre if there is nothing to be the centre of. In other words, the existence of centres requires that there is something outside them from which they can be distinguished. There is thus outside and inside of a centre. The inside is defined in terms of familiarity; centre is the familiar as contrast to less familiar, or unknown domain outside. Home is a good example of this; we know well what is going on there, but as we leave through the door, the surrounding suburb may hide things we are not aware of. This is often a matter of scale; it is possible to be thoroughly familiar only with a limited entity. Thus compact firsthand experience is more likely to promote insideness than the vicarious or fragmented experience of larger domains of which just parts can be encountered at a time. Therefore the constitution of larger far-away domains of our existential space is different from the one of the smaller immediate ones (Paasi, 1984, p. 30). The former is characterised by increasing abstraction whereas the latter is familiar. On the other hand, we imagine what is elsewhere on the basis on what is here (Relph, 1976, p. 53), but because there is no immediate involvement, the 'elsewhere' cannot be characterised by an equally dense web of meanings.

A centre can appear at various levels and scales. At the largest levels of 'geography' a centre may be our own country, maybe even the earth. In this respect the centre as a place of familiarity is relative; it is familiar compared to the outside. In the same way insideness and outsideness is felt in relation to the situation. When we think at the global level, we can feel insideness in relation to our home country although it is not small enough for us to experience first hand as a whole. At the global level it becomes home, compared to the strangeness of the rest of the world and the outsideness felt there. What at some level could seem too large a domain even to experience first hand, may at another level be a centre with lots of meanings attached and to which we project our feelings of insideness. Thus the centres are not fixed; home is the centre when I am having my Sunday afternoon walk, town is the centre when I travel in the countryside, and my country is the centre when I visit distant countries on the other side of the world. Of course none of the centres at different scales disappear, but their stay in the 'background' until the situation makes them acutely relevant.

Centres are what we know directly in contrast to what we do not know, or know less directly. Thus a centre is home which we compare to a place far away, a travelling companion who feels familiar compared to the people of a foreign country, and our own culture that makes sense in contrast to the culture of an alien people. While the spatial component in the concept of centre is strong, it is also a spatial metaphor applied to other aspects of existential space. Centres represent at least relative familiarity compared to the Other elsewhere.

Paths are routes that connect the centres with each other and with the surrounding domains. In this way paths give our existential space continuity (Nordberg-Schulz, 1971, p. 22). They facilitate movement and are the expression of that movement. In this role paths mediate the tension between inside and outside. Movement between centres and domains outside them creates a continuous variation in the degree of familiarity felt as well as variation of the levels of existential space. New centres are also created in the process. Paths are a means to leave, a possibility to something (Heikkinen, 1993, p. 9).

Centres are the places of meaning and knowledge, but as we go further from them the meanings and knowledge become more abstract, finally passing into realms of ignorance (Ley, 1979, p. 226). However, existential space is not homogeneous, therefore meanings and knowledge do not get equally thinner everywhere. The familiarity remains greater where we have lots of paths, thus revealing the directions of our relations, the domains where our interests reside. The partiality of existential space is visible in the sense that paths do not lead everywhere. They only 'open up space' (Bollnow, 1967, p. 183; Relph, 1976, pp. 20-21) depending on our intentions. The domains beyond our paths may be irrelevant to those intentions and we do not confuse ourselves by paying attention to them.

A familiar example of a way to work can illustrate the point: We may have used that very same route daily for years, but still we may not know what lies behind the buildings along the route. It is simply irrelevant to us in the context of getting to work. Our familiarity with the immediate surroundings of the route is enough and we naturally suppose that the area beyond the buildings is similar to the one we see. It is simply not necessary to open up paths to that area, quite the opposite; it might mean arriving late at work. We can do that at another time, but then our situation and consequent intentions are different; then the space does not actualise through the situation of going to work any more. To expand this spatially orientated presentation of existential space we could imagine a similar example from the social dimension. We can also think of communication as a path. In formal situations for example, we have paths that are well structured and 'mapped' by conventions of good manners. Departing from such conduct may, in a given situation, make it impossible to reach the intended goal. Not to mention the situation which often takes place in travel; the paths of the participants from different cultures are altogether incompatible.

Paths imply movement, interaction, and relation. Along the paths we reach out from centres, but equally importantly, the same paths also allow us to return. In this sense the tension between centre and the Other, mediated by paths, forms the basis for feelings of longing for distant places and homesickness (Bollnow, 1967, p. 182). In a more general sense, we use paths when we balance between the desire to feel security provided by familiarity and our desire to explore unknown domains. The use of paths is also an expression of our need to 'take possession' (Nordberg-Schulz, 1971, p. 21) of our environment by reaching out and returning. Travel is an example of this; home is left temporarily for new experiences, thus travel is a path.

Path clearly illustrates the literal and metaphorical nature of the elements of existential space. Path as a metaphor is by no means purely just an academic illustration; it is also a very common everyday metaphor for example for life (life is a way) and doing things (Is this the right way to do it?). This reflects the fact that we understand our existence spatially. We exist in relation to space, and express this relation in our language (Heikkinen, 1993, p. 9).

Domains' role in existential space is to 'fill out' spaces where centres and paths do not reach, thus creating coherence, as well as logical continuity. This coherence is often achieved with typifying the domains and making them fit to a particular world-view (see Schutz and Luckmann, 1973, pp. 8-15, 138-139). The domains on the level of 'geography', beyond our personal experience, are especially susceptible to this, as it is possible to accord them whatever characteristics we like. This is the domain of the Other. Domain is often so large an element that it remains rather unstructured 'ground' on which centres and paths appear as more pronounced 'figures' (Nordberg-Schulz, 1971, p. 23). Relph (1976, p. 20) calls domains districts or regions.

Domains are regions that we define, using certain characteristics in defining them. Within a domain, we *believe*, that characteristic is homogeneously distributed. Thus we define the domain between the roads we use when going to work as certain kind of blocks ('This block is an industrial area, the one on the right houses mainly working class people'). A domain may contain a centre or centres that represent the domain. For example, in a map of most international airlines we can see that the domain of Philippines is represented by Manila (Figure 2.1).

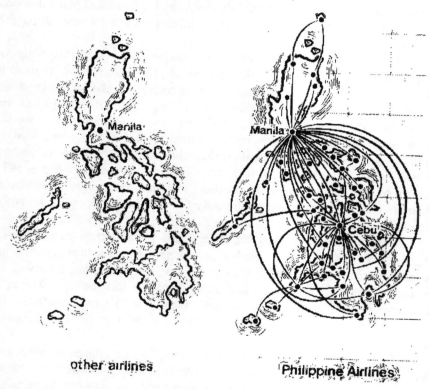

other airlines   Philippine Airlines

Figure 2.1 An example of centres in domains

Increasing familiarity with the domains inhabits them with more and more centres, as illustrated in this airline advertisement (Time, Aug 21, 1995, p. 65). The discussion about existential space has indicated a tension between the familiar and the level of 'geography', the Other, between the centre and outside. The tension is an important aspect of what travel is all about. The outcome of that tension and the interaction it initiates is largely determined by how the paths involved mediate that interaction. Thus travel is a path that mediates between the experiences of home and the Other. In chapters to come the conceptualisation will be specified further.

Place as Lived World

Location as a concept means a point where something is situated. As such it is an element of analytic space concepts, and may thus be considered an objective entity. In contrast, the notion of place refers to the lived, and thus subjective quality of location. While location sets out important elements that are part of what place is, place eventually arises only from human experience. Agnew and Duncan (1989, p. 2) write about *location, locale,* and *sense of place. Location* characterises e.g. 'the spatial distribution of social and economic activities resulting from between-place factor cost and market price differentials'. *Locale* is the concern of microsociologists and humanistic geographers. It is 'the setting for everyday routine social interaction provided in a place'. Finally, *sense of place* is the 'identification with a place engendered by living in it'. In my own discussion I have combined the latter two, when I write about place as lived. Places are characterised by meanings we give to them. Such an experiental phenomenon is as complex as life itself.

Gibson (1978, p. 138) starts his paper about the subjective meaning of places by claiming that the concept of place is so self evident that it is a waste of time to define it: 'any time we speak of geography we are already speaking of places'. I believe that Gibson did not want to try to define place because any definition easily leaves some aspects of such a complicated concept without consideration. In general, humanistic geographers seem to think that it is wiser to remain content to analyse the meaning of place rather than try to struggle against its tendency to slip through the web of definitions. There are numerous attempts to define the concept of place: Place is 'a fundamental expression of man's involvement in the world' (Relph, 1976, p. 44). 'Place is always an act of referencing, and "places" are nothing more or less than reference points in someone's projections' (Samuels, 1978, pp. 30-31). Place is 'a product of experience' (Paasi, 1986, p. 113). In the end we have many definitions which each capture a part or parts of what place is, but none of which properly expresses all aspects involved. In short, no list of humanistic (or any other) definitions can provide a conclusive definition of place. The point in humanistic definitions is however, that place is portrayed as something that receives its constituents through human beings. It is not a neutral and objective segment of space.

In existential ontology, place is a result of our spatial self-definition and the consequent emergence of our selves. According to Heidegger place is 'that which places man in such a way that it reveals the external bonds of his existence and at the same time the depths of his freedom and reality' (cited in The Dictionary of Human Geography, 1986, p. 346). If we thus understand space as both possibility and restraint, then place is what we make of them. In a similar manner, Karjalainen considers space as something that 'permits growth, expansion and freedom, whereas place becomes a "room", a constraint' (Karjalainen, 1986a, p. 121). Sometimes we may feel that there is not enough room and we want to break free from the constraint of our place. This is evident in numerous 'on-the-road' movies and in our occasional urge to get away from home.

Someone advocating a viewpoint on the middle ground between objective and subjective view of place (Entrikin, 1991) could say that overt emphasis on the subjective characteristics of place is just another deviation from its holistic character: While humanistic geographers criticise objectifying science for reducing place to mere location, in the same way they sometimes themselves downgrade place by disregarding the objective qualities inherent in it. Place is always the relative location of the objects in the world while also being a meaningful context of human action (Entrikin 1991, p. 10). 'To ignore either aspect of this dualism is to misunderstand the (...) experience of place' (Ibid., p. 134).

However, this critique misses its target in the eyes of those who have adopted existential ontology. Concepts like neutrality and objectivity require us to operate in a highly conceptualised realm, which in itself is already a human construction. Therefore there is nothing defined as objective or neutral, unless those meanings are given. However, what human experience adds to a mere location does not take away the location's qualities that are *perceived* as 'objective'. They always mean something when encountered. Thus the climate of this place means that I need to wear warm clothes in winter.

The structuralist critique maintains that the humanistic portrayal of place is overly individualistic. According to them place is a result of structures and processes which govern the way the place is constituted. However, Paasi (1986, p. 112) explains that to understand place through an individual experience does not contradict this; 'these structures are reconstituted precisely through the agency of individual practices'. I'd be willing to take this still basically structural claim further towards the interactionist position. We could say that individual experience of place is, not a result of, but indeed strongly affected by structures and processes that govern the way the place is constituted. At the same time these individual experiences not only *re*constitute the structures; there is always a possibility to contribute something new to them (although the contribution of a single individual is likely to be small).

Places are reference points in our existential space; they are thus parts of a bigger referential totality. This can also be seen in an expression of English language: things, events and experiences 'take place' (Pocock, 1981, p. 12). To 'take place' means that something positions itself (or is positioned) in such a way that it integrates into a bigger whole. In these wholes the distances between places have to be evaluated (Karjalainen, 1986a, p. 129). It is done by weighing the meanings of the places in the context of the present situation. This accentuates the lived quality of places; the distances between them are not measurable in metres and kilometres alone. Here humanistic geography goes beyond what behavioural cognitive mapping can (or attempts to) achieve. The distances are primarily considered on the basis of the question: 'What does it mean to overcome them?' The answer may naturally involve aspects that can be measured such as time, money, energy, but it often contains values like affection or social decency. Thus, for example, the distance to a country that has totally alien culture may be perceived greater than to the one that feels more familiar, irrespective of the actual distance in kilometres.

Places as centres lead to interesting dynamism in which the interplay between movement and pause defines what is a path and what is a centre. While moving, centre is something anticipated. The end of movement fulfils the anticipation. In movement the world appears as scenes that are continuously changing and thus not centring anywhere. Stopping allows us to sketch a place that is the present centre of our existence. Mere scenes transform into a place. Travel expresses the dialectic between directional paths and places as centres, movement and pause. Driving on a highway does not make the highway a place, instead, the vehicle in which we travel is one. But when we stop and step out of the car we find ourselves in a place, which from within the moving car was only a changing landscape. All this happens because movement implies reach and the expression of that reach is a path, not a centre. Place is not directional like path (Tuan, 1979, p. 411). While driving on a highway we are on our way to and from somewhere. In movement the concerns we have appear in relation to the reach in which we are involved, whereas stopping makes those concerns appear in relation to the location in which we are. Suddenly our situation is defined in this particular location. It starts to mean something to us; it becomes the place where we stopped to change a blown out tyre. The very place becomes the centre of those meanings. Thus such a place is both an objectifiable, physical centre in the sense that we can point to it as a cluster of things, but it is also a very personal, subjective centre of meanings that may be the property of just one, a handful, or a lot of people. This takes place in bus travel, when the group stops to see a sight.

According to Nordberg-Schulz (1971, p. 20) place includes the components of centralisation, proximity and closure. Centralisation reflects the fact that place is where our consciousness focuses. Proximity implies that we have some meaningful concern that makes the place relevant for us. Closure indicates that the place is at least approximately possible to define in contrast to the domains outside it, although this is not always easy.

The scale of places can vary greatly. Thus inside a city there can be an endless number of smaller places. Centrality and proximity of such differently sized places arises from the level of personal involvement; the involvement is centred 'here' and is concerned with something that is within our relative reach (thus even the city is central and close in contrast to the whole country). Closure similarly arises from the limits of our involvement. Thus the closure arises from negation of places, i.e. what is contrasted as being outside their often vaguely defined limits.

Sometimes the place of our concern is on the level of 'geography'. This happens when a dream of a distant paradise island is entertained, for example. We may imagine a place to which we have never even been; how can such a place be a centre and how do proximity and closure occur? By imagining a place we invest it with qualities derived from those we imagine the surrounding domains to have. The nature of such a place is hence representational; it becomes a symbol and the centre of the surrounding domains, irrespective of the 'facts' relating them to the place. In this way the domains beyond our direct experience become charted by using centres to create the necessary order in arranging our existential space. Proximity is apparently very hard to associate with places that are far away and which are only imagined. But the involvement with the place is still there as a creative processing of the knowledge and impressions of the far place. Imagining the place brings it mentally close and the consequent emotional proximity can be *felt* strongly as in reading a book. Closure of the imagined place is a consequence of the fact that in order to imagine it, we have to detach it from its surrounding domains. This is used in travel advertising, which encourages us to detach places from their 'real' contexts and place them into ones of our dreams.

Important elements of places are their people. Not every place is inhabited, but where this is the case, it is impossible to separate the people and the place in any other than conceptual terms: 'People are their place and a place is its people' (Relph, 1976, p. 34). This is the result of place being a setting for human involvement with the world. The people have created a considerable portion of the meanings and physical features of the place. Tuan (1979, p. 387) writes:

> Place incarnates the experiences and aspirations of a people. Place is not only a fact to be explained in the broader frame of space, but it is also the reality to be clarified and understood from the perspectives of the people who have given it meaning.

Any difference in socio-cultural heritage between the inhabitants and the visitors is likely to create difficulties in understanding these meanings. In travel, a mediator is needed to interpret and carry those meanings to the visitors.

There are many similarities between the concepts of place and landscape. They both are more than collections of sensory data; they have meanings attached to them. Every place has a landscape that is the exterior appearance of the place and which generates interpretations according to perceivers' background and situation. On the other hand every landscape has places within it. They are inseparable. The underlying difference between place and landscape is that the latter refers to the area that is defined by what can be observed at once whereas place is an entity that is defined by centralisation, proximity and closure. Therefore a place can be larger or smaller than a landscape, depending on the criteria. We can never be *in* the landscape we see because it is always something that unfolds before our eyes. Thus we are not a part of *our* landscape. The ontological distance between it and us remains. Instead, we can be in a place as well as a part of it; ontologically we can be much closer to it.

Humanistic geographers' definition of place has its implications for tourist's experience of place. When tourists experience places, their experience is not so much directed by what they encounter, but by what meanings they give to whatever they do encounter. That in turn, derives from their intentions towards the places, the framework within which they understand them, their situation as visitors, and the extent and nature of their involvement. Here again, humanistic portrayal of place requires a preceding post-structural analysis of the structures of politics and power that guide the tourist's intentions, situation and involvement. Without such an analysis, the meanings revealed have little connection to the world that surrounds the tourist.

Place as Symbol

It is considerably easier to attach meanings to places that are more or less directly perceptible portions of space, than into a domain that is often too large to have much perceptual unity (Paasi, 1986, p. 111). Indeed, place can coincide with such a domain as in the case of a nation-state, but in many cases place is a smaller entity. Place is a centre where the characteristics of the surrounding domains are perceived to be represented, hence places become symbols. This applies not so much to a place where one lives or otherwise knows well. Such a place is characterised by the immediate involvement and familiarity that allows one to see the place presentationally; it presents itself as an integral part of daily involvement with the world. Instead, a distant place that one knows only vicariously lacks this immediate, palpable relation to us. Therefore it appears more as a symbol of the images attached to the domains around it, than as a 'real' place where 'real' people experience their daily involvement with the world. Of course a familiar place can also be perceived as a symbol, but in a distant place the element of being a symbol is emphasised by the fact that there is no immediate first-hand experience of it. The image of such a place tends to be characterised by increasingly abstract and stereotyped ideas of what there is, based on socially transmitted information about the place. It is thus directed by the discourse of the Other.

For Parisians, the city indeed symbolises the whole country, but more importantly for them, it is a place of their daily existence. Instead, for someone who has never been in the city, it is primarily a symbol of France. When personal acquaintance with the city increases, new meanings are added to the symbolic meaning. The place starts to get meanings derived from the more immediate first-hand experience, but it still retains the former symbolic meanings, perhaps in an altered form. This quality of places as being symbols of something else is exploited by travel advertising. Its intention is to turn destinations into symbols of images and ideals that respond to our wishes and dreams. Thus we become lured to those destinations.

Public and Private

Place has a dual character; on one hand it is something that has very personal subjective meanings (evolved in personal involvement with the place), on the other it also has meanings that are shared by whole societies (place as symbol). The contrast between personal and social meanings of place has produced several attempts to conceptualise them. The underlining principle is to distinguish between public and private spheres of meanings. Tuan (1979, p. 412) uses the terms 'public symbols' and 'fields of care', the former being 'places that yield their meaning to the eye', the latter 'places that are known only after prolonged experience'. Relph (1976, p. 56) writes about 'horizontal' and 'vertical' structuring of the image of places'. Horizontal structure of the image of a place is public; the one shared by the group, and the vertical structure is 'the one of intensity and depth of [personal] experience' (Ibid.). Houston (1978, p. 226) describes verticality as the character of place that provides roots, gives direction and accompanies personal memories. According to him, our identity is rooted to the vertical structure of the image of place. Horizontality, in turn, is the more objectifiable character of the identity of place.

The public meaning of places is expressed, for example, in architecture and monuments, in the official information about the places and so on. Public meanings are 'horizontal' in the sense that they are shared by a large part of the society. Personal meanings develop in the context of personal experiences of places, as described earlier.

Personal and public meanings are both historically bound and change through times. Physical objects, events, people, and human meanings change during the lifetime of any one person. In this sense Pred (1986) writes about 'becoming' of places. He connects the structuration theory with the concept of place and demonstrates how 'people produce history and places at the same time as people are produced by history and places' (Ibid., p. 198). As a result from these processes place is both an individual and more or less shared concept within a socio-cultural group. The processes in which the structures that affect the place are internalised (structuration process) are a result of the dialectics of the physical characteristics of places, activities taking place there, and the meanings inherent in them. According to Relph (1976, p. 47) these are the three basic elements that constitute the identity of place.[8]

It is interesting to compare this structuration theory to the social construction of the Other. The latter process takes place much the same way, just that the direct contacts with the place are replaced by indirect secondhand, more or less significant meanings. As a result, the public, intersubjective and stereotyped meanings characterise our relation to the Other. In this case the private meanings have little chance to differ much from the public ones due to the lack of personal firsthand involvement.

The people that inhabit the place do not always unanimously share the public meanings. Societies are often multicultural and each group may have its own code of interpreting the meanings of places:

> Places signify both social and personal experiences. The memories bound up in a particular place may be the property of one, two, or handful of people. Places may act as signs, but the messages they communicate will not be the same for everybody who reads them (Keith, 1988, p. 42).

The historical situations in which places get their meanings vary for different groups at the same time. The consequent intentions of the groups toward the place may vary enormously. In the Australian context a good example is the coexistence of Aboriginal and European communities in the same place. The long local history and distinct culture of Aboriginals put them in a different situation from the other cultural groups. The public meanings change with the historical situation of the group and the private ones with the accumulation of personal experiences. In travel, public meanings of places are mediated to a tourist by travel advertising and other markers. The trip becomes then a process in which private meanings are accumulated and in which they interact with the public ones.

Place Identity

The markers that mediate the public meanings of other places appear in the familiar socio-cultural framework we have internalised in the place or places we have lived. Thus our place is an integral part of our identity. The fact

---

[8] Relph (1976, p. 48) distinguishes yet another basic element of this identity of place: the 'spirit of place', or *genius loci*. However, I fail to see how this differs from strongly established meanings.

that we have experienced a lot in our places means that we attach ourselves emotionally into them. What we are is for a large part the result of our past experiences;[9] our identity is tied into them. People and events, feelings and emotions of the past experiences originate an emotional bond with the places where they took place. The most important feature of place that can be singled out as promoting identification with it is, that place and its people are part of each other. Thus social relations as an extremely important part of the experience of place play a big role in how they are lived.

Personal and socio-cultural identities meet in place identity (Buttimer, 1980, p. 167). We are what we are largely because of where we are from. But place identity is not only a result of our socio-cultural heritage and the consequent personal development being located and situated in a certain place. The attachment derives from the feeling that the place is a part of us and we are a part of that place. Our place identity embraces the meaning of the place(s) to us. In the case of very strong place identity, the feeling of oneness with the place can even have spiritual aspects that are impossible to explain analytically; it is a sphere of human experience that is only approachable by the experience. That we identify with places is evident when we are homesick. Ley (1979, p. 228) writes how a person removed from his own place has an 'uncertain identity'. We only have to visit a home of migrants to see that the place where they came from is indeed a big part of their identity (Kallio, 1994). This kind of portrayal of place identity is however, problematic in today's mobile societies (Relph, 2000, p. 619). However, while I acknowledge the 'homelessness' or 'placelessness' of many people, I concentrate on the people who clearly identify with their place.

Our identity is *not* something that is defined when we are young and then crystallises into a stagnant form. Whether we have lived in one place for a long time or not, the places we have lived in nevertheless leave their marks on our identity. The identity thus evolves in the course of our life, and the impact any single place makes to it depends on the intensity of our involvement with the place. In travel, the places that have made an impact on our identity form the experiential background from which we apprehend new experiences in new places. If we have a strong place identity with a particular place (home), it becomes the measure against which the new

---

[9] This is again a statement that arouses controversy. The relative importance of our genetic and socio-cultural heritage (nature versus culture) was the topic of debate in cultural anthropology of the first decades of this century already.

places are compared. However, if the intensity of our involvement with these new places is strong enough, they will also contribute at least a little to our identity. This is one of the ideas I am going to deal with later in the work.

3 Travel Research and Humanistic Geography

Humanistic Geography and Travel

The analysis of the experience of an unfamiliar place is a way to do the connection between humanistic geography and qualitative travel studies. The concepts of existential space and place as discussed above, point in the direction of contrasting the experience of a new place to the experience of home. The nature of the experience of everyday has its implications in the experience of travel.

According to Minca (2000, p. 389), travel is above all a spatial phenomenon. As such the pivotal issue is the change of place. The resulting interplay between home and away is naturally most striking and obvious when the home place is experienced as something deeply familiar in contrast to the totally alien 'away'. Tourism is thus a suitable forum to study this interplay. Of course, many people travel to places to which they have been before, but I leave this kind of travel outside the scope of this thesis. Another thing is that nowadays hardly any place is completely alien any more; there is little chance of not knowing at least something about destinations in advance. Few destinations are so totally alien that we would not have formed a some kind of impression of them in advance already. We have done this on the basis of whatever kind of information we may have received about them. Nevertheless, from commonly shared experiences tourism comes closest to an extreme variation in the degree of homeness and 'awayness' over a short time period. One could study migration, but I want to analyse the experience of being away from the perspective that one is destined to come back. The need to experience more while still safely anchored to the home place reflects the dual character of the (home) place as being the actualisation of both the constraints and possibilities of life. Thus it can be a battleground of the feelings of security and imprisonment.

Life-world and Natural Attitude

The experience of everyday life is the background against which the decision to travel and the eventual travel experience must be compared. The experience of everyday life takes place in our everyday environments and situations. In phenomenology this everyday life realm is called life-world (lebenswelt). It is the world of our direct and immediate everyday experiences, our physical and social environment. Our life-world is largely shared; it is intersubjective. It is filled with meanings and functions that make sense not only for us but also for the others who belong to the same socio-cultural group. Thus it is a social reality (Luckmann and Schutz, 1973, p. 243). During socialisation we become familiar with its features and internalise its meaning-contexts. Because of internalisation it becomes our world; it is our uniquely personal construct, while it still mostly has meanings and functions shared by others. The strictly personal elements of it are based on our personal histories, experiences and knowledge, which nevertheless have most of their origins in the intersubjective sphere of living in a social world.

We tend to take our life-world for granted. It is our daily world without any scientific interpretations, our world as we live it (e.g. Gurwitch, 1970, p. 35; Luckmann and Schutz, 1973, p. 3; Entrikin, 1976, p. 620). As such it is the object of phenomenological study that attempts to understand our experiences that are grounded in the prescientific contexts of our daily world. Our life in our everyday life-world is thus characterised by what in phenomenology is called *natural attitude*. It is an attitude in the sense that it characterises our everyday living. It is natural because we have inherited it in our socialisation and therefore it naturally becomes the way of apprehension of our everyday life. We usually live our everyday lives without deeply reflecting on its constituents; we naturally assume that what we see is what is there and that everyone else sees the same as we do. We take things and experiences for granted (Phillipson, 1972, p. 127; Luckmann and Schutz, 1973, p. 3; Duncan, 1978, p. 270; Bullington and Karlsson, 1984, p. 52). Natural attitude is thus a mode of our consciousness that enables us to act in the familiar environment without having to carefully reflect on everything.

This applies primarily in the everyday-life situations in which our interest in new experiences and knowledge is largely pragmatic; we learn 'the "relevant" elements and aspects of the world only insofar as it is necessary to master the situation' (Luckmann and Schutz, 1973, p. 139). We do not want to make practical things belonging to our everyday lives unnecessarily complex. For example, if we need to do something with a computer, we want to know what to do to perform the task, not how the computer works. The things we do are characterised by familiarity, and unless there is a deviation from the usual, we do not reflect on them. Only if something unexpected happens, may we be forced to reflect on things and see them with 'new eyes'. We may, for example, realise one morning that a building in a certain place has been demolished, but find it impossible to recall what it looked like. The building had been an unreflected aspect of our familiar environment that we only noticed it after it wasn't there any more. This implies a character of natural attitude; the state of affairs is unproblematic 'until further notice' (Luckmann and Schutz, 1973, p. 4). In the example, the disappearance of the building was a 'further notice' that forced us to bring something taken for granted into question.

Speaking in existentialist terms, the things encountered in our daily lives belong to familiar reference complexes, within which things make sense and exist without our reflection on them. Heidegger uses the example of the hammer and how it is naturally understood in the context of hammering (e.g. Pickles, 1985, p. 160; Karjalainen, 1986a, p. 90). The hammer makes sense as a piece of equipment in the act of hammering, more than as an object of its own right. Its 'hammer-ness' is most naturally met when we use it in hammering. When hammering, we do not pay attention to its superficial qualities like colour or material, the most relevant aspect of it is how good it is in serving the end of hammering. The hammer is 'ready-to-hand' (zuhanden); it is apprehended through its use. When things are ready-to-hand they are so familiar to us that reflection on them is unnecessary in the context of performing the acts we are supposed to carry out in our everyday lives. Ready-to-handness of things is the realm of natural attitude. Instead, if we gaze observantly at the hammer we detach it from the reference complex in which it receives its ready-to-hand character. It is no longer something we use quite unconsciously in order to accomplish a task of hammering. It's taken for granted nature has got a 'further notice'; it becomes an object. Now we apprehend the hammer from outside, it becomes 'present-at-hand' (vorhanden). 'The "use of the hammer" turns into the "look at the hammer"' (Karjalainen, 1991, p. 13).

Karjalainen (1986b) shows that the context pair of insideness and outsideness is closely connected to the notions of ready-to-hand and present-at-hand. Readiness-to-hand appears as the deep familiarity associated with everyday life. We can apprehend things without reflecting carefully on them every time. When aspects of the world are ready-to-hand, they are often lived intimately; we are insiders in relation to them. If the aspects of the world are present-at-hand, we see things as if from a distance, we are outsiders. In the case of a landscape, the local inhabitants apprehend it as something ready-to-hand; it is very familiar and may consequently act merely as a background to the daily tasks they are performing. For the outsiders the landscape is primarily the object of gaze, something that is consciously looked at. Thus for the local insider the place and the landscape appear as ready-to-hand whereas the visitor, an outsider, encounters them at least initially as something present-at-hand. This does not mean that the local people could not, when the daily routines do not prevent them, gaze at the landscape and detach themselves from its readiness-to-hand to experience its beauty or hideousness. In other words, we are able to detach ourselves from the natural attitude that normally is our everyday mode of being when we go about our daily tasks. It can be done in our familiar environment by consciously reflecting on the things we see, rather than just accepting them in the usual way. This necessarily happens when a change in the familiar draws our attention to itself, or when we go into another, altogether unfamiliar place.

The natural attitude of readiness-to-hand and the need for paying attention when something becomes present-at-hand is an interesting dialectic that takes place in travelling. Much of our travel experience can be understood from this perspective. The following discussion introduces some of the ideas that implicitly include the dialectic of ready-to-hand and present-at-hand.

Home and Reach

Travel is primarily an attempt to extend the external bounds of our existence without sacrificing the possibilities actualised at our home place. We balance between our desire to feel secure and our desire to reach out to the world. This leads us to an important pair of concepts, namely 'rest' and 'movement' (Seamon, 1979) or 'home' and 'reach' (Buttimer, 1980).

'Rest' is associated with the familiar order present at home; it is the familiar life-world with its conventions that derive from the past, a feeling of being at home (Seamon, 1979, p. 132). Movement links with horizon, reach and unfamiliarity, it helps us to assimilate places and situations into our familiar world (Ibid., p. 133). Seamon studies our relation to the world from the perspective of how conscious of our environment we are. In the more unconscious end of the continuum there is 'obliviousness' which means that 'the experiencer's conscious attention is not in touch with the world outside but directed inwardly' (Ibid., p. 104). A more conscious mode is 'watching'; we look 'attentively upon some aspect of the world for an extended period of time' (Ibid., p. 105). Both of these modes are still habitual, and characterised by natural attitude; the environment at large is not seen as new but as ready-to-hand. As contrast, the modes of 'noticing' and 'heightened contact' open up new insights. On those modes we are conscious of our environment. When we notice something 'a thing from which we were insulated a moment before flashes to our attention' (Ibid., p. 108). This is exactly what happens when something in our familiar everyday environment changes so that we suddenly pay attention to it. Our usual natural attitude becomes disturbed by the change and we are forced to consciously reflect on things. Seamon's 'heightened contact' approaches a spiritual experience in which 'the person feels a serenity of mood and vividness of presence; his awareness of himself is heightened, and at the same time, the external world seems more real' (Ibid., p. 111). These are the rare moments of vision and insight (see also Relph, 1981a, p. 178) we sometimes momentarily experience. These latter modes of consciousness about our environment are opposed to our everyday natural attitude mode. Using the terms of Heidegger, the environment is not ready-to-hand any more; it is experienced as present-at-hand instead. Thus 'rest' is characterised by a habitual way of experiencing the environment while 'movement' facilitates the creation of openness (Seamon, 1979, p. 139).

Buttimer's (1980, p. 170) 'home' and 'reach' express a very similar idea. 'Home' is where we live, and 'reach' is the (physical or mental) movement outward from that home. Our life is dialectic of the two as in 'rest and movement, territory and range, security and adventure...'. If our centre of home and paths of reach in various aspects of existential space are not in harmony (we are, for example, forced to live away from our family and friends, in a place where we do not feel at ease), our sense of the very place is weak. In the opposite case the home place provides *the* centre for the various interests of our life. We could say that then the home place is *the* centre for our values. The life-style of a particular social group strongly reflects its values, and much of the identity of the place as they experience it arises from this life-style, thus creating 'our place'.

Schutz too uses similar terms to chart the spatial arrangement of our personal world. While the terms used are primarily physical, they readily apply also in other aspects of existential space. Schutz divides our world between the world within actual reach and the world within potential reach (Schutz and Luckmann, 1973, pp. 36-41). The world within the actual reach refers to 'here'; it is accessible to our immediate experience at the very moment. The world within potential reach subdivides into two different parts: restorable reach and attainable reach. Restorable reach implies the part of our world that has previously been within our actual reach, i.e., the places of which we have first hand experience. Temporally such reach thus refers to both past and future; the immediate contact has been there, and can be restored. Attainable reach is the part of the world that can be brought within actual reach, so temporally it refers to the future. It belongs to the level of 'geography' in existential space. All these modes of reach are in a dialogue. To a large extent, the actual and restorable reach are together quite equivalent to our life-world in which we usually operate. Some part of it is usually transformed into actual reach by our bodily presence. When we go somewhere where we have never been before we establish new places of restorable reach and thus widen the area of our first hand involvement with the world.[1]

Ideally, there should be a balance between home and reach so that one of them does not start to dominate our life and thwart the need for the other. What the 'right' balance is naturally varies from person to person. Too much reach can mean rootlessness, loss of identity and security, whereas too much home gets simply boring.

Reach appears not only as a dramatic craving for distant and exotic countries, but also as more modest goals to provide opposites to everyday routines. Saturday night fever in a local disco is an example; it is an attempt to reach beyond the everyday relations with people to the new spheres of social interaction (the adventure of flirting and possible prospect of a 'one night stand'). Travel is thus just one expression of reach. Nevertheless, it is easy to see travel as materialisation of our need to balance our familiar home place with some less familiar experiences of different places.

The need for both home and reach constitute the tension in our home place: the tension between wanting to stay and the desire to escape (Relph, 1976, p. 42). In a way, the place gets the blame for not providing us with what we desire. Our intentions towards the familiar home place are associated with the tasks of our everyday life so that the place can take on the exaggerated character of being a prison of routine. Since it seldom appears as exciting or full of adventure it is easy to make it guilty of producing the overwhelming feeling of everydayness that may sometimes overcome us. So in our minds, to achieve variety equates to a 'change of scene'. We think that since this place is routine, a place away could offer something different.

> But the king too couldn't think of anything better than to live like that, and however one lives, whether in great style or in poverty, whether in Madrid, Barcelona or anywhere, in the end it's the same daily routine, and one gets bored with it. People who live anywhere, for example, imagine that

---

[1] For a different version of how these terms are applied see Rose, 1988.

Barcelona is a fine place, and the people of Barcelona want to travel Anywhere (Bichel, 1971, p. 22).

Space and time are the ultimate frames of our existence that define what we can do. We cannot do anything about time, 'it thrusts us forward from behind, blows us through the narrow funnel of the present into the future' (Sontag, cited in Robinson, 1987, p. 187). Only space as places is left to us to manipulate and so we change places in order to achieve the experience of variety that we desire. Later we will notice that this movement in space can also be used to facilitate a perceived change in time.

Travel to an alien place removes familiarity. As Tuan (1977, p. 146) writes: 'In a new setting they [tourists] are forced to see and think without the support of a whole world of known sights, sounds, and smells - largely unknowledged - that give weight to being'. Our natural attitude is no longer capable of handling the things that now surround us, and which may be beyond what we have experienced before. What was ready-to-hand at home is now present-at-hand; suddenly the everydayness we were so fed up with has at least temporarily gone. Presence-at-hand here indicates that the things are there as objects that we may contemplate, but whose meanings in their original local context (that is, meaningful to the local people) we cannot grasp. We can and we do attribute different qualities to them, but in a 'wrong' way; the qualities we give are not compatible with the totality of equipment to which those things in their original local context belong. We ourselves create these contexts, but since we do this on the basis of our own background, the result may be totally alien to the original local context as perceived by the local people. This is even more likely when we remember Schutz's idea that new elements we encounter are incorporated into our existing knowledge base with the least possible effort (Schutz and Luckmann, 1973, p. 139). We may have managed to create contexts for the things we encounter that gradually make them become familiar, ready-to-hand, for us, but this readiness-to-hand seldom derives from the original contexts of those things. Instead it is often incorporated in what Bruner (1991) has called the '*tourist discourse*', the way of seeing things in the framework of tourism.

Tourist Discourse and the Other

The tourist discourse is the whole of both individually and socially constructed ideas and practices of (and relating to) tourism; it contains the ideas of how to be a tourist. As a discourse, the tourist discourse is in a continuous process; the ideas and practices of each individual tourist contribute to it. Because tourism largely works in the framework created by the international travel industry, also the tourist discourse is greatly affected by this industry. This is evident in travel advertising in which the basic tenets of the tourist discourse are expressed. However, as any discourse, it also has its established conventions which change slowly, and which have strong impact on every single experience that takes place within the discourse. In other words, these established conventions, if not determine, at least direct the ways in which the individual experiences of tourists form. In this way tourist discourse is a form of cultural production. It places its actors, tourists, operators and locals (the Others) in their clearly defined roles. It constitutes the culture of tourism and hence 'sets the frame of (...) tourism, at least for the tourists, and provides the lens through which the entire experience will be viewed' (Bruner, 1991, p. 240). The tourist discourse is one form of *xenology*,[2] 'the conventional ideological structure placed as a frame on all experience of the other' (Harkin, 1995, p. 651). It originates from our Western culture that imposes itself on the Other through the practices, meanings and values of the very discourse. 'It can be seen as much as a structure of power as it is a structure of meaning' (Bruner, 1991, p. 240).

Speaking of the tourist discourse does not mean that there is only one discourse of tourism, however. There are many different tourist discourses, for different types of tourism. The discourse of a resort holiday trip differs from the one of an Interrail trip, for example. All discourses of tourism nevertheless share the idea of providing a framework within which the Other can be related to the tourist's own stock of knowledge.

In tourism the distance and difference (spatial, socio-cultural, ontological, and experiential) between home and the Other is what appeals to potential tourists. Otherwise they would prefer spending their holidays at home. The distance highlights the difference between readiness-to-hand at home and the presence-at-hand in the Other. Naturally the use of the term Other is most appropriate, when we discuss travel to third world countries, or to countries where culture is very different from our own. The Other is the domain in which we can find the presence-at-hand we are after. The contrast between home and the Other is made clearly visible in the tourist discourse, which, according to Duncan (1993, p. 46), still has traits from the nineteenth century discourse of the Other. He distinguishes two such

---

[2] Xenos (Gk) = strange(r); logos (Gk) = reason, discourse, word (The Oxford Handy Dictionary, 1991).

traits: Firstly, the Other is located in the past. Often this implicitly involves the perception that this is also the case in terms of human evolutionary development (i.e. the societies - maybe even the people - of the Other are less developed than our Western societies). Secondly, it is characterised by exoticism. In relation to the former the tourist discourse tells us to travel to experience ancient lifestyles of peoples who still live as they have through past centuries. In relation to the latter it presents places as unspoiled paradises with exotic peoples and their quaint customs. If we do not have first hand experiences of the Other, or if our experiences of it are shallow, it is easy to attribute whatever characteristics we like to the Other. The existing tourist discourse is an important source of those characteristics.

In travel the relations between people, others and us, are particularly unclear, because what is perceived may differ drastically from what the others perceive in similar circumstances. Experiences in an unfamiliar place get this new dimension; the new place challenges our senses to open up to things to which we did not usually need to pay attention at home. Things that were the most ordinary at home, like walking on the street or having something to eat, become an adventure where we have to come to terms with things that we may not have been in contact with before. We have more distance between the things that aren't ready-to-hand any more and us. We become temporary outsiders for whom it is a relief to be able to just look at everything without having to be involved. As outsiders we can marvel at things without having the burden of being concerned with all the possible responsibilities that involvement could bring with it. For example, we might find it interesting to walk through the meat market in Bali and see all the meat and flies in the heat of the sun, but we would not buy our meat from such a place.

This is a lure of reach: to be able to temporarily switch the readiness-to-hand of home into the presence-at-hand of reach. Instead of familiarity there is an adventure of negotiating in unfamiliar circumstances. But there is also the other side of the coin; while new places provide elements that satisfy our need for reach, they also take away the security provided by home. In an alien place we are vulnerable to crime and all sorts of menaces resulting from the fact that we may not know how to act properly. Home and reach thus complement and suggest each other as safety and adventure, rest and movement (Seamon, 1979, p. 136). Lutwak (1984, p. 59) has noted than in literature:

> a new place means new adventures, new people for the hero to encounter, new objects to handle, new ideas to contemplate. Free movement opens up

the world with a variety of interests, whereas restriction to a single place is more consonant with tragedy and death.

Luckily our home place seldom gets that bad, but the analogy to everyday ruts remains.

To be able to carry out a particular act of reach, the assessment of what aspect(s) of home the reach is supposed to complement, and consequently, what kind of reach is desired, is needed. Most of the time this is by no means a conscious process, but in any case, the existing existential space is very important in guiding this assessment process. This is because it contains the impressions of what kind of possibilities various centres and domains may offer in the sense of accommodating the particular expectations of the reach. It is an indication of the strength of the spatial dimension of our existence that the assessment often leads to the conclusion that it is our place that is responsible for the need for reach. Of course this is also an indication of the important meaning of place. The reason for the need to reach derives from our place; leaving is meaningful only because something else, the Other, is contrasted with this place (Heikkinen, 1993, p. 14). Whether reach is sought through new relationships in a night-club, stretching our mental horizons by doing meditation, or travelling to a new place, most means of reach are socially formed. Many are even institutionalised to the point that there is a large industry providing services that facilitate reach. In other words, the need to reach is utilised to make profits. This creates a paradox; while reaching becomes more available, it simultaneously loses some of the elements that constitute reach.

Our experience of our life-world, home, is characterised by natural attitude in which everything is normally encountered as ready-to-hand. The familiarity of home and the craving for change is the impulse to reach for something else at least temporarily. Travel is a path we take to reach for new experiences. We want to experience something new, the Other, that is present-at-hand to us and thus stimulates our consciousness by making us marvel about things. Travel is a response to this craving for the openness of reach to contrast the habitual home. The travel industry has an important role in providing the framework for that reach. While it provides possibilities to reach spatially further than ever, it also institutionalises that reach and thus directs it. It becomes reach that is satisfied within the framework created by the conventions of the tourist discourse. Once again, the humanistic concepts meet the post-structural ones. The reach desired is channelled through the discourse of tourism with its own structures of politics and power. Based on these ideas, tourism in this work is considered as reach.

4 Qualitative Traditions in Travel Research

Three Traditions in Qualitative Tourism Studies

Qualitative tourism studies started initially as cultural critique against the perceived superficiality of the tourism experience. One of the best-known example of such critical writing is Daniel Boorstin's book 'The Image; A Guide to Pseudo Events in America' (1972; orig. 1961) in which he dedicated a chapter to the subject. His aim was clearly to show how spurious those experiences were. Even the title of the chapter: 'From Traveler to Tourist: The Lost Art of Travel' suggests his view that tourism is not to be compared with the glorious travels of the past. According to him, tourists are wrapped inside the touristic infrastructure and thus separated from their destination. He also claims that tourists actually want to see features that *confirm their expectations.*

Boorstin's central idea is that for the tourists the reproduced or staged is better than the 'real thing' because it is easier to grasp and it makes sense as a sight; it does not have to be understood in any other but the tourist's own familiar terms. In Boorstin's framework what is reached for in tourism is the confirmation of beliefs and images of the Other, and most importantly, the supplementation of those images with experiential first hand involvement that gives weight to them.

Boorstin's approach has been blamed for underestimating travellers and for suggesting that all travellers actually want spurious experiences instead of the authentic ones. For example MacCannell (1976, p. 104) states that: 'None of the accounts in my collection support Boorstin's contention that tourists want superficial, contrived experiences'. Also Jokinen and Veijola (1990, p. 150, my translation from Finnish) comment on Boorstin: 'Boorstin's perspective was by no means the one of a scientist's, but a very common prejudice against modern tourism, in which scientific analysis was replaced by the rhetoric of moral superiority'. It does indeed seem that Boorstin's writings weren't even meant to be scientifically based analyses of clearly defined phenomena, but rather expressed his own critical perspectives on the ever-increasing pretentiousness of modern life in general. Despite its largely anecdotal nature the chapter contains valuable insights and has been regularly cited ever since in academic writings on tourists' experience. Many later writers have given some of the issues Boorstin raised (often without conscious reference to Boorstin) a conceptual framework and developed them further (environmental bubble by Cohen, 1972; semiotics of attraction by MacCannell, 1976; placelessness by Relph, 1976; encapsulation by Weightman, 1987; tourist discourse by Bruner, 1991).

Another major work from a different point of view is Dean MacCannell's 'The Tourist; A New Theory of the Leisure Class' (1976). Like Boorstin, MacCannell too wrote about tourists in general, without paying much attention to actually defining them more specifically. However, while Boorstin stated that tourists want superficial experiences, MacCannell saw them as seeking for authenticity. The importance of this search to the tourists is a result of alienation from one's society and the assumption that travelling brings one closer to authenticity. 'For moderns, reality and authenticity are thought to be elsewhere: in other historical periods and other cultures, in purer, simpler lifestyles' (MacCannell, 1976, p. 3). In other words, the Other is invested with the ideals we would like to encounter in it. According to MacCannell, tourists are after some kind of connection with the authenticity they perceive is lacking in their own society and life.

For MacCannell much of this perceived lack of authenticity and the resulting alienation from society is a product of advanced differentiation found in today's societies. The alienation for MacCannell is based on a similar view to that of Marx. There is no more connection between workers and the product their work produces. People are separated from the immediate first hand feeling of being directly involved with society through their work. This may also take the form of a feeling that our life is guided from the outside, and we have too little say in it. It seems impossible to be in control of much that affects on our lives. People find it hard to get first-hand experiences of life and they have to rely on vicarious experiences. Travel becomes a way to overcome this by allowing one to reconstruct the differentiations into a whole. 'Modernization (...) brings the people liberated from traditional attachments into the modern world where, as tourists, they may attempt to discover or reconstruct a cultural heritage or a social identity' (MacCannell, 1976, p. 13). But MacCannell argues that for tourists this can only be an attempt; they are bound to be separated from the 'authentic' meanings of the things they encounter. Furthermore, they cannot escape the fact that the differentiation in our society is an integral part of the way it works.

I agree that travel may provide some kind of coherence to our existential space. In travel we may not be able to overcome the differentiations of society, but the context of travel provides a coherent framework for everything we encounter. While the structures of travel pay tribute to the differentiations (unique, quaint, exceptional), these differentiations also become meaningful parts of a whole through these very structures. This happens as the structures of travel allow us to see all the differences tied together into a meaningful string of experiences. Tourist experience reveals that no matter how quaint things seem, they still make sense. We separate things from their original contexts; they are just on display for us, tourists. This is greatly helped by the travel industry, which encourages and effects the separation by often presenting the Other as displays and performances. There is no need to understand the things in their own terms any more, the fact that they are on display itself explains that they are significant, and for tourists they make sense as sights, not as what they originally were. Now they are ready-to-hand as items of a display, although the travel industry attempts to present these items as present-at-hand.

So in fact, MacCannell's views about how much a tourist can understand about what he sees aren't very different from Boorstin's. Boorstin (1972, p. 102), too, suggests that what the tourist sees 'is seldom the living culture, but usually specimens collected and embalmed especially for him, or attractions specially staged for him'. The main difference between Boorstin and MacCannell still remains their disagreement on the tourists' desire to look for authenticity. The quest for authenticity is also the reason for what MacCannell (1976, p. 10) calls touristic critique of tourism:

> The touristic critique of tourism is based on a desire to go beyond the other 'mere' tourists to a more profound appreciation of society and culture... *All* tourists desire this deeper involvement with society and culture to some degree; it is a basic component of their motivation to travel (emphasis added).

There is no agreement on MacCannell's views. For example, Bruner (1991, p. 240) states:

> The data gathered for this paper suggest the contrary [to MacCannell], that most tourists are quite satisfied with their own society, most are not alienated, and they are not necessarily seeking an authentic experience elsewhere.

This view seems to be more accordant with what Boorstin wrote. The arm wrestling about whether or not tourists search for authenticity seems rather pointless; some probably do seek it, others do not care.

Cohen (1988a, p. 38) finds further complaints about the incompleteness of MacCannell's view:

> ...MacCannell's approach necessarily leaves unexplained an essential aspect of behaviour in touristic situations: the suspension of everyday obligations, the freedom enjoyed by tourists, and their licence for permissive and playful 'non-serious' behaviour in the Far Place.

The 'Turnerian' perspective approaches tourism from exactly this direction. It is based on the analogy between initiation rituals and travel. The original contexts were formulated already in Arnold van Gennep's study 'The Rites of Passage' (orig. 1908) about the structure of initiatory rituals. Anthropologist Victor Turner later used those concepts in studying anti-structure in rituals (1974, orig. 1969) and pilgrimage (Turner, 1973; Turner and Turner 1978). The most important concept is liminality, which is a stage in the general structure of initiative rituals, rites of passage. Cohen (1988a, p. 37) describes Turner's approach to ritual:

> 1) Separation: both spatial and social. The individual is taken to an unfamiliar place, peripheral to his original place of abode, and separated from his ordinary social group.
> 2) Liminality: Through the separation, the individual has crossed the threshold (Latin *limen*) of his ordered world, and finds himself in a state of 'anti-structure', 'out of time and place', where his ordinary role and status obligations are suspended and where general human (rather than particular social) bonds are emphasized.
> 3) Reintegration: The individual is reintegrated into his ordinary social group usually in new roles and at a higher social status.

Liminality in a ritual is thus anti-structure to the normal everyday state of affairs. It is 'an interval between two distinct periods of intensive involvement in structured social existence' (Turner, 1973, p. 199). It 'represents a negation of many of the features of preliminary social structures, and an affirmation of another order of things, stressing generic rather than particularistic relationships' (Ibid., p. 214). It is the anti-structure for the everyday. In travel this facilitates the removal of restraints of the responsibilities and roles one may have at home. Travel becomes a play in which we can act out new roles. Thus a pizza-delivery man can act like the owner of the world, and a shy housewife transforms into a seductive manhunter. Of course, such play may not always go to such extremes; the anti-structure of travel is utilised just by sleeping late and in not having to do any work.

The persons who share the common state of liminality may also have a feeling that Turner called 'communitas' (Ibid., p. 192). It is a feeling of common consciousness, even brotherhood that draws from being in the same situation and sharing its experiences, whether strange, uplifting, scary or interesting. In the tourism context this, of course, depends a lot on the nature of the trip. If there are strong ties already in the group that travels, the feeling of communitas may become stronger. Organisations and groups often organise an excursion ta achieve this. However, Jokinen and Veijola (1990, p. 120) refer to the tendency towards the opposite: While travelling, we live a holiday version of our normal suburban life. There is no attempt to seek any kind of communitas, neither anti-structure. This again illustrates the fact that not all tourists are similar; one seeks for the possibility to act out a role, another wants to have feeling of togetherness, yet another is happy just to sleep late and enjoy the afternoon sun. Not to mention that some people do all this on a same trip.

In its original meaning the term liminality it is strictly connected with the rites of passage. 'When liminality is applied to cultural phenomena of leisure in industrial or postindustrial societies, we must clearly realize that its use is metaphorical, carried over from its primary sphere to another' (Turner, 1978, pp. 286-287). Liminality was a natural part of initiative rituals in tribal and early agrarian societies. Thus experiencing it was an obligation for all the members of a society. In industrial and post-industrial societies these rituals are separated from the sphere of work and obligation and are thus more or less based on voluntary participation. Thus Turner and Turner prefer to use the term 'liminoid' in the context (Turner and Turner, 1978, p. 231). The transformation from compulsory rituals involving liminal stages to voluntary rituals with liminoid ones has happened simultaneously with the change from tribal communities into the more complex and differentiated societies (Ibid., p. 280). 'Perhaps we could use "liminoid" for the modern symbolic inversions and expressions of disorder, and reserve "liminal" for the ritual, myth-telling contexts of less complex societies' (Turner, 1978, p. 287). So there is a distinction 'between liminal situations which are obligatory and typically appear in a religious context, and liminoid situations, which are optative, and hence characteristic of modern secular contexts, such as leisure' (Cohen, 1988a, p. 38).

Turner saw pilgrimage in complex societies as a successor of the initiation rites of tribal ones. He wrote, 'there is a *rite de passage*, even an initiatory ritual character about pilgrimage' (Turner, 1973, p. 204). The difference between pilgrimage and tribal initiation rites is pilgrimage's non-obligatory nature that transforms its liminality into liminoidity. Sometimes pilgrimage can have quite playful aspects as markets, bazaars, and fairs may operate close to the shrines (Ibid., p. 205).[1] Also the trip itself may contain several different intentions, of which the pilgrimage is just one. Thus in pilgrimage some elements of tourism are often present. Since pilgrimage is a voluntary social phenomenon, it is rather 'liminoid' than 'liminal' in van Gennep's full sense (Turner and Turner, 1978, p. 35).

Pilgrimage has some of the attributes of liminality in passage rituals: there is a separation from the familiar place, a liminal stage away from it, and finally reintegration, returning from a far place, ideally changed or enlightened, to the familiar place (Turner, 1973, p. 213). But while pilgrimage has lots of common features with passage rituals, some of them are also common with tourism, like release from mundane structure and homogenization of status (Turner and Turner, 1978, p. 34). Naturally also the pattern of leaving the familiar place behind and going away to a far place and coming back to the familiar place is exactly the same as in tourism.

Like the pilgrim the tourist moves from a familiar place to a far place and then returns to the familiar place. At the far place both the pilgrim and the tourist engage in 'worship' of shrines which are sacred, albeit in different ways, and as a result gain some kind of uplifting experience (Urry, 1990, p. 100).

Also the feeling of 'communitas' among the travellers has been considered an important common feature between pilgrimage and some types of tourism (Turner and Turner, 1978, p. 34). However, the coherence of comparison between pilgrims and tourists has been questioned on the grounds that the framework from which they see the place can be completely different (Eade, 1992, p. 32; Cohen, 1992, p. 49). 'At Varanasi, the pilgrim perceives the city as one of the most beautiful in India, while the tourist considers it one of the dirtiest' (Smith, 1992, p. 12). There can indeed be a fundamental difference between what the destination represents to pilgrims and tourists, but not necessarily. For pilgrims the place as a whole can be quite incidental, they are primarily interested to be involved

---

[1] Already in 'The Canterbury Tales' the pilgrims entertain themselves by telling stories which are not likely to be revered for their piety.

with shrines that commemorate important events or are otherwise important in their faith. The location is important, not the place *per se*. While tourists are often interested in seeing a particular place, there are many to whom places are equally incidental from the point of view of the purpose of the trip as they are to pilgrims. A holiday week in a sunny beach resort can be anywhere as long as the requirement of sun and sea are met. There can be a lot of diversity in the ways different tourists see the same places because of their different frameworks. Thus the difference of seeing the place from a different framework appears not only between pilgrims and tourists. Both pilgrimage and tourism can be seen as reach for the Other. The former seeks it primarily within the spiritual dimension, the latter within other dimensions. Both ways of travel provide anti-structure for our everyday living; whether we travel to seek spiritual enlightment or to indulge ourselves into immoral vices, it differs from our everyday.

In Turner's approach pilgrimage in many features bears resemblance to tourism. It does not need much modification to apply Turner's description of the central idea of pilgrimage to tourism in general. 'The point of it all is to get out, go forth, to a far holy place approved by all' (Turner and Turner, 1978, p. 7). If the word 'holy' is removed, what else is there but the idea of a tourist trip? Even Turner (1973, p. 196) himself indicates that many visitors to shrines 'should perhaps be considered as tourists rather than pilgrims *per se*'. Not to mention that countless shrines are tourist attractions themselves. The central idea of this Turnerian tradition in qualitative tourism studies is that travel is a liminoid period between leaving home and returning there. It is anti-structure for our everyday living. It is notable that although Turner himself did not study tourism particularly, he still happened to formulate a theoretical background for an important tradition in tourism studies.

As both Boorstin's and MacCannell's tourists leave a familiar place, go to a far place, and come back to the familiar place, the Turnerian tourists do the same. Furthermore, in a far place they encounter great sights that have important meanings, just as MacCannell's tourist does. The difference lies in the idea that travel is anti-structure, it is a liminoid period between leaving home and returning when the usual everyday norms of behaviour can be abolished. Unlike MacCannell's approach, this explains the playful aspects of a tourist trip. Travel is free time and voluntarily obtained anti-structure that temporarily 'relieves' from rigid obligations of seriousness and decency of everyday working life. The playful activities at a far place can be seen as 'compensatory' (Cohen, 1988a, p. 39), anti-routine, thus giving a general framework for understanding what tourists do. Travel as anti-structure also enables us to use it in seeking enlightenment and experiences that the everyday life (perceivedly) cannot offer. Whether we search for authenticity or fun, in any case we have a 'legitimate' possibility to satisfy our need for reach by straying from the norms of the life at home.

Some Turnerian Offspring

One example of Turnerian approach in which the idea of compensating everyday with anti-structure is clearly present is Gottlieb's study of 'Americans' Vacations' (1982). She roughly divides travellers so that they either want to be 'peasant for a day' or 'king for a day' (Gottlieb, 1982, p. 173). She suggests that upper middle class travellers want to experience something that they do not experience at home, thus playing at being a peasant for a day. Similarly, lower middle class and working class vacationers play being king for a day. Hence by travelling people want to experience temporarily what they do not experience in their everyday life. In those cases travelling is anti-structure in which the reversal of the world occurs and thus it is a liminoid period breaking the everyday existence. By no means does Gottlieb mean that the strict division exists that sharply in reality. She writes that 'the division of travellers into two polar types, as suggested in this essay, is merely heuristic' (Ibid., p. 178). The obvious problem with Gottlieb's division is that it adds little to our understanding of travellers who do not change their behaviour while on travel.

Graburn (1983, p. 12) distinguished two categories of tourism: first the '*modal*' category, i.e. cyclical, recreational tourism and secondly, '*rites-of-passage*', i.e. travel that occurs with the changes in life situation. In *modal* tourism travel is anti-structure for the sake of it. It is sought because of the recreational effects that temporary reversal or modification of roles can offer. It can be said to be liminoid only because it facilitates anti-structure between periods of normal everyday life. In *rites-of-passage* tourism travel comes closer to van Gennep's original meaning of liminality. Just as in rites-of-passage, travel is a liminal stage that separates two different stages of life, two different social statuses. A young person travelling after finishing studies is a typical example.

In Murray's study about the role of travelling in personal change 'Life as fiction; the Making Sense of Personal Change' (1990, pp. 124-132) '*vision quest*' and '*pilgrimage*' derive from Turnerian tradition. 'Vision quest' for Murray is a way of travelling in which travellers seek to encounter 'events with special meaning' for their personal life (Murray, 1990, p. 127).

The name 'vision quest' comes from a rite of passage of Thomson Indians, who sent their pre-pubescent male adolescents alone to the wilderness to get a vision that is supposed to give direction into their lives. Similarly, modern travellers who travel at the stage of their life when their status in their home society is changing (e.g. after finishing studies, having ended a long relationship), are at a liminal stage while away from home, and may obtain a direction for their life. Thus this type of travel closely resembles the rite of passage of Turnerian tradition. The element of reach is strongly present, often as an attempt to explore one's physiological and psychological limits.

Murray's 'pilgrimage' can be seen as another straight derivative from Turner's studies. Murray (1990, p. 129) arrives at the conclusion that much of the modern tourism is successor to pilgrimages because the structural similarity of each, namely that pilgrims as well as tourists are 'escaping from the hierarchical forms of normal life'. Also both are making a journey to a sight, looking at objects, and interpreting them as traces of glorious days of the past. The main difference between Murray's 'vision quest' and 'pilgrimage' is that the latter as primarily anti-structure, usually contains few elements that would give a direction to the life of a traveller.[2] The obvious motivation to the kind of travel is mostly a need for recreation, not necessarily any quest for meaning, as it often is in the former case. The traveller reaches for the anti-structure for the sake of it.

None of the traditions introduced here alone are sufficient to understand tourism. Each of them is useful in understanding some tourist experiences, but each also omits significant aspects of tourism. According to Boorstin, everyone wants fabricated reality. MacCannell says the opposite. Turnerian tourists want whatever is opposite to everyday. What if someone's travel is just a holiday version of everyday life? The problem would not exist if the traditions did not try to extend their claims over all tourists.

Integrating the Traditions

Instead of treating tourists as a homogeneous group, Cohen (1972) proposes a classification that addresses the differences in tourists. He divides travellers into four different groups according to the extent to which they require and seek familiarity. He explains that:

---

[2] Here Murray's 'pilgrimage' must not be confused with pilgrimage as such. The latter can indeed be a strong source of direction for life.

> many of today's tourists are able to enjoy the experience of change and
> novelty only from a strong base of familiarity, which enables them to feel
> secure enough to enjoy the strangeness of what they experience (Cohen,
> 1972, p. 166).

It is notable that he speaks about 'many tourists', not all of them, even
though what he writes obviously applies to the most of the contemporary
tourists. His classification allows for another kinds of tourism by dividing
tourists into two main groups: institutionalised and noninstitutionalised. The
former main group includes 'organized mass tourists' and 'individual mass
tourists', the latter 'explorers' and 'drifters'. The vast majority of tourists
belong into the first group; they are the ones that rely most on the travel
infrastructure created by the travel industry. Some of them are also the ones
that Boorstin (1972, p. 85) meant when he wrote that tourists expect
everything to be done to them and for them. Toward the drifter end of the
spectrum this reliance decreases, as also does the proportion of tourists
travelling that way. This division also reflects the different balance of home
and reach which each individual needs. Organised mass tourists are happy
when the home element is prevalent, whereas a drifter prefers a lot of reach.

Apart from the above typology, a further significant contribution is
Cohen's (1972) concept of 'environmental bubble'. The term is in fact, an
attempt to understand the role of the travel industry in mediating the
experience of tourists, the theme that was so important already for Boorstin.
Cohen sees the amount of familiarity in tourist's experience as an essential
characteristic of that experience, and this familiarity is achieved within the
environmental bubble. 'Often the modern tourist is not so much abandoning
his accustomed environment for a new one as he is being transposed to
foreign soil in an "environmental bubble" of his native culture' (Cohen,
1972, p. 166). The environmental bubble is thus the 'homelike'
infrastructure that more or less provides the physical frames for the tourist's
experience. The element of reach is apparently great because we can travel
far away, but in practice the travel industry provides us with means that
diminish it and create a substitute 'home'. The term environmental bubble
has later transformed into the concept of 'tourist space' (Cohen, 1979b, p.
20; Weightman, 1987, p. 231; Urbain, 1989, p. 110; Minca, 2000). Also this
term illustrates how tourists occupy a space that is in certain ways (e.g.
ontologically, culturally, conceptually) distinct from the space that the local
people inhabit. The idea has been developed further by Hottola (1999, pp.
111), who writes about metaworld into which the tourist escapes for the
confusion that the strangeness of the Other causes.

The role of the travel industry is especially central in forming the travel experience of institutionalised tourists. The tourists are converted into consumers who express themselves by purchasing a product (the travel package) that reflects their needs and intentions. It is the result of the need of travel industry to provide travel as commodity, as something that tourists buy and pay for. According to Cohen (1972, p. 170), this is achieved in two ways: by transforming the attractions and by standardising the facilities. The attractions are transformed into commodities and facilities are standardised according to agreed conventions. New attractions are also created. A trip is planned and sold as a package. The institutionalised tourists buy not only the travel ticket, but also the accommodation, at least some of the meals, and a pre-arranged programme like guided tours and performances. During their trip the tourists are enveloped with these elements provided by the travel industry that are separate from the 'reality' of the destination and that are already familiar to the tourists from home. This is how travel as a means of reach becomes institutionalised. 'The tourist comes home with the illusion that he has "been" there and can speak with some authority about the country he has visited' (Cohen, 1972, p. 174).

In 1979 Cohen wrote an article 'Rethinking the Sociology of Tourism' in which he altogether questioned the justification of considering tourists as one homogeneous group. Referring to the previous works of Boorstin and MacCannell he writes: 'It seems obvious by now that there is no point of search for "the tourist". Rather, there exist different types of tourists that are distinguishable by a wide variety of characteristics' (Cohen, 1979b, p. 21). He continues: 'Since tourism is evidently a multi-dimensional phenomenon, it would be senseless to search for *the* typology of tourists as it is senseless to talk about *the* typical tourist. However, this does not mean that for each empirical purpose at hand a special typology shouldn't be constructed...' (Ibid.). Cohen emphasises that different typologies are just conceptual tools to aid understanding, not 'real' divisions among travellers. I think we should concentrate our efforts in understanding some particular type of travel that does not even try to represent all tourists. These particular types are part of the whole scale of different tourists. If a typology is then desired, it is constructed in order to be able to relate the studied tourist type to other types of tourists.

Obviously influenced by the works of MacCannell and Turner, Cohen developed a new typology. MacCannell's generalizations apparently convinced Cohen that his own approach of not considering tourists as a homogeneous group was adequate and worth developing. In his article 'A

Phenomenology of Tourist Experiences' (1979a) he brought up a new classification that recognizes the relation between a person's experience of life and mode of travel. The Turnerian view of travel as anti-structure or as a rite is connected with Boorstin's and MacCannell's views so that the resulting classification gives room for a wide range of differing modes of travelling. In relation to MacCannell, his point is that 'Assuming (...) that not *all* moderns are equally alienated, one can hypothesize that they also will not seek authenticity with equal intensity' (Cohen, 1988a, p. 35). In the Turnerian tradition it is easy to get carried away with Boorstin's critical views by concentrating on the playful aspects of tourism and stressing how it is an inversion of everyday life. In relation to this Cohen reminds: 'not all tourists are "ludic"'[3] (Ibid., p. 40).

Cohen's (1979a) idea is to link the notions of authenticity and centre. It is not entirely clear how this linking is done, but it seems that the search for authenticity transforms into the search for centre, which perceivedly represents the authentic. Cohen uses the term ''spiritual' centre, whether religious or cultural, i.e. the centre which for the individual symbolizes ultimate meanings' (Cohen, 1979a, p. 181). These ultimate meanings are obviously supposed to be the fulfilment of authenticity. Spiritual centre is something we would like to identify with, and the possibility or impossibility of doing so may determine the meaningfulness of our lives. This idea is strikingly similar to Buttimer's notion of centredness, which is the measure of how well the different dimensions of a people's home and reach (i.e. spatial, social, spiritual, etc.) are harmonised with the place where they live. However, the terms have a slight difference in the sense that Buttimer's centredness requires a certain spatial location, whereas Cohen's spiritual centre does not. The sense of place is thus connected with one's values; the more strongly the place and values coincide, the better the place provides a centre for one's life interests. The ultimate values determining the centre can often be connected with the life-style of a particular social group living at a certain place. The very essence of the centre is therefore metaphorical rather than geographical, even though there may be a place or places where one's ultimate values are given a manifestation like for example Mecca and Jerusalem. It is more usual, however, that the spiritual centre is more like an idea of ideal way of life than a specific place. 'The centre, of course, symbolises an ideal. Ideals are not fully realizable, but can only be approached "asymptotically"' (Cohen, 1979a, p. 195). At the

---

[3] *Ludere* (L) = to play (Webster's New Collegiate Dictionary 1980).

metaphorical level the centre represents the ideas of how one (or the whole world) should live.

According to Cohen, tourists' mode of travel depends on whether their spiritual centre is inside or outside of their own society. On this basis Cohen (1979a) divides modes of travel into five groups; *recreational, diversionary, experiental, experimental* and *existential*. Although this typology of different tourists attempts to portray the wide variety of tourists, I think it still leaves many kinds of tourists outside its scope. It overestimates alienation in determining the mode of travel and makes travel appear as a serious business in which the meaning of life is at stake. According to Cohen's classification people who are not mass tourists are necessarily alienated from their societies. I find this very hard to believe. An additional problem in Cohen's classification is that each individual trip does not always reflect the innermost needs and aspirations of people. Even true seekers of alternative values may sometimes travel purely for fun to a destination they know won't offer them their spiritual centre. This is what Cohen does not mention clearly enough. Furthermore, 'one's purpose as a traveler varies from one locale to another' (Riley, 1988, p. 323). In Singapore we may happily engage in shopping and usual sightseeing and after a couple of days seek for a deeper cultural insight in a remote Sumatran village. Still another point is that the way we travel often changes during the course of our lives; from subsequent travels we may require different things than from our first ones. Thus typologies describe practices rather than types of people (Edensor, 2000, p. 322).

A productive source of tourist typologies is the travel industry that has realised the importance of recognising different marketing segments. The number of typologies constructed for this purpose is stupefying and their elaboration high (see e.g. Lowyck and van Langenhove and Bollaert, 1992; Heath and Wall 1992, pp. 92-102). Numerous different typologies are based on geography, socio-economic and demographic position, psychography (personality) and behaviour. Plog has summarised all these typologies in a new typology that consists of eight categories of tourists: venturesome, pleasure-seeking, impassive, self-confident, planful, masculine, intellectual and people oriented (Lowyck et al., 1992, p. 27). These typologies are to be applied in marketing research and they are based on largely quantitative criteria. As they are designed for marketing purposes, their usefulness for this work is so limited that I am not going to introduce them here in more detail.

Postmodern Travel Studies

While Cohen's typology provides interesting insights for some experiences of tourists, as a typology it is incomplete. In fact, in any typology there is always something that causes someone to see faults in it. The point is that we can exhaust ourselves in indulging in definitional exercises and taxonomy, but still come up with partial results (Berghe, 1994, p. 7). Thus I am not going to attempt a single interpretation of 'typical' tourist, nor a comprehensive typology of different tourists. However, in trying to understand a particular kind of tourist, it is useful to devise a typology to help locate that particular kind of tourist studied in the wider context of different kinds of travel. This clearly reflects the current hermeneutic and postmodern tendency to avoid metatheories. With historical hindsight we could say that Boorstin already saw the first symptoms of this tendency. He complained that the focus of writers had been changing from what he saw as important, into something he thought was less valuable: 'Travel books have increasingly become a record not of new information but of personal "reactions". From "Life in Italy", they become "The American in Italy"' (Boorstin, 1964, p. 116). This illustrates the epistemological shift from 'truths' to interpretations, from metanarratives to points of view.

Along with these changes in the way in which different theories about tourism are assessed, scholarly perspective on tourists has also changed. In the spirit of 'democratising' different discourses 'the rigid separations that modernism insisted upon between high and popular culture' are also relaxed (Shapiro, 1990, p. 1). A reflection of this in tourism studies is that generally the critical attitude towards the perceived spuriousness of mass tourism has made room for the acceptance of playful aspects of it. An anecdote describes that well:

> A guest to the hostess of cocktail party: 'I find the whole situation absurd, no one seems to realize the silliness, the grotesque artificiality of their behaviour.' 'Ah', said the hostess, 'you must join the sociologists in the far corner. The rest of us realized all that long ago but decided to ignore it and enjoy the party' (Cohen and Taylor, 1976, p. 45).

For the postmodern tourists, travel is a game and they can freely admit that they are just playing and having fun without intentions to seek anything more (Urry, 1991, p. 100). 'Thus, holidays have become less to do with the reinforcing of collective memories and experiences and more to do with immediate pleasure' (Ibid., p. 102). Here Urry obviously refers to Turnerian concept of communitas. The feeling of sameness among fellow travellers ceases to be one of the most desired experiences. Instead, mere fun becomes more important. This development is characteristic of our time; as the meaning of community ties for an individual wanes, individualism flowers. This contradicts Turnerian anti-structure by emphasising how travelling is a holiday version of normal suburban living (Jokinen and Veijola, 1990, p. 120). While Turnerian tradition stressed the tourists' quest for anti-structure that differs from their everyday life, the postmodern tourists are left with a paradox. While they seem to be looking for anti-structure, they also want it to be like everyday life. They want the 'fun' -part of the former, and the 'security' -part of the latter. This is a very clear expression of the need to balance home and reach.

> [Inter]railers want everything from life: continuous travel while having a career, individualistic experiences and long term relationship, they want to live abroad but also own a secure home in Finland (Malmberg, 1990, p. 14; my translation from Finnish).

The essential contribution of postmodernism to tourism studies is that travel has started to be seen as a game in which the quest for authenticity is not necessarily important. According to Urry (1991, p. 100) 'the world is a stage and the post-tourist can delight in the multitude of games that can be played'. The whole idea of authenticity in the context of tourism has become questioned because the tourist experience operates primarily through reproductions. Authenticity, or more often perceived authenticity, is just an aspect of the game that makes playing more exciting for those who seek for it.

Just one way of seeing travel does not provide a comprehensive understanding of it. None of the perspectives described in this chapter are alone sufficient for the apprehension of the wide variety of touristic phenomena. The image of tourist emerging from each is hardly more than a caricature (Cohen, 1988a, p. 43). Also Urry (1991, p. 135) has noted that 'it is inappropriate to think that it is possible to devise "the theory of tourist behaviour"' in the sense that it would never be comprehensive. As we saw, many of the perspectives are even contradictory to each other. The caricatures emerging from the perspectives, however, taken together do cover quite a wide variety of touristic phenomena. The obvious mistake has generally been to claim that a particular perspective can represent all travellers, or to present the perspective as if it would. Rejecting one perspective in favour of another is not the answer if we are to gain new understanding of tourism. Instead, each one has its own particular strengths on the specific areas of the subject. Boorstin's critical view cleverly illustrates the spurious aspects of tourism that nevertheless exist. MacCannell has explicated some tourists' quest for authenticity. Turner's writings about rituals appeared afterwards to be allegorical to the organisation of tourists' experience and Cohen gives a typology that interestingly relates travel with our experience of our own society.

Cohen (1988a, p. 43) later writes about typologies:

> Typologies (...) do not resolve the problem, precisely because they reduce to a common ground the essential differences in analytical focus characteristic of each approach. Hence, an alternative strategy appears to be more appropriate: a research programme which would simultaneously take account of, and compare, the tourist's psychological needs and experiences, the socio-structural features of tourist settings, and the cultural symbols expressed in the touristic process.

Cohen suggests that his typology of different modes of travel (1979a) would be such an alternative strategy. However, I think that his comments above applies equally well to his own typology. Instead of a typology, the way in which our relationship to places has been portrayed in humanistic geography provides the alternative strategy Cohen is after. After all, it encompasses all the aspects he wants to include in a research programme. The fact that there has been little interchange of ideas between humanistic geography and travel studies has so far prevented such place-centred strategy. However, this may well change soon. The use of some literary metaphors like 'text', 'narrative' and 'discourse' has become a common practice in both fields. From shared vocabulary with shared meanings there should be a short way to the exchange of ideas, especially since the interests of both fields are quite similar (see Daniels and Cosgrove, 1993, p. 57).

Typical Tourist?

Above I have distanced myself from the types or typologies of tourists, especially if they are claimed to be comprehensive, which they never are, nor can be. However, if a study of tourist's experience is attempted, there have to be some criteria according to which it is possible to define who to study. Therefore I will introduce a simple typology after all, but I readily admit that it will not even attempt to be comprehensive.

According to the definition by the World Tourism Organization, a tourist is 'a temporary visitor staying at least 24 hours in a country visited for the purpose of leisure or business' (The Dictionary of Hospitality, Travel, and Tourism, 1990). Alternatively, according to the United Nations a tourist is 'one who spends more than one night and less than one year away from home for business or pleasure, excepting diplomats, military personnel, and enrolled students' (Ibid.). Definitions like these are designed to facilitate uniform administrative and statistical handling of tourism. Thus the concept is defined in terms of the quantifiable characteristics of tourists that are of little use here. Many studies referred earlier try to describe what a tourist is in qualitative sense. The result is more a characterisation than a definition; it is ultimately a futile search for the typical tourist.

Here I am going to distinguish between two kinds of tourists. These types arise from the largely anecdotal distinction between 'tourists' and 'travellers'. It is usual to use this distinction like this happy customer of a travel agent:

> At the end of this trip I feel I have *travelled* the Silk Route - at no time did I feel like a tourist (The Trans-Siberian railway and The Silk Route by rail 1996, p. 12; emphasis original).

In a guidebook for backpackers the same distinction is characterised as follows:

> *Tourists* stay in Hiltons, *travellers* don't. The *traveller* wants to see the country at ground level, to breathe it, experience it - live it. This usually requires two things the *tourists* can't provide - more time and less money. If you're going to *really travel*, it's going to take longer and on a day-to-day basis cost less (South-East Asia on a Shoestring 1992, p. 35; emphasis added).

This distinction has also been used without much reflection in some academic writing (e.g. Boorstin, 1972; Seamon, 1985, p. 242). The distinction underlines the critical attitude towards tourists as mere consumers, in contrast to travellers as adventurers. According to Bruner (1991, p. 247) 'this distinction between tourism and travel is a Western myth of identity and should be analyzed as such'. He illustrates this with an example from Bali:

> In Bali, an individual traveler who takes great pains to distinguish him- or herself from the hordes of mere tourists will be catered to, for the Balinese are as sophisticated at marketing as the tour agents. However, from the native perspective, a self-declared traveler is simply another variety of foreign visitor (Ibid.).

The distinction implicitly arises from some of the previous discussions. Graburn's (1983) modal and rites of passage, Gottlieb's (1982) peasant and king for a day, and Murray's 'vision quest' and 'pilgrimage' -travel all share this opposition of two different modes of travelling. The same could be said about Cohen's (1972) categorisation of institutionalised and noninstitutionalised tourists. Instead of using the terms 'tourists' and 'travellers', I'd like to call these two different kinds of tourists *'conventional tourists'* and *'backpackers'*. This terminology reflects the visible differences in the appearance of them; the former are often characterised by caricatures, the latter are predominantly young and carry a backpack.

Conventional tourists are modal tourists, who want the relaxation and fun that the anti-structure of travel brings with it. Cohen's (1979a) 'recreational mode' of travelling and 'institutional tourist' (Cohen 1972) depict conventional tourists. Their 'spiritual centre' is within their own society; hence they are not travelling to find any particular deeper meanings. Anti-structure for them means simply different conditions from home. In the most common cases it equals being king for a day instead of working from nine to five. They are also allowed to participate in somewhat frivolous activities that would not be considered 'proper' at home, like getting drunk and sleeping late. They are modal tourists because they have only their periodical holidays from work to use for travelling. Due to this they have a considerable amount of money to spend during their short vacation. Conventional tourists are institutionalised in the sense that while travelling they are completely dependent on the touristic infrastructure that has been specially created for the purpose. For example, they live in a hotel, eat in restaurants, and take part in sightseeing excursions.

Backpackers are usually young travellers who travel for longer periods, months, sometimes even years on a relatively low budget without being on an organised tour (for a more detailed definition see Loker-Murphy and Pearce, 1995, pp. 826-831). They are in Cohen's (1972) sense noninstitutionalised. In Riley's (1988, p. 318) study, 'most expressed a desire to "see the world" before settling down to the responsibilities of children, careers, home ownership, and so forth'. Also travel as 'an opportunity to experience real freedom, to seek adventure in an exotic, or at least different, setting, and to satisfy curiosity about foreign places' were expressed (Ibid.). This strongly suggests that Turnerian anti-structure very well describes what backpackers are after. They stay in cheap accommodation and try to become familiar with some of the local culture. Cohen (1972) called some of these travellers 'drifters'[4] and describes them in a way that clearly fits into the idea of rites of passage:

> He [drifter] is young, often a student or a graduate, who has not yet started to work. He prolongs his moratorium by moving around the world in search of new experiences, radically different from those he has been accustomed to in his sheltered middle-class existence. After he has savoured these experiences for a time, he usually settles down to an orderly middle-class career (Cohen 1972, p. 175).

The anti-structure enables backpackers to be Gottlieb's peasant for a day. In fact, not only is travel time anti-structure for them, it is a real rite of passage, from one social position to another. The trip is a 'ritual play with separation and social distance' (Adler, 1985, p. 351). Backpackers travel at a period of their life when their life situations change. The most typical example are young travellers who travel after graduating from school or university. In this kind of travel it is easy to distinguish the different components of a rite of passage. Separation occurs when backpackers leave their familiar place and its conventions. While away they are in a liminoid state; in relation to home they are not (for example) students any more, but do not have careers yet either. They are something between, something that is easy to see as a period of life when by leaving the familiar behind, they learn who they are and what they want. Finally, after the travel they are reintegrated into their society and they find their own place in it. Backpacker travel thus is not only structurally similar to rites of passage, it *is* a rite of passage. In it identity and maybe even future direction of life are modified.

Qualitative travel studies have evolved from cultural critics through attempts of metatheories to the present situation in which the justification of

---

[4] At the time 'flower power' was in vogue and drifting was an expression of this alternative life-style and values. Drifters were associated with the Hippie-culture. They travelled to form communities of alternative life-style and thus displayed Cohen's existential mode of travel.

such theories is questioned. It does not mean that the suitable elements of such theories should not be used when the context for them is right. However, it has proved futile to try to construct a theory that would comprehensively understand all kind of tourism. I have introduced the central elements of the past discussion in order to provide a broader context for the types of tourists whose experiences my work represents. This distinction between conventional tourists and backpackers, like any distinction, is only an analytical tool to examine various experiences.

5 Charting Shared Experiences

Material

In this work I am doing interpretations based on the experiences of my own travels accumulated during my adult years. The material includes memories, countless unrecorded discussions with fellow travellers, my own travel diaries, recorded informal interviews, a collection of travel advertisements and travel guidebooks. In order to provoke I'd say that I am the material. I am not going to separate my experiences from the experiences of the people who have been travelling with me. The experience on travel is typically shared with your fellow travellers. You must understand your travel companions to be able to travel with them and enjoy their company. Thus the way I understand an experience cannot be completely alien to those who have been with me. I think that it is pretentious to try to detach oneself too much from one's own experience and claim some sort of cool authority over the 'material gathered'. I do not accept the view that in trying to understand experience of place, somebody else's experiences would be somehow more valuable than mine. To judge this view unscientific is to say that one's own experiences do not count in a scientific inquiry. This would take us back to the times of positivistic hegemony. I am willing to grasp any available source that adds to the understanding of a travel experience, without the initial concern of whether it is methodically respectable. If such methodical anarchy should be named, it would probably come closest to triangulation: a potpourri of methods that approach the topic through different sources and angles and thus give a holistic picture of it (Hottola, 1999, p. 24). This chapter introduces the interview material. The other material speaks for itself in the course of the work.

I have been strongly influenced by the seven and half months trip around the world I made with a friend in 1988, when I was 22 years old. It was my first real trip overseas and it included five days in Singapore, three months in the east coast of Australia, a month in Fiji, and three and a half months in Western Samoa. During the trip we kept a daily diary (there are some lapses). We wrote not only about the events and people, but also about the feelings and reactions we had. On this trip I was forced to reflect on my reactions in strange environments and I became conscious of my feelings and emotions in a much more tangible way than before. Thus without

71

realising it, I engaged in what could be called a phenomenology of everyday life. Later, during the course of my studies, I realised the connection and became interested in applying this phenomenological method to the study of tourists' experience. I feel that the Turnerian idea of travel as a rite of passage very well describes at least that first big travel experience of mine. The experience was definitely different from what my life was like at home, and it was indeed reach for novel experiences that would (and did) provide meaning for life. Later I have travelled numerous shorter trips, like taken part in travel on bus tours in Turkey (ten days with my student colleagues in April 1989) and Estonia (a week with my student colleagues in May 1990). Both of these trips were characterised by a strong feeling of belonging within the group. I also spent four weeks backpacking in Bali (May 1993), where I interviewed sixteen people in eleven interviews.

The people I interviewed are drawn from two groups: my student colleagues who have participated on the above bus tours and various tourist trips; and the backpackers I met in Bali. These groups represent the distinction between conventional tourists and backpackers. The intention is to discover whether it is possible to see similar themes arising from these different modes of travelling or whether the experience of place is totally different between the two. Also methodologically it is interesting to compare the differences in the extent to which it is possible to penetrate the subjective experiences of others within each group. It could be expected that studying familiar people from my own socio-cultural background as an existential insider provides deeper insights than the study of strangers who have different background and language.

In the case of the friends of mine the language we used was totally familiar to us all and we were able to use expressions that conveyed meanings beyond the words. Also the cultural differences were reduced to the differences in personalities, and because I had known the participants for seven years (before the interviews), I was familiar with those differences and knew what they meant. Furthermore, the familiarity and common experiences promoted a strong extent of intersubjectivity. All this facilitated extremely easy potential sharing of these peoples' experiences. It also helped to overcome any possible shyness about recording. But most importantly, as we shared many of our lives' recent experiences and knew each other well, it was easy to read between the lines. Not only could I raise many issues that in other circumstances could be considered sensitive, but I could also make informed interpretations of what they said. I had myself been a part of some of their experiences. I also heard several versions of the same events so that I could see some differences in the ways in which different individuals experienced the same things. In attempting to connect everyday experience to the experience of travel (Squire, 1994, p. 12), my technique of studying people with whom I have shared everyday experience and some travel experience felt appropriate.

I interviewed ten people in December 1993, while I visited home from Australia. These were the people I could catch at the time; additional possible interviewees were scattered around the country. I used a tape recorder to record the interviews that lasted from 40 to 90 minutes. I had a list for myself of themes I wanted to cover, but I intended to let the interviewees to tell as much as possible. Most of the time I wasn't as much interviewing as listening. While some topics on my list may not have always become covered in an interview, I saw it more important to get an account that was to the least extent influenced by my questions. With four of the people interviewed I had shared a bus tour in Turkey and two others had made a similar trip to Portugal (a trip in which I had inadvertently participated vicariously through numerous conversations with many people already before these recorded interviews). One couple showed me their holiday slides from bus trip to Ireland and from a trip to the Czech Republic, another showed photos from their honeymoon in Dominican Republic. I also saw pictures from Turkey and Portugal. In addition, I interviewed a carpenter in his late fifties who also showed me his photos and whom I knew well. Thus I saw photos from all the trips that were covered in the interviews. Going through the photographs proved very helpful in bringing back the events and feelings that took place at the time of the travel. Apart from the Eurail trip to the Czech Republic, all these trips represent the trip of a conventional tourist and lasted two weeks at most.

On the trip to Turkey we flew from Helsinki to Istanbul, stayed there for five days and then drove by bus to Bursa, Kusadasi (at the time a strongly developing new beach resort), Izmir, Canakkale and back to Istanbul. The trip took ten days and we were a strongly cohesive group with few contacts with the locals apart from shopping. From all I heard about the trip to Portugal, it was very similar, except that only one day was spent without sitting in the bus. As geography students, this group of people may not be the 'average' people because they are highly educated. However, the trips were conducted in a 'holiday mode', i.e. the activities hardly differed from the activities of any tourist group; bus tours, shopping, lying on the beach. In our trip to Turkey I was fully participating, without the slightest idea that some day I would use the trip as a material for my thesis. Thus the problem of balance between participation and observation appears now as the need to rely on a memory of the events that took place long ago. This difficulty is lessened by the existence of photographs and collective memory of the participants I have interviewed; someone always remembers something that another one cannot recall properly. Becoming familiar with the literature of tourism studies afterwards has made it possible for me to 'step back from the inevitable personal involvement, so as to see more than does the mere participant' (Smith, D., 1988, p. 263). In my opinion, this is what phenomenology is about; to be able to disclose the elements of one's experiences. The experiences can be deconstructed and reconstructed with the aid of phenomenologically orientated hindsight. Hindsight can be exploited because it offers the possibility of reconstituting the experience in terms that were not known at the time of the experience (Daniels, 1985, p. 153). Thus it becomes easier to 'step back' from the experience and have some detachment through the conceptualisation emerging from all the literature studied afterwards. In the process, it is important to be aware of the distinction between the original experiences and their later interpretation.

Table 5.1   Interviews in Finland in December 1993

Interviewee*	Sex	Age	Trips covered in the interview
Martti	m	29	Turkey, Estonia
Kaapo	m	27	Portugal, Estonia, Lanzarote
Arvo	m	26	Portugal, Estonia
Satu	f	28	Turkey, Interrail in Europe
Minna	f	28	Turkey, Canary Islands
Sari & Olavi	f/m	28/32	Ireland, Czech Republic
Raili & Markus	f/m	25/25	Turkey, Portugal, Dominican Republic
Erkki	m	58	USSR, Morocco, Tunisia, Canary Islands

*Ages at the time of the interview. All the names have been changed.

The difference in language and socio-cultural heritage between my backpacker interviewees and myself are naturally thicker. As English is not my first language, I sometimes found it hard to convey my meaning. Nine of the sixteen backpacker interviewees had the same problem as they were Danes, Dutch, Germans and a Norwegian. Conversing in a language that is not mastered perfectly necessarily means that all the connotations and delicate meanings of words are not understood.

Coming from within a Western culture, my cultural background is in some extent similar to that of the backpackers I interviewed. However, there are also differences, relating for example to the colonial past of some European countries and the consequent multiculturalism of their societies that Finland does not share. There is little tradition of travel in Finland.[1] Also the harsh conditions of the northern country together with the strict Lutheran working ethic have meant that travelling has been seen as something idle, something that suits only the rich and lazy. This apparently started to change from the end of the 1960s when charter travel to Spanish destinations (Majorca, Canary Islands) became possible for the working class people. During the early 1970s travel became an instrument in 'keeping up with the Joneses' and many people feel inferiority in relation to the others who have been travelling more than they. In terms of home and reach, I think that Finns have traditionally emphasised home more than most other European nations.

In Bali I was able to interview people in the middle of their travel experience. It was natural to interview the backpackers because I was perceived to be one of them; I stayed in same places and was about the same age. I interviewed backpackers who I met in accommodation, restaurants and places frequented by them, so that the normal exchange of conversation between fellow travellers initiated the recorded interviews. This made the interviewees feel that they helped me, their fellow traveller, to fulfil the purpose of my trip, rather than participated an academic study. Thus I attempted to conduct the interviews as much as possible in the context of the natural exchange of conversation between similarly minded travellers. Of course, this technique brings bias to the sample; my analysis on backpackers is based on the experiences of people who are much like me.

With one exception the interviewees were between 20-30 years old. I interviewed 16 people in 11 interviews that lasted from 35 to 90 minutes. I used a tape recorder to document the interviews (in hostel room, veranda or restaurant), but a lot of discussions took place outside the recording process. Sometimes the tape run out, other times the conversation opened when the recorder was not present. It would be probably better to describe the encounters as discussions rather than interviews. However, given that the interviewees were not very familiar to me as the Finnish respondents were, in a couple of cases the tape recorder caused some initial tenseness. I had the

---

[1] Apart from the sailors of Åland and the Swedish speaking coast. However, their travels have not become a largely shared tradition within the Finnish-speaking majority.

same list of topics for myself as when interviewing the Finnish respondents, but I often set it aside when people started to talk about travel-related things that they were seemingly enthusiastic about. Initially I thought I would tape record the conversations without the people knowing it, but I abandoned the idea for four reasons. First, my tape recorder was not quite inconspicuous, second, hiding would produce poor quality of the recording and third, to get a good sample of the topics I would have wanted to cover I should have to have used copious amounts of tape. Finally fourth, befriending a person and secretly taping a discussion would become awkward since the purpose of my travel would have surfaced anyway. The number of interviews is not large, as I first tried to befriend the interviewees to be able to better understand their situation. This usually happened within a time period from a few hours to a couple of days, but in two occasions I travelled with the interviewees for a few days.

The small number of interviewees (total of 26) is compensated by a strong degree of familiarity with ten of them (the Finnish participants), and at least some sort of acquaintance with the rest. The fact that I shared the situation of the latter by being one of them (just another backpacker) usually facilitated mutual understanding; there was a strong sense of sharing a common experience. However, sometimes the differences in thinking opened my eyes to see larger perspectives.

The techniques I have adopted are thus quite similar to those of ethnography. Central to ethnography is to concentrate on the perspective of the researched, to understand their everyday life. There should be no methodological restrictions in doing so. Participant observation and un- or semi-structured interviews are typically used in ethnography, and generally the idea is to somehow become a part of, or at least to be involved as much as possible with the studied group. The idea is that the researchers learn from the participants, without imposing their own ideas on them (Donovan, 1988, p. 190). Thus the material has the chance to speak for itself, and the danger of imposing of researchers' own ideas on the participants is diminished, as there are no restrictive hypotheses. There are however, risks associated with doing this. It may be that the material the researchers gain by just gathering all sorts of data they think somehow relates to the topic they are studying, appears to be too unspecific. It may consequently happen, that they must go back to the field with more detailed ideas of what they really want to know. It is thus advisable to know already beforehand what kind of information we are after, but not to let that knowledge interfere with what the participants report from their own perspective. This is why I let people talk about what they felt was important, rather than trying to force them to respond to a certain predetermined schema.

Table 5.2   Interviews in Bali May 1993

Interviewee*	Sex	Age	Length of the trip**	Nationality	Countries covered on the present trip by the time of interview
Sigrid	f	21	1y	Norwegian	USA, NZ, Australia, Indonesia
Kathy	f	28	4m	British	India, Thailand, Malaysia, Singapore, Indonesia
Jim	m	29	2m	USA	Taiwan, Thailand, Malaysia, Singapore, Indonesia
Alice	f	47	3w	USA	Indonesia
Inge	f	30	2.5m	Danish	Nepal, Singapore, Indonesia
Torsten	m	21	3m	Danish	Thailand, Malaysia, Singapore, Indonesia
Tina & John	f/m	24/26	6m	British	Australia, Indonesia
Anne & Heidi	f/f	22/22	2m	German	NZ, Australia, Indonesia
Lis & Hanne	f/f	20/20	3m	Danish	Russia, China, HK, Thailand, Malaysia, Singapore, Indonesia
Mary & Roy	f/m	28/30	21m	British	USA, NZ, Australia, Indonesia
Denise & Aron	f/m	22/23	8m	Dutch	USA, Surinam, NZ, Indonesia

*Ages at the time of the interview. All the names have been changed. **y=years; m=months; w=weeks; Length of trip prior to interview.

It would, however, be dishonest to claim that I did my fieldwork without having any preconceived ideas about what I was after. Having formulated some ideas based on my own experiences, my aim was to see whether those ideas also emerged from the experiences of others. Thus I would not call the method a grounded theory (Donovan, 1988, p. 186; Hottola, 1999, p. 26). In all, my method is a blend of different techniques ranging from analysis of my own experiences as a tourist through eliciting accounts of others' experience by informal interview, to discourse analysis of travel brochures and advertisements. I have tried to be sensitive to my own experiences.

Validation?

My methods are somewhat similar to what MacCannell (1976) did: 'I undertook to follow the tourists, sometimes joining their groups, sometimes watching them from afar through writings by, for and about them' (Ibid., p. 4). It seems that MacCannell was trying to create a theory of all tourists and thus he received criticism based on the informality of his methods:

> MacCannell's collection, however, was hardly systematic or representative, being based on informal methods. (...) Such informal methods may be highly useful to gain basic insights. They do not, however, lead to balanced conclusions any more than Boorstin's spirited quotations (Cohen, 1988a, p. 34).

Graburn (1983, p. 18) has noted that if we remove the attempt to apply MacCannel's analysis in all tourists, there should be no concerns about the approach's validity in dealing with certain kind of tourists.

It is usual to criticise these informal methods for their subjectivity and limited representativeness. Thus it has been lamented that '...it is difficult to see how the account of a single journey, even though comprising a multiplicity of experiences, can be generalized inductively from all observed cases of phenomenon to all cases of phenomenon' (Dann and Nash and Pearce, 1988, p. 15). This is true, it cannot do it *inductively*; in dealing with individual experiences such generalisation is not possible. But inductive generalisation has little to do here in this work. Of course it is necessary to gain understanding of the studied phenomena that goes beyond the 'sample', especially since my own experiences are so central in it. However, representativeness in statistical sense is not essential; the most important thing is to understand whatever 'sample' we have, be it just one person. Indeed, it would not be even possible to empathetically explore the experiences of a large number of people; the individual accounts of personal experiences and their empathetic appreciation would dissolve into more or less stereotyped mass of generalisations. Achieving the kind of understanding that I am after in this work is not at all dependent on the number of people involved, but on the empathetic ability to relate to those peoples' experiences. Therefore the depth with which I can analyse my own and the participants' experiences, not the number of various experiences, becomes crucial. Naturally the consequent claims cannot, and are not intended, to provide a metatheory of all tourism.

Even if I only had studied one experience, it would reveal something of that particular experience. The idea is to find themes from experiences - even if only one or few - which can then be reflected to experiences more generally. This reflection includes the comparison to one's own experiences, and is the very key to increased understanding. This increase in understanding involves one's personal experiences and the experiences of others, not only the experience or experiences that are studied. Thus achieving this does not require the study of as many experiences as possible (as does induction). It constitutes of the approach from particular to general, not through induction, but through empathetic understanding.[2] This understanding is valuable, although necessarily more or less subjective. Such subjectivity, however, should not deny us the benefit of this kind of understanding.

A lot of (human) science is handicapped by the obsession with objectivity, verification and representativeness. I think this happens because of the misunderstanding that this kind of study is just a weak form of induction. This handicap makes it impossible, or at least extremely difficult, to make scientific statements about, for example, some immensely personal experiences like religious awakening or appreciation of arts. In this way it restricts the sphere of phenomena that can be studied. Olsson writes how some methodological requirements force us, as researchers to be more stupid than we actually are (Olsson, 1982, p. 227). Relph writes in a similar vein: 'The measure of any work is whether it adds to our knowledge of the world or our understanding of ourselves or enhances life, not whether it follows methodological rules precisely' (Relph, 1981a, p. 112). Much of the delightfully vivid insight we gain from our usual everyday involvement with the world and our involvement with what we study is rejected, because it

---

[2] As ideally happens in interpretation of literary works and art more generally. The expression of an artist contains his or her version about the phenomenon the work describes. The others then attempt to decode that version into something that makes sense to them and reveals to them new insights about the phenomenon. Personal experience of the artist and its expression may thus, once interpreted, create new understanding and insight also for others (of course a mystic could argue that an insight should be attained without interpretation, which is necessarily bound to the limits of conceptualisation).

does not conform with the scientific criteria of what constitutes scientific knowledge. This is probably why Olsson (1982, p. 224) provocatively writes:

> Read less what I am sufficiently ignorant to write and more of what you know so well that it must be passed over in silence! Deafen yourself to the noise of the expressible! Listen instead for the whisper of the taken-for-granted!

The result of a good interpretative study is that it adds to our understanding. This criteria is, however, problematic because it is not always easy to see this at once. It is immediately possible to see whether the research is carried out cogently from the perspective of theoretical reasoning. But the assessment of whether there is any addition to understanding of the phenomena requires that it is proven in the experiences of those who familiarise themselves with the results. Besides, the two do not always guarantee each other. Thus the success of a study depends on first, how well the communication between the researcher and the researched works and second, how well it works between the researcher and the reader (Johnston, 1983, p. 59). The first is facilitated by appropriate qualitative techniques that allow good adaptation to the living context of the situations in which the research is being conducted. The second is possible when the researcher provides analysis that allows the readers to reflect on their own experiences against the framework provided in the analysis. This requires sensitivity and skill in transcending the meanings of the experiences studied so that they apply also more generally. Success in this is the mark of a good qualitative study.

6 Travel as Reach

Motivation to Travel

The motivation to travel draws from the difference between the mundane everyday home with its familiar daily chores and the perceived possibility of the Other to satisfy the need for reach. This difference makes the change of place appear meaningful because the Other is compared to the everydayness of home. What is anticipated from the Other thus relates to what is known of home (Heikkinen, 1993, p. 14). Thus in motivational analysis the relationship between the everyday at home and the perceived excitement of being away should be central. This relationship translates into the dialectic of home and reach. In the kind of travel analysed in this work, this dialectic takes the form of leaving home, being in contact with the Other, and coming back home.

Motivation to travel thus has deep roots in everyday life and society's influence on it. We do not want to travel simply because of one or several reasons, but because of an underlying theme behind these reasons. The dialectic of home and reach is such a theme. Reach may involve many aspects of life, not only the spatial aspect of wanting to be in some other place. But because place is such an all-encompassing entity, reach for something in these non-spatial aspects often takes on a spatial expression. Therefore travel can be an expression of reach in which changing place may be quite incidental, but nevertheless necessary in order to achieve what is reached for. It is thus only conceptually possible to distinguish between reach in which place itself is quite incidental (e.g. wanting to participate in an event) and reach that is concerned particularly with place (e.g. wanting to visit one's former home). Reach in any aspect of life easily translates into the desire to at least temporarily get away from our home place.

Examination of existing classifications of different travel motivations suggests that they are mostly constructed to serve market research for commercial purposes of the travel industry (e.g. Crompton, 1979, pp. 408-424; Yan and McDonald, 1990; Clarke, 1992; Eagles, 1992; Ross, 1994, pp. 14-19). These kinds of studies are often little more than lists of possible reasons to travel. Together with classifications of different kinds of tourists, they are designed to be helpful in recognising marketing segments. A problem with these listings is that they are neither exhaustive nor mutually exclusive. From the perspective of this work, they do not add to the goal of

81

understanding the connection between travel motivation and the experience of everyday life. Naturally the travel industry wants to know which strings it has to pull to make people purchase its product. However, here we have to go beyond single identifiable reasons and recognise patterns in the way the desire to travel is constituted.

From Push and Pull to Escape and Search

The dialectic of home and reach is illustrated in analysing motivations in terms of push- and pull-factors (Dann, 1977, 1981) and as escape and search (Urbain, 1989). Push and pull conceptualisation is adapted from migration studies (Herberle, 1938; Lee, 1966). Expressed simply, the idea is that there are (often perceived) push- (-) and pull-factors (+) both at home and in a destination, and when the sum of these at home becomes clearly negative, one decides to go somewhere where the sum is perceived to be positive, if there are no insurmountable obstacles in doing so (Lewis, 1982, p. 101). Adapted to travel this view is problematic because in migration the movement is (mostly) one way, whereas, by definition, a tourist intends to return home. Therefore, if the destination pulls and home pushes, why would travellers return home at all? After all, travel is a cyclical phenomenon in which we reach for change in the form of the contact with the Other, and then return back home (Figure 6.1).

Figure 6.1   Travel as circle from home to the Other and back

This is a basic conceptional characterisation of travel, which will be developed further in the course of this work. This cyclical pattern differentiates tourism from migration or drifting. It also illustrates the dialectics between home and the Other, and our balancing between home and reach.

In marketing studies, 'push motives have been useful for explaining the desire to go on a vacation, while pull motives have usefully explained the choice of destination' (Goossens, 2000, p. 301). Dann (1977; 1981) considers the push-factors only as anomie and ego-enhancement, which makes the conceptualisation even more artificial. Furthermore, push- and pull-factors as behaviouristic categories indicate a somewhat mechanical view of people. Such terms imply that we are pushed or pulled by something, and in our motivation to travel we only respond to some external stimuli. Of course we often do so, but we also have the possibility to act from our own initiative. This simplifying tendency is recognised nowadays by the marketing researchers and new aspects like hedonism and psychological processes involved are taken into account (Goossens, 2000). Dividing motivations into push- and pull-factors nevertheless illustrates the dialectics between home and reach. The division points to some connections between everyday experience and motivation. But at the same time it simplifies the connection too much by reducing a decision to travel to a simple mathematical equation.

A somewhat parallel pair of concepts is escape and search. However, they imply that people themselves are the actors who do something instead of just responding. Need to escape indeed arises from certain circumstances, but we still have the freedom not to escape; nothing pushes us to travel. Similarly, we are actively searching for something instead of just allowing something to pull us. This conceptual difference (push-escape; pull-search) may sound slim, but it significantly reflects the different positions of behaviouralism and humanism. In the present discussion my purpose is to start the analysis using Dann's application of push- and pull-factors, but then depart from them and proceed towards the concepts of escape and search. Despite the deficiencies of Dann's approach, it is useful as a starting point; as we proceed, the deficiencies are addressed and an alternative approach developed.

Sometimes both of the motives of push and pull are present; travel is a 'response to what is lacking yet desired' (Dann, 1981, p. 190). Dann maintains that often push-factors are prior to pull-factors; first we have to have a need to travel, and only after that do we decide the specific destination. 'By examining "What makes tourists travel", one is looking at a more elementary (and by implication, causally prior) need than a specific reason for choice of resort' (Dann, 1977, p. 186). As far as normal holiday travel is concerned, this is usually true, but naturally there are also situations where people travel somewhere just because there is something that makes them want to do so. A particular place or sight so strongly attract the people that they set off to see it. In other words, pull factors too, sometimes determine the decision to travel.

Push   According to Dann (1977, pp. 189-190), anomie and ego-enhancement are the underlying push factors. Anomie (the lack of common social or moral standards in one's society because of two or more competing ones) creates the need to reach for something where such fragmentation is absent. Thus anomie easily prompts alienation, since an individual can feel that the society is felt to hinder the possibility to live up to his/her values and ideals. There is no harmony between them and the perceived lack of values in the society as a whole. For most people, this does not apply to everyday life, which many of us are quite happy with and do not feel alienation caused by anomie. Among my respondents, such alienation did not seem to be a problem (on the other hand, for the one to whom it clearly was, it was a big one). While many expressed a need for change as a strong motive to travel, that by no means necessarily implies a fundamental disagreement between the set of values of the people and their society. Anomie is thus too strong a concept to describe a normal need to balance home and reach, a need for variety.

Ego-enhancement in Dann's vocabulary seems to mean status acquisition by travelling. Following his logic, those who want to travel and do not feel anomie are in some degree self-centred egoists. While ego-enhancement in this sense can indeed be an important factor in motivations to travel, I do not believe that the feeling of anomie is the only alternative motivating travel. Even if we agree with the values of our society, it is obvious that sometimes we just need some change. That need does not have to have anything to do with anomie or ego-enhancement (in Dann's meaning). However, we should not limit ego-enhancement to mere egoism. What Dann calls ego-enhancement, I'd consider as showing off. Healthy ego-enhancement is for personal satisfaction and self-development rather than for impressing others. It is necessary for the maintenance of a healthy self-esteem. Therefore the need for change may well arise from the anticipation of great personal satisfaction resulting from a deviation from everyday life. However, having an outgoing and wealthy image, 'keeping up with the Joneses' (Dann, 1981, p. 190), and using travel as a means to demonstrate that one can 'break the bonds of their everyday existence and begin to "live"' (MacCannell, 1976, p. 159), are surely parts of the reasons for travel. We might not be fully aware of these reasons; or we just might not be willing to confess them, and react by actively ignoring them. What travellers say are their motivations may only be reflections of deeper needs which they do not understand, nor wish to articulate (Lundberg, cited in Dann, 1981, p. 189; see also Crompton, 1979, p. 421; Smith, 1979, p. 54;

Culler, 1981, p. 129; Riley, 1988, p. 318). Relph points out that 'for many people the purpose of travel is less to experience unique and different places than to collect those places'. This is social tourism; travel for social ends rather than for the experience (Relph, 1976, p. 85; Tuan, 1974, p. 95). The goal of showing off may thus sometimes be at least semi-consciously present in decisions to travel.

There is a tendency of the younger, idealism-filled travellers to emphasise the difference between them and tourists. In my own first big trip I remember having strongly detested being called a tourist, as did a couple of my younger backpacker respondents:

I am not a tourist; I am a traveller (Sigrid, 21).[1]

The discourse of backpacking is about personal development, and it is perceived that there is little room for personal development in mass tourism. Thus these kinds of comments are meant to be declarations of identity. On this stage of life the young travellers are eager to define their identities, and thus it is important to distinguish oneself from the mass tourist: the epitome of being middle-class.

In this kind of sharp distinction there is also the sense of elitism and ego-enhancement. Sometimes it seemed that the status gained in the eyes of others after having completed such a trip was also influential in deciding to travel. In some sense a certain kind of superiority is sought, as noted by Helms (1988, p. 4): 'intangible knowledge of distant realms and regions can be politically valuable "goods"'. In a more sophisticated and apparently not so overt form, expectation of recognition by others may relate not directly to the fact of having completed the trip, but indirectly through the personal development expected to be gained. Maturity becomes a 'good' obtained from the travel, something for others to acknowledge. This kind of motivation does not always seek superiority over others, sometimes just perceived equality. It is a matter of unspoken peer group pressure. Having friends with exciting accounts of their backpacking adventures, one may feel inferior without having experienced all that him/herself. With age and maturity the need for this kind of ego-enhancement diminishes; maturity does not have to be proved for others any more.

---

[1] The extracts from the interviews are presented in indents. I attempt to use the exact words of the interviewees, although in the case of those who do not speak English as their first language, I may have paraphrased the expressions. The translation from Finnish naturally involves some interpretation also.

The conventional tourists' way of displaying identity and ego-enhancement differs from the backpackers. The discourse I could read from between the lines indicated that superiority in relation to others is sought either in frequency of travel or in destination selection. Especially the latter is important. This is the interpretation I gave to the detailed justifications of travelling to those specific places. Although the destination may be the same as the destination of thousands of others, the choice is held to represent an idea that addresses something in the person's identity. It is as if the perceived desirable qualities of destinations like exoticness, uniqueness, etc. somehow transmitted from the destination to the tourists. The potential tourists anticipate this transposal so that it becomes part of their motivation to travel. Thus places, as symbols of something desirable, become fetish-like 'goods' that increase the power of their possessor, i.e. the person who has 'collected' these places. I could discern this, because I knew the interviewees so well and we shared similar social conventions regarding the social meaning of travel in our society.

Thus, instead of being exclusively a push-factor, ego-enhancement in the sense of personal development can be understood as something that is searched for, especially for backpackers. Dann is partially right in that home may be a push-factor when it gives us the feeling that in order to gain personal development we have to travel elsewhere. Staying at home is then perceived as an impediment to such development. But more important is the pull of the prospect of self-development in travel. We are drawn to travel by the desire to attain something that we perceive we cannot get at home.

Pull Pull factors for Dann relate to the reasons why tourists want to travel to a particular destination. They are the things that attract us somewhere in particular. A place or a sight, about which we have read a book or seen a movie, may fascinate us. We may have been there before and want to go again because we liked it. The pull factors of places where we have never been are based on the images we have of those places. Therefore an essential character of these pull factors is that they are perceived. This is exploited in travel advertising where images that easily transform into pull factors are boldly brought on our eyes. Heavenly beaches, luxury resorts and exotic customs are used to allure us to travel to a destination. It is hardly surprising then, that the images forming the pull factors are distorted and biased. Travel advertising (dealt with in more detail in the next chapter) is by no means the only source of such bias, albeit the most obvious. Our knowledge of places where we have not been is always mediated through the mass media, arts, education and other people who have been there or who have some knowledge of them. In other words, the 'pull' of a destination is mediated through markers that point to the place. These markers are based on all the information (and misinformation) we have about the place. On the basis of markers we place the destination in the 'geography' level of our existential space.

The most influential marker that can attract people to a particular destination is the positive opinion of other people who have been there. The fact that someone had recommended the place was often the decisive impact that made people to want to go to this particular destination. It can be a (good) novelist, travel writer, friend or relative.

> My brother had been to Bali and he said it was great. I also read a book by a famous Danish travel writer who said that Bali was very interesting (Torsten, 21, a Dane).

In the case of a writer, the account has power because it is written by someone with recognised authority to make such claims. When we face someone who has had first hand experience of a place, the aspects of the account that are impossible to communicate in words become more meaningful; the enthusiasm can be seen, heard, felt and even shared. Vividness of expression and the fact that we meet the person face to face makes it easier to imaginatively transpose ourselves to the destination. Exchanging comments with someone in person means at least some degree of empathy. This again translates into feeling that it is possible to get oneself into similar kinds of situations, and therefore experiences, as the other person. We expect that if we travel to the same destination, we will most likely experience the place similarly to the person who told us about it. This imaginative self-transposal is an important part of motivation (and the advertisers know it well). The more the people who tell about the place are similar to us - fellow countrymen, same age, similar lifestyle, etc. - the more attention we pay to what they say. This is because then the account we get is readily incorporated into our own familiar socio-cultural framework.

Thus what we know about distant destinations is a socially constructed narrative. One of the most important results from this is that we are given a perspective on Other places through a primarily Western framework. Places and the meanings in them are brought to us in such a way that they make sense in our world view. Even if the local perspective is attempted, it is bound to be an outsiders' view of what the insiders' view would be. Thus, the pull-factors are always our own, outsiders' interpretations, and they reflect the hopes and fantasies we project to the places that are elsewhere. We can do so because our first hand involvement has not 'rationalised' our image of the place; actual experience does not interfere with imagination.

Through the entire history of popular music in Finland many of the most popular songs tell about distant, exotic places and the desire to get there.

> Beyond the ocean, in the distance somewhere is a land
> on its shores of happiness the waves whisper on the sand
> there the flowers beautiful eternally shed their light
> and the sorrow of tomorrow can be left aside.
>   Oh only if I once were able to enter that wonderland
> never would I leave its shores like the swallows in a band
> But without wings I cannot fly, I'm earth's unhappy heir
> Only my thoughts, unbounded, can carry me there.
> (Unto Mononen, translated from Finnish by L. Suvantola)

Distant places of those songs are not so much 'real' places as the geography of dreams, wishes, and adventure (Jokinen and Veijola, 1990, p. 37). Often also the distant places in our existential space, the ones on the level of 'geography', are equally marked by impressions which may have little to do with the realities of those places. We could perhaps argue that the motivation to travel to a particular destination is propelled by the imaginative self-transposal, rather than its pull-factors as such. Thus the motivation to travel is understandable as a search for something perceived to be fulfilled at the destination. Our motivation is based on the geography of dreams (Suvantola, 1999).

From the accounts of the travellers I distinguished three ways in which people end up to a destination. The first is when we become mesmerised by our mental image or memory of the place so that we want to go there. We may have more than just one of such desired places. It is important that we go particularly to these places; the pull there is a strong part of our overall motivation to travel. As an example, I met a Dutch girl who had always wanted to visit Indonesia because her grandfather was born there. In the second way the place just happens to be on the route. This often happens in the form of stopovers; the primary destination is somewhere else, and the stop is just a necessary part of getting there. In the third way of ending up travelling somewhere the destination itself is not so important as long as it meets certain requirements. Here we have a prior need to travel, we are not pulled by a particular place, but pushed by a need for change. So, when deciding where to go, we may have several possibilities, and the choice is made on the basis of cost effectiveness. A pull-factor of a destination is thus the perceived value for money it can offer. This tendency is very clear among the Finnish tourists, who are typically pushed to travel by the long, cold, dark and gloomy winter. When asked what would you like from your holiday destination, the majority wanted to travel to places where it is warm and the price of the trip not too expensive.

> All I want is that it is cheap and warm; the purpose is just to relax. Of course I'd like to see the local sights if there are any (Kaapo, 27).

The obvious pull relates to sun and warmth, it is quite incidental where these can be acquired. Consequently the destinations with proven record of such qualities and competitive prices are chosen. This means that in the winter the destinations where the operators have well-established infrastructure and therefore are able to offer cheap prices are popular. Thus Finns customarily go to the Canary Islands in the winter months and summer vacation is reserved for more elaborate destination choices. In terms of motivation; the desire to escape is prevalent in gloomy winter months, but during the summer vacation the need to escape is not so pressing and a greater degree of search can be accommodated.

Here the 'pull' has little to do with the characteristics of a particular destination (contrary to Dann's meaning of the concept). We are pulled to travel by something associated with travel itself, rather than with particular destinations (see Selänniemi, 1992, p. 40). Travel is active reaching for new experiences, therefore the term pull is misleading, because it gives the impression of treating humans as if we were just particles which are pulled by forces beyond our control. Thus it is better to conceptualise travel motives in terms of escape and search. The terms indicate that we ourselves are the actors in the process.

Escape and Search

Escape I interviewed a person who has a degree from a university, but who, prior to the interview, had been unemployed for over a year, since his graduation. He felt that he was useless for society; that it had dropped him off. For him, living in the same place for day after day (a financial necessity) became utterly meaningless and the only ways to ease the feeling of alienation were drinking and travel. It is just that the latter option was too expensive. In fact, drinking may be an alternative strategy to 'travel' away from the realities of home. Since being under the influence of narcotics is described as a 'trip', then being intoxicated by alcohol may well generate similar connotations.

The term escape expresses the need to lessen the weight of home. In extreme cases, the reason for the desire to escape can be anomie and the consequent alienation. If the degree of alienation from one's society is overwhelming, only the consciousness of the possibility of occasional breakout and escape can make everyday life tolerable (Dann, 1977, p. 188). Possible sources for such alienation include unemployment, or the constant need to suppress one's intentions and ideals because of some external pressure.

A more common and less dramatic motive to escape the home place is simply a need for a little bit of change.

> The most important thing in travelling is to get away, somewhere else... The routines of everyday are here in this place; even being free from work does not release you from them... If you have a holiday and you spend it at home, you do not consider it as a holiday. Immediately when you change place the homely tasks fade away, you change the topics you think about, work issues and things like that just vanish (Martti, 29).

There is the desire of getting at least temporarily away, without reference to a specific destination. This equals to travel into an 'anti-destination' (Urbain, 1989, p. 112; Krippendorf, 1987, p. 29). We want to get away, we want antistructure for the everyday. We are convinced that it can be achieved if we leave home.

Beside routines and alienation, the need to escape may also arise from unhappy events. The home place embodies the events that have taken place there. I met a woman who had lost her child and had immediately wanted to travel away:

> It did not matter where, as long as it was far away and I could leave right away (an unrecorded comment).

She told me how changing place helps to forget the sorrow, sorrow stirred by the familiar places that stand as constant remainders of the lost child. Three other backpackers (of the 16) were travelling to forget a broken relationship:

> I got to get away and get her out of my mind (Jim, 29).

Travel provides the necessary disengagement from familiar places so that through the travel experience it is possible to try to eradicate some of the old associations they embody, and invest them with additional new meanings. These can, to some extent, eventually soothe the painful association between the familiar places and the unhappy events that took place there. In this way the motives to escape arise from routines, alienation and mishaps. Naturally, travel can also be motivated without anything negative to escape from. We may have always wanted to see a particular place, while still being completely happy with our home place.

Search Without any necessarily dramatic events at home, the new impulses, presence-at-hand, is often expressed as the desire to seek novelty; the mere difference from home appeals:

> To get to a new place is always nice for a moment, even if the place was totally miserable. The fact that people act differently there from what they do here in the familiar environment is interesting... There is always something new when the place changes (Martti, 29).

> You see new places and people and it is more exotic to be away than in the familiar environment. Experiences are new and you look at things differently. It is change; [after that] you appreciate your home differently (Minna, 28).

These are rather sophisticated views of geography students, who can reflect (on the basis of previous travel experiences and education) on the notion that a new place makes them perceive differently. In the latter comment the idea of changing attitude to the things home is also present. In Seamon's terms, going away changes the mode of merely 'watching' the environment into a mode of 'noticing' it.

In this way the dialectics of home and reach create the simultaneous desire to escape and search. Even though escape is the desire to get away without any special destination necessarily in mind, getting away always provides something instead. In other words, if we escape something, we also want something else (better) instead; there is thus a fine line between escape and search. So, rather than being alternative sets of motivations, escape and search are successive or coexist (Urbain, 1989, p. 113). The examples of escape demonstrated that an escape becomes a search for relief from what was escaped. Thus, for example, marvelling at the architecture of a Balinese temple may help us to forget daily routines back home, or even the loss of a loved person, granted that we have achieved some degree of recovery already.

Novelty is often associated with specific features of the destination; these features resemble what were called pull-factors earlier. Novelty is sought not only for its own sake but can also serve as a means for personal development. While we may

> want to see India because of the culture (Denise, 22),

the motive arises from the desire to experience more than is possible at home. Here reach in its spatial sense is very concrete:

> If you never go anywhere, your sphere of life is quite limited. Of course, some are satisfied with little (Martti, 29).

Novelty of the things encountered is thought to put oneself in a situation where one has to re-define one's relation to things. This redefinition is thought to bring personal development. Especially among the backpackers, personal development was the single most important object of search. Many expressed the idea that travel was their quest for direction in life:

> I wasn't sure where I was heading [in my life] (Jim, 29).

> [On this trip] we look for future direction, for self, for confidence (Denise, 22 and Aron, 23).

In the pursuit of this

> the destination is less important than being on the way, it is interesting to see people and places, but more importantly, travelling helps you to put things in your own life in perspective (Tina, 24 and John, 26).

Thus, while novelty is part of what is sought, it is the act of travel, irrespective of the destinations, which allows the detachment from the usual everyday life at home. This detachment facilitates reflection on what that life is and how it relates to what we would like it to be. This is summarised by Craik who writes: 'tourism is a secularised experience of locating oneself in the world' (Craik, 1991, p. 31). This supports the idea that backpacking travel especially for younger people is a form of rite of passage. A British couple felt that it is becoming a norm in Britain for young people to take time off and travel (Tina, 24 and John, 26).

A theme closely related to personal development is the search for freedom. The perceived freedom to decide what we do is seen as providing the detachment we need to be able to have a new perspective on our life. Being free from the restraining commitments of everyday life is supposed by the traveller to facilitate the true expression of self. It also forces the travellers to take responsibility for themselves, which teaches self-confidence. It is probable that while the prospective backpackers anticipate the personal development that the experience of freedom is supposed to generate, the process in which this takes place becomes meaningful only in the experience (all the references above are, indeed, recorded either on the trip or after it). The pre-travel expectation of personal development derives from the experiences of others who have told about the impact the travel had in their lives or who are perceived to have changed as a result of a trip.

Searching for freedom for its own sake, rather than knowing that it will also be an element in bringing personal development is surprisingly more often implied than clearly stated. Two respondents told how they wanted to travel while the opportunity was still there:

This is my last chance to do some real travelling (Jim, 29).

I wanted to go before I got too much older (Roy, 30).

They explained that when they go back home, it is likely that they will have to settle down and start to pursue their careers. The long-term travel could be their last opportunity to taste freedom from the responsibilities of working life. It would be easy to imagine that the search for such temporary freedom is an important motive to travel and that people would express it clearly, especially in backpacking context, but it seems to be somehow shadowed by the search for self-development. Reasons for this may be that these people did not feel imprisoned by their home. Thus they do not have to escape in order to search for freedom, something that they felt they have achieved at home already. On the other hand, limited time and heavy dependence on the touristic infrastructure do not necessarily bring about a feeling of freedom on a conventional tourist trip, let alone on a bus tour. This is probably why the motive of freedom did not appear at all in the conversations with the conventional tourists. In their situation freedom appeared from a different perspective. Their travel had little to do with searching for personal development, but the motives were associated more with escape from routines and winter. The freedom sought was freedom from routines and cold, not freedom for its own sake. Here the interconnection between the motives of escaping and searching is especially clear; the tourists seek release from what they escape.

Nowhere is the fact that the reach in travel also involves dimensions other than spatial as clear as when people who are well acquainted at home set out to go on a bus-tour trip. The main motive is not to become familiar with other places and cultures; it is to reach for new contexts of social interaction within the group, togetherness:

> Always when you tour in a group of students like us, it has nothing to do with travelling, you just move to new places to have fun between yourselves (Martti, 29).

Our bus trip to Turkey was seen as a forum to expand the extent of mutual interaction with friends by providing new situations in which our friendship could be expressed. There is also a lot of anecdotal evidence of holiday romances; the possibility of such a romance must be a part of the motivation to travel for some. Travel is an opportunity to indulge in the reach for new emotional experiences. Readiness-to-hand of the relationships at home and its established situations turns into presence-at-hand in new places - themselves maybe incidental - but nevertheless conducive to new kinds of situations in which new relationships can emerge and the existing ones get new aspects. This kind of reach is thus not primarily spatial, even though it involves moving from one place to another.

Authenticity is commonly cited as an important motivation for travel (MacCannell, 1976; Cohen, 1988b; van den Berghe, 1994; Waitt and McGuirk, 1994). Waitt and McGuirk (1994, p. 5) for example describe the 'post-modern tourist quest' as tourists 'seeking heritage (real or perceived) to counteract inauthentic postmodern life'.[2] It is a quest for continuity in this fragmented world where many feel that the firsthand contacts with the events of life are getting buried beneath an increasing amount of spurious experiences, produced by various industries (there is a telling paradox here; the travel industry provides the supposed means of release from these second-hand experiences).

---

[2] This is quite exactly what MacCannell (1976) wrote about modern tourists, and quite contrary to what Urry (1990) wrote about post-modern tourists for whom travel is a game in which authenticity is largely irrelevant.

This description is a gross overstatement of the extent of spuriousness the people I interviewed felt in their everyday lives. Most of them were quite happy with their lives. But there is a kernel of truth in it; the home place is not always perceived to provide all the desired experiences that are felt important in gaining personal development. A large part of this may be the feeling that our lives are directed by structures and events bigger than ourselves, and that we consequently have too little control on our own lives. A backpacking trip is seen as an opportunity to take charge of our own life. Travelling with a backpack gives the feeling that all the things in life are right here, right now. We feel that we have more than usual control of our lives. This relates strongly to the motive of being free, however, before the first backpacking trip this motive of searching for authentic first hand experience of life cannot be well articulated. It can only be anticipated on the basis of vicarious experiences. Thus part of the motivation to travel is precisely this search for authentic, immediate hold on life, which is hard to experience at home. The authenticity is not sought in the destination, but in the act of travel itself. The search for authenticity from travel is thus merely instrumental in search for personal development.

If authenticity is sought in the features of the destination, it may be hard to distinguish this desire from the desire to seek novelty. The desire to see India because of the culture implies that the culture has a certain novelty value, which is increased if it is perceived as authentic. Thus the anticipation of seeing authentic local cultures is effectively a quest for novelty, and thus presence-at-hand. Of the two groups I interviewed, most backpackers expressed the desire to see authentic cultures and customs, while for the conventional tourists the authenticity of the destination was largely irrelevant. They were more concerned with having fun and some change from their home environment.

These findings do not support the notion of 'travel career' (Pearce, 1988, pp. 27-34). The concept is based on Maslow's hierarchy of needs. It is assumed that people's preference of how, and to what kind of destinations they want to travel, changes during the course of their lives. Early in our travel career we are supposed to be content to satisfy our basic physiological needs (such as rest, food, drink, sex), but later we seek the fulfilment of higher needs (such as self-development and self-actualisation). With the young backpackers in my material the opposite seems to be the case; their first backpacking trip is strongly motivated by the search for self-development. Also the 'Interrail' travels of teenage Europeans are search for identity for many.

In all, I was able to discern two main search-motives, under which other motives can be grouped. These main motives are search for presence-at-hand, and personal development. Not even these are always separable from each other, as it is possible to search for personal development through presence-at-hand. Search for novelty, authenticity, freedom, and social interaction can all be seen as components of the two main motives. All the things searched for represent the attempt to reach beyond what is ready-to-hand at home. Usually the motivation for travel is a complex mix of escape- and search motives. We can travel without necessarily escaping anything, but voluntary travel without search for something is inconceivable.

Reaching for a Centre

In Cohen's (1979) typology of different modes of travel the central feature determining the type of motivation is the extent in which authenticity is sought. Although I have rejected the search of authenticity as an independent source of motivation, it is indeed a component in some of the search motivations. Thus as opposite to Cohen's typology, what is expected to be authentic varies; it can be the experience of having control of life, or a people living 'unspoiled' by tourism or development. I want to relate my findings to Cohen's typology, because it helps to understand where the types represented by my respondents belong in the field of different modes of travel.

The conventional tourists belong clearly to what Cohen (1979) calls recreationary mode. Their spiritual centre is clearly in their home society and they feel that their lives there provide them with a reasonable amount of authenticity. Only the unemployed interviewee expressed ideas that would depart from the recreational mode. His emphasis on the escape-side of motivation as the desire to get away from the feeling of alienation is clearly diversionary in Cohen's sense. The experiental mode of travel describes MacCannell's tourist and neither group of people I interviewed fits into this category. Here the desire to escape moderate alienation is balanced by the desire to search for authenticity in novelty. I found little evidence of alienation from the backpackers, although many of them were searching for authenticity. A further difference is that the experiental tourists tend to remain tightly within the frameworks the tourism industry creates while the backpackers intend to be less dependent on them. The experimental mode of travel would otherwise describe my backpacker respondents well, except that in Cohen's typology such travellers are necessarily alienated from their own societies. Like Cohen's experimental tourists, my backpacker respondents were clearly in search of personal development. These people are developing, extending, and testing their existing spiritual centre, rather than looking for a new one. The aspect of search in experimental motivation rather than escape from alienation should be emphasised. Among my interviewees there was only one person, the unemployed conventional tourist, who displayed feelings of alienation.

To say that our spiritual centre is within our society does not necessarily mean that it is physically a certain place there; it is first of all the socio-cultural adherence in which we organise our thinking in a way we have learned. To search elsewhere for more elements to use in that thinking does not mean that the centredness of the thinking is moving away from one's own society. It is just gaining depth from the experience of presence-at-hand. Thus while seeking personal development, places - while instrumental - can be quite incidental to what is searched for. Hence it is not always relevant to talk about searching for a spiritual centre outside one's society in spatial sense, because this centre is often existential rather than spatial. It is sought from the experience of the Other (presence-at-hand), rather than from the Other as such. For the people I interviewed it is the experience of being on the way, travelling, which is important, not so much the places visited.

The fact that my interviewees were predominantly happy with their lives at home supports the idea of seeing travel as reach. 'To reach' implies search rather than escape. The escape motives found (release from routines, alienation, and mishaps) are not so significant as the search motives (the search for presence-at-hand and personal development). This does not mean that there would not always be some unfortunate individuals for whom one of the escape motives is predominant. However, my interviewees were more motivated by the anticipation of what they could find on their travels, rather than by the need to escape something at home.

Advertising: Geography of Dreams

In balancing between home and reach, travel becomes an expression of reach. It allows us to balance familiarity and excitement, the readiness-to-hand of home and the presence-at-hand of the Other. This need has become so common and compelling that market forces have realised the huge potential for profits in providing people with the means which appear to widen their horizons of reach. There is now an industry providing the reach; reach through travel has been commercially institutionalised.

A lot of reach is pursued in leisure time. Most imaginable forms of reach, and consequently our use of leisure time, have been largely institutionalised. We spend our leisure time by consuming. There are businesses catering to every possible aspect of our leisure time. It is difficult to think about any sport, pastime or hobby without commercial connections; even walkers are offered special shoes, clothes, accessories, and magazines. Businesses have processed people's need to have 'anti routines' (Jokinen and Veijola, 1990, p. 104). In our leisure time we try to pursue our dreams, but now, according to Adorno, businesses are turning our own dreams back on us, in the form of commodities (Ibid., p. 144). Travel is one of these commodities and our dreams are the material that the travel industry utilises in advertising it. Travel advertising is the means through which the travel industry tries to create motivations for travel, and convert those motivations into actual travel. Travel is 'society's institutionalized means of enabling fantasy and reality to be imperceptibly mixed' (Uzzell, 1984, p. 85). The travel industry 'packages the image, or dream, into a whole, and markets it as a single basket-full of leisure experience' (Reimer, 1990, p. 503). Thus travel is a commodity that is made tempting to us by using elements of our own daydreams and fantasies and also by creating and enhancing our stock of them.

This kind of portrayal of travel advertising is especially applicable in the case of conventional tourism. Backpacking as such has rarely been advertised by the travel industry since the very idea of this mode of travel has been to avoid the structures of conventional tourism. Thus there has been a perception within the travel industry that there is limited commercial potential in backpacking, although this attitude is changing fast[3] (more about this in a later chapter).

Markers of a Destination

A travel advertisement is a marker of the destination or the act of travel; it directs our attention to it. Markers are things, ideas and narratives that point to what they mark; they contribute to our image of the marked. Of course

---

[3] The impact of backpackers on the national economy at least in Australia demonstrably exceeds that of the conventional tourists (Loker [no date], p. 55; Haigh, 1995; Loker-Murphy and Pearce, 1995, pp. 836-838). This happens simply because they usually stay in the country much longer than the conventional tourists. Although they spend less on a daily basis, over time their cumulative expenditure is greater.

advertising is not the only creator of markers; markers of a destination or a travel experience can be, for example, postcards, posters, books, news, advertisements and even our daydreams. All the information and misinformation we have about places and peoples can be used in creating markers. Significant producers of markers, apart from deliberate advertising are travel literature, movies and art. Pocock (1992, p. 239) noted that for visitors, the essence of a region about which a famous author had written, was the image that the author had created. For example, in the USA the fame of the movie 'Crocodile Dundee' aroused a lot of American interest in Australia and increased travel there (Riley and van Doren, 1992). Australia's image as having interesting exotic natural environment and indigenous culture was enhanced. This imagery also implied that Australia would satisfy the need for adventure. This suggests that an image created and enforced by sufficiently powerful markers and sustained by the travel industry, defines a destination more than any 'realities' of the place. Powerful markers promote matching images. The consequent image of the place is vivid and therefore powerful, and acts as a new marker in turn. It is easy to empathetically live a narrative description provided by a good book or a movie, instead of scattered pieces of information. Furthermore, these kinds of markers are often the main sources of information we have about the places.

In this way a vivid description of a place (whether the place is real or imaginary) can give a strong feeling of insideness towards the place, thus marking it. This insideness is vicarious; it is not mediated through our bodily presence, but through imagination that gives us the feeling of intense involvement with the place. In our imagination we project ourselves there and vicariously live through the experiences of the characters (Relph, 1976, p. 52). Adventures and exotic places may even mesmerise us to the extent that they turn into daydreams. Reading Tarzan books as a child left lasting image of jungle in my mind, and seeing a movie about Robinson Crusoe made me imagine what it would be like to live on an uninhabited island. Later, Gauguin's paintings of Tahiti and stories of missionaries and anthropologists among distant peoples created curiosity about how those peoples really live. The desire to find confirmation to these markers was indeed an important part of my motivation to set out for my first big trip. Thus our image of the place in our existential space is based on its markers. Not all markers are equally powerful in contributing to this image, however. Travel advertisements actively try to utilise the effects of the other powerful markers that favour the destination.

This is aided conceptually by distinguishing between 'organic' and 'induced' images of travel experiences (Gunn, 1988, p. 24; Echtner and Ritchie, 1991, p. 3; Fakeye and Crompton, 1991, p. 11). Organic image means the accumulation of mental images about travel experiences that happens before the person has encountered any commercially orientated sources of information, i.e. advertising (a situation, which nowadays is quite inconceivable). An induced image results when we have become interested in a specific potential travel experience (or a destination) and actively search for information about it. The organic image then becomes modified by the addition of the impact of commercial information into it. The concept of organic image in its fullest sense is clearly an abstraction: among the markers we encounter there is always also some commercial material that refers either to the attraction, or at least to a similar type of attraction, thus altering the image by bringing some induced elements to the otherwise apparently organic setting. Surrounded by the mass media which continuously feeds us with images of products, and thus also images of travel destinations, there is little chance that our consciousness would not be influenced by these images. The threshold between organic and induced images is therefore our conscious effort to seek information: While we are indeed likely to encounter commercial material among other markers, only after the decision to seek more information about a specific travel experience, does that material receive special attention from us. This is when the organic image gives way to the induced one.

In order to be effective, these induced images have to be understandable to the people they are directed to. Therefore the symbols and reference structures used in them have to be based on the public's common stock of knowledge. It is little wonder then, that they are full of stereotypes and images that reinforce our existing impressions. They provide us with depictions to which we can relate on the basis of our experiences, imagination and needs. The depictions mirror the values and aspirations of our culture, not the culture of the destination (Hanefors and Larsson, 1993, p. 32). The important role these images have, is illustrated for example in a study which found that of the British tourists interviewed, over 50% based their choice of the destination solely on the information provided in travel brochures (Mansfeld, 1992, p. 407). Thus the actual decisions to travel to a particular destination are heavily based on these induced images. It follows that the proportion of people who choose the destination using the brochures at least to some extent, must be even larger.

Barthesian Myths

Markers, by definition, are signs and signifiers of what they refer to, which is signified. An elementary example of the relationship between signifier and signified is language. A word is a sign for a thing or a meaning, which the word is not in itself, but to which it refers. Barthes (1972) calls this first order semiotics. The second order appears when the totality of signifier and signified is formed into a symbol that again points to something else. Thus, for example, the word 'beach' refers to a certain kind of piece of landscape. Through some complex social processes, the word and its meaning have together begun to signify other concepts, e.g. relaxation, leisure, etc. The result is what Barthes (1972, p. 109) calls a 'myth'.[4] Of course, these myths are not limited to just two orders; there can be indefinite number of these symbolic layers. The tourist discourse, and especially the advertising element of it, is an excellent breeding ground for myths. In advertisements the signs which are familiar to us and which provide pleasant connotations with what is advertised, are brought upon our eyes. The advertising message is 'full of implicit references: beneath its enunciation it is a representation' (Urbain, 1989, p. 108).

We are offered vacation images that are supposed to confirm the sweetest images we may hold already. What was initially part of our imagination, becomes marketed as reality. Travel advertising utilises our tendency to project our dreams on the level of 'geography' of our existential space and tries to make us believe that the product it sells conforms exactly to those projections. This possibility arises from the quality of places as symbols. The destinations advertised are turned into symbols of images and ideals that respond to our more or less real needs. Thus travel advertising creates and sustains myths (in Barthes' sense) by using the existing semiotic connotations and creating new ones within which the prospective tourists place themselves in the semiotics:

> Not far away in the blue seas of the South Pacific are the beautiful islands of Fiji - truly a paradise, a kaleidoscope of experiences to replenish the spirit (Qantas Jetabout Holidays; Fiji 1993-1994, p. 4).

Here the South Pacific and its islands signifying paradise are a well-established semiotic connotation (geographical location and features are substituted for an ideal). In the terms of semiotics, the beautiful islands in

---

[4] The meaning of myth in this context differs from the anthropological meaning of the concept. In anthropology myth is a narrative that explains the existing social realities.

the South Pacific (signifier) stand for an ideal habitat where living is exclusively a joy (signified). This is already a myth far beyond the first order semiotics. The accumulation of Barthesian myth continues when the semiotic connotation of the islands and the paradise is transferred to the role of signifier in a next order semiotic (Uzzell, 1984, p. 86). Now the prospective tourists place themselves in the framework provided and create that next order semiotic – see Table 6.1.

Table 6.1   Accumulation of myths

	Signifier	Signified	
(N)th order	South Pacific +	Beautiful islands =	Paradise =>
(N+1)th order	Paradise +	Buying the trip =	The experience of paradise

When travel advertising sustains myths and creates new ones it actually only provides the elements for the prospective tourists who each individually do the creation for themselves. The step from signifiers to signified is not big. Often it is possible to separate them only in conceptual analysis. The established semiotic connotations the advertising utilises are a part of our socio-cultural heritage and because of that, their interpretation by us in a way that suits the purposes of the advertisers comes naturally. This means that the features used (like the four s's: sea, sun, sand, sex) 'have powerful semiotic function in their own right' (Uzzell, 1984, p. 97).

Escape

It is hardly surprising that the theme of escape, while being a part of motivation for much travel, is also well recognised by the travel industry as worth exploiting. There is a big travel agency called 'Swingaway', another's motto is 'The greatest escape' (Viva! Holidays), a catalogue of a third is 'Escape' (STA Travel), and innumerable holiday packages are sold as a 'Getaway'. Thus travel advertising has evolved into an art that is able to increase our perceived need to escape our everyday life and convince us that the travel industry has the means to provide this escape.

Emphasising the negative attributes of our everyday life is a carefully calculated method to make us feel out of place at home (MacCannell, 1976, p. 154). This kind of advertisement promotes release from the rules and codes of our everyday life (Craik, 1991, p. 34). Our everyday life is described so that the words stressful, mundane, dull, and artificial come to mind. Then again, this must be done in a delicate way so that we do not get offended by advertising that we feel is underestimating our way of life. A clever advertisement only gives a hint of what we may have had in our minds already; we are supposed to arrive spontaneously and 'independently' at the final conclusion that is, to see our 'need' to travel away. A typical way to achieve this effect is to use expressions like 'Getaway', 'The greatest escape', 'escape from the dreariness of the winter to the...', and so forth. These expressions are entirely or in part signifiers of something negative. Once we have seen the signifier we do the semiotic interpretation and construct a whole in which we place ourselves into the situation where our 'need' to escape becomes 'obvious'. 'Getaway from your place!', implies the advertisement, and we inevitably continue in our minds: '...to experience something different'. The 'dreariness of winter' reminds us about our everyday routines associated with our place without even mentioning them. The word 'winter' is enough to create a negative image in our minds as follows: winter = cold + dark + routines = this place => need to escape, to 'get away'.

Urbain (1989, p. 115) shows how some travel advertisements that use the escape-theme connote travel as a departure from home 'with no specific quest or new referent'. This requires playing down the home, while the destination is kept as a vague image of something alternative, an anti-destination. Urbain's example is an advertisement by an airline: 'From Grey to Blue Without Stopping' (Ibid.). Here the motives of escape are utilised so that it is not so much the matter of what specific features there are in the destination as far as the image created of it responds to our psychological needs (Pearce, 1982, p. 65; Uzzell, 1984, p. 80). The Finnish tourists who want to travel to southern destinations in order to escape the wintertime are typical prey for this kind of advertising. As it appeared, the qualities of the destinations do not matter as long as the requirements of warmth and relaxation from everyday routines are satisfied. I'd imagine a similar sentiment is held by Britons who travel to destinations in Spain, commonly referred as 'Costa del Anywhere' or 'Costa del Whatsit'.

Communicative Staging

The attention catching slogans described here (like 'Getaway!', 'The greatest escape') are used mainly in posters and titles of price lists in order to evoke interest. Obviously advertisements about particular destinations or travel experiences have to provide a more concrete picture about the product.

Travel brochures provide more or less detailed descriptions through which the image of the destination is consequently formed. It is all about creating favourable images of the destinations or travel experiences and the possibilities for 'discovery' in these. This process of image making by travel advertising involves purposeful simplification, exaggeration and misinterpretation. Applying theatrical terminology, originally applied to social science by Goffman, Cohen (1989, p. 49) calls this process 'communicative staging'. His context was local staging that was used in jungle trekking in order to give the tourists the impression that they really are encountering traditional tribal people and their truly 'traditional' life style, quite spontaneously. Tourist brochures communicatively stage the destination and the travel experience and create images designed to meet the psychological needs of potential tourists. The image of the place has to appear simple so that it is easy to grasp, it has to be exaggerated to catch attention, and finally, it has to include at least some measure of misinterpretation in order to be able to achieve either of the former two.

Simplification consists of forming a stereotypical mass identity for a destination by selectively emphasising elements that appeal to potential tourists. The destination has to appear as a comprehensible whole whose qualities are in harmony with the touristic infrastructure offered there. Thus the role of the information provided about environment, climate, people and culture is to facilitate the imaginative transposal of one's images and dreams to the destination.

> Travel to a land where gilded spires and jewelled Buddhas shimmer against afternoon skies; where classical Thai dancers enchant with their grace and exotic festivals fill the streets with colour. The magic of Thai culture is rivalled only by the beauty of its sparkling beaches, tropical rainforests and warm, hospitable people. So discover the treasures of Thailand and you'll soon see why they call it the Land of Smiles (an advertisement by Tourism Authority of Thailand in Time; August 7, 1995, p. 9).

By exaggerating some qualities of the destination it is possible to capture our attention. It is also an attempt to persuade us that the imaginative transposal of our dreams and ourselves is justified; the destination lives up to those images. The most commonly exaggerated quality is authenticity, it is conveyed in terms like 'ancient', 'traditional', 'untouched', 'best kept secret', etc. It has to be that way in order to allow us to 'discover' and 'explore' the places.

Tavanipupu is such a paradise, I almost regret revealing its existence (Australian, 25-26 March 1995, p. 16 of the travel section).

My friend and I promised we'd keep it a secret from our friends (Escape, 2/1995, p. 29).

The secret sells. In this way the supposedly 'unspoiled' nature of a place becomes institutionalised. This eventually leads to the loss of that quality by luring masses of tourists, who seek authenticity, to the place.

To facilitate a plausible touristic presentation in which peoples, sights and activities form a neat tourist system around the facilities offered, it is often necessary to misinterpret some of the local realities. Of course, simplification and exaggeration are misinterpretation already, but other forms of misinterpretation also occur. Mostly the objects of misinterpretation are the local customs and conventions where treatment as an important guest is applied to tourists.

It has been only in recent years that visitors have been *invited* to share the thrill of the Pentecost leap (Vanuatu brochure, emphasis added).

One doubts, whether visitors have been invited to share the thrill. Rather, I suspect that persuasion on the part of the travel industry has been so strong that tourists have been admitted. In everyday language communicative staging would be called selective, partial and decorated truths, or even outright lies. But as Krippendorf (1987, p. 22) has noted, even if we can see beyond the clichés and lies of those advertisements, it is nevertheless, pleasant to become seduced by them again and again. Clever communicative staging creates an interesting framework for a trip. As long as all participants play their role in that framework, the actual truthfulness of the communicative staging is incidental, because the play itself is enjoyable.

Marketing Personalised Daydreams

While travel advertising indeed uses our own daydreams to sell its product, it more importantly provides further material for those daydreams (Reimer 1990, p. 503; Urry 1990, p. 13). Krippendorf (1987, p. 22) noted how people describe their motivation to travel by reiterating all the reasons that feature in advertising. Travel advertising has managed to create public meanings for destinations. To be effective, advertisement has to cause us to internalise those public meanings so that we imaginatively place ourselves into the milieu it depicts. Without this imaginative self-transposal the advertisement cannot address us personally. The internalised public meanings created or affected by advertising are material for us to create our own private meanings. Thus, in the case of an effective advertisement, we are not just passive receivers of it. On top of the (often unconscious) process in which we make the semiotic interpretation of the message, we also expand it to be applicable to our own situation. Successful advertising makes us to dream about: 'What if I...?'.

> The clear hues of blue sky and seas of Greece are renowned. But *when you are there, its other colors will awe you* - the flaming reds from a setting sun, the gold when it rises, the rich green of the olive trees, the stark white of the buildings on the Aegean Islands and the ochre of those on islands anchored in Ionian. Each color *speaks to your heart* in a different way. GREECE Makes your heart beat! (Olympic Airways; advertisement in the Australian Travel Section, March 25, 1995, p. 15; emphasis added).

Thus our fantasies are not necessarily entirely our own creation, but personal versions of images created or at least focused by advertising. Advertising tries to make us think about our possibilities and ourselves in the world of travel that is based on images. We can transpose ourselves into that world without considering the everyday roles and rules that restrict us in normal life. The possibility that we could actually do what we wish in the world of travel should be a clear implication that such a world is a world of fantasy (Dann, 1977, p. 188). Travel advertising causes us to fantasize about finding something valuable or exciting in the destination. At the surface level (Urbain's enunciation) of the advertisement we are sold the pull-factors of the place, but at the deeper level of representation we are offered our dreams. This way the potential travellers project their travel according to those fantasies and form their expectations beforehand (Dann, 1981, p. 201). Advertising gives us a mental framework for our journey and for our appreciation of the destination already before we depart.

An important way of promoting travel destinations and experiences, in which our daydreams play an important role, are travelogues. They appear in newspapers' travel sections and in popular magazines, and are a mixture of travel description and advertising. Nowhere else it is so easy to see how the language of advertisements is incorporated into travel writers' accounts of a trip. This is largely due to the fact that the writers are frequently sponsored by the travel industry and therefore they have to promote their product. However, sometimes the writers write from a genuine desire to share their great experience, and usually these accounts incorporate quite similar repetition of the themes of advertising. Whether this is conscious or not is not always obvious, but it nevertheless indicates that in any case advertisements contribute to the actual experiences and on how people report them.

> From its palm garden setting, Kota's Ding Dong restaurant presents a view to soothe any soul. Over succulent serves of fresh crab, king prawns and lapu-lapu fish, you gaze in meditative bliss at the shimmering lagoon, white sandy beach, turquoise waters and a sister island, Cabaliad, beyond (The Advertiser Weekend Magazine, April 1, 1995, p. 39).

Thus, while the above account is a part of an advertising feature, it could be hard to distinguish it from an account of any traveller who has personally lived such an experience and who is capable of such vivid literary expression. This kind of advertising makes the imaginative self-transposal easy, and is thus efficient.

In all advertising it is important to facilitate easy imaginative self-transposal by recognising various market segments. Thus the same operator offers tennis, scuba-diving, golfing, fishing, boating, adventure, exploring, and indulgence holidays, as well as something for singles, families and honeymooners (Qantas Jetabout Holidays; Fiji 1993-1994, p. 5). This is designed to appeal to our need to be recognised as an individual. The expressions of advertisements are calculated to make us feel that they are speaking to us in our situation; they seem to have something just for us. It gives us that flattering feeling that we as persons are the focus of their attention.

> While in Bali you'll be very well looked after... Tour East will meet you on arrival in Bali, transfer you to your hotel, and take care of any sightseeing arrangements you may require during the course of your holiday (Jetset Bali 1994-1995, p. 2).

The advertisement plays on our natural need for recognition. By addressing us personally,[5] the advertisement also tries to direct our imagination towards the self-transposal.

Search

In its attempt to present travel as an answer to psychological needs, travel advertising depicts travel as a horizon of reach in all imaginable aspects of life.

> Exciting cultures, breathtaking scenery, inspiring new friends, endless variety (Club Med; New Caledonia, Tahiti 1992, p. 5).

Thus travel advertising turns the purchase of the trip into an endeavour to enlarge one's restorable reach. It facilitates the transforming of the level of 'geography' in one's existential space into the sphere of personal first hand involvement. Mostly the search involves some kind of novelty that provides change from the everyday. However, even in the advertising directed to the mass tourists, there also emerges the theme of personal development. According to some advertisements, the travel experiences they offer can result in transformation of self (Bruner, 1991, p. 239). Urbain (1989, p. 116) refers to the same thing by characterising some vacation experiences as identity adventures. An advertisement suggests that the product gives new perspectives, and that the experience will make us different (implying 'better') people.

> However you spend your holiday in Fiji, the spirit of the islands will transform you (Qantas Jetabout Holidays; Fiji 1993-1994, p. 4).

> And perhaps above all, you may make an important rediscovery. Yourself (Club Med; New Caledonia, Tahiti 1992, p. 5).

---

[5] Sometimes the advertisers bend over backwards to address as wide as possible a segment of potential tourists and individuals at the same time: You may be young, or as young as you feel. You may want to do everything. Or nothing at all. Whatever holiday you're thinking of, at Club Med we've probably already thought of it. There are sports of all sorts, clubs for kids, activities for the active and the inactive, night clubs open till the next day, traditional cultures, modern conveniences, and staff to take care of everything. Especially you. (...) And unlike other holidays, the package cost doesn't mean we treat our guests as a package too. You are an individual, free to do as you choose (Club Med; New Caledonia, Tahiti 1992, pp. 2,4).

The communicatively staged image is created so that it is supposed to bring about this self-transformation. To underline this the advertisements give the idea that the impetus for self-development has to come from the outside. The need for self-development is thus institutionalised. This is quite natural; otherwise there would be little need to use the services of the travel industry in pursuing it. Another way to self-development as implied by the travel advertising is through the experience of novelty as adventure. The travellers are made to feel as if they were some kind of heroes, adventurers, who dare to break the boundaries of normal everyday living. MacCannell (1976, p. 159) writes about authenticity and how it is 'available only to those moderns who try to break the bonds of their everyday existence and begin to "live"'. Some advertising portrays adventure travellers as present day heroes who can achieve something more than everyday life and conventional tourism are able to offer.

> Far away or near, Discovery holidays start where the package tours stop and the crowds thin out (Exodus Discovery Holidays 1994-1995, p. 3).

Marketing the Infrastructure

Communicative staging of the destinations arises from the need to cater for tourists' different psychological needs. One escapes boredom at home, another seeks for experiences that inspire the spirit. However, whatever their psychological needs, the basic physical needs of all tourists are more or less the same; that is, holiday destinations everywhere have to provide accommodation, food, activities, accessibility, etc. Consequently, the infrastructure of the travel industry is basically very similar, whether it is located in Australia or the Bahamas. Of course, there are significant differences in the extent of luxury and affordability, but if the infrastructure within a certain price range is compared, the similarities usually far exceed the differences. Differences are merely results of adding some 'local colour' to the otherwise similar infrastructure. In the advertising it can be seen at first sight, that the potential tourist is not so much offered a particular place, but the image created about that place and the infrastructure located there to serve him. Browsing through any travel brochure gives the impression that hotels and swimming pools are the single most important features of the destinations (see Cooper and Ozdil, 1992, p. 384).

> A deluxe hotel enjoying a convenient location overlooking Lumpini Park. A minute's walk away is Bangkok's major commercial, shopping and

entertainment district. Every guestroom combines modern 5-star luxury with the *opulence of Traditional Thai Style*. Colour TV, air conditioning, hairdryer, safe, swimming pool, restaurants, bars, fitness centre, tennis and squash courts (Creative Tours; Thailand Apr 95-Mar 96, p. 12; emphasis added).

From the conventional tourist's perspective differences of the destinations are largely the differences in how the touristic infrastructure is presented (Holloway and Plant, 1992, p. 150). The role of communicative staging is to emphasise those differences by trying to unite the 'local colour' with the infrastructure. Thus it creates an image of the 'spirit of place', albeit within the part of the tourist discourse that has been generated by advertising. Combining the infrastructure with the local colour is important because the latter represents the Other; often the very justification of travel. In the above advertisement this is emphasised by capitalising 'Traditional Thai Style'. The style is presented as if it was a distinguished and clearly defined autonomous style rather than a collection of stereotyped features that, for the tourists at least, represent 'traditional' Thailand.

Travel Advertising as a Part of the Tourist Discourse

The conventional tourists I interviewed used primarily newspaper advertisements as their sources of information for the decision of where to travel. As they want to escape the dreariness of winter and know well what they want from their destination (warmth), they seek for the most cost effective destination. Thus the most relevant information at that stage does not need to describe the specific features of the place (insofar as they know it is somewhere warm) but the price of the trip. Once the decision to travel to a particular destination was made, then more specific information was sought. A large portion of such travel related information is found in the advertising material and is thus an integral part of the tourist discourse. Most people see through the phraseology of the advertisements, but even then the images they create are very real in our minds. The power of this material in shaping our perceptions does not primarily reside in the phrases and pictures of a particular advertisement. Rather, it is present in the tourist discourse that is represented in the advertisement. The tourist discourse is thus a collection of powerful myths (in the Barthesian sense), and a single travel advertisement is a representation of those myths. We may well be aware that travel advertising is just a play with more or less biased images, but nevertheless, we still want to take part in that play. Thus travel advertising wants to direct our framework for travel into the established conventions of the tourist discourse. These conventions are created, sustained, and used by the travel industry.

> There's the Pacific. And then there's Club Med's Pacific (Club Med; New Caledonia, Tahiti 1992, p. 1).

The wording of this advertisement implies that the realities of this destination for the tourists can be quite distinct from its other realities.

Travel creates a framework within which expectations are formed and which directs the experience. The myths and images created and sustained by the travel industry are designed to become self-fulfilling prophecies. This works in at least two ways. First, the advertisements' expressions become elements of language used in describing travel experiences. Second, whether we see through the biased images the advertising tries to create or not, we easily compare and apprehend our experience in relation to those images, thus creating the framework for our experiences. Hence, travel advertising is an integral and influential part of the tourist discourse.

7 Tourist Discourse and Tourist Space

The Travel Industry and Standardising

The Travel Industry

An early definition for the travel industry is given by Likorish and Kershaw (1958, cited in Gee, Choy and Makens, 1989, p. 4): The travel industry is 'that part of the national economy which caters for the traveller who is visiting places outside the locality where he resides or works'. At present the definition is somewhat outdated because it only includes so called 'direct providers' (e.g. travel agencies) who are dealing directly with travellers. Later-developed sectors of 'support services (e.g. hotel management firms) and 'developmental organizations' (e.g. planners, government agencies) are ignored (Ibid., pp. 5-7). Also the days when the travel industry was restricted to the level of national and local economies are far behind; trans- and multi-national companies now have a lion's share of the tourist dollar. However, while acknowledging these limitations, the definition is suitable for the purposes of this work. As the purpose here is only to analyse the personal experiences of the travellers, the deeper exploration of support services and developmental organizations of the travel industry go beyond the scope. Naturally even the most personal experiences may be *indirect* consequences of the acts of those sectors, but the sector of direct providers has by far the most influential effects. After all, they are the ones that eventually deliver whatever the other sectors may have provided. For present purposes, a comprehensive and precise definition of the travel industry is not necessary. It is enough that the travel industry is seen as the provider of goods and services the travellers are willing to pay for.

Commodification The travel industry has made travel a commodity (see e.g. Boorstin, 1972, p. 85; Greenwood, 1977, p. 130; Pi-Sunyer, 1977, p. 155; Craik, 1991, pp. 87-88; Britton, 1991, p. 454; Pretes, 1995, p. 2). Cohen (1988b, p. 380) calls this 'commoditization' (I prefer commodification):

> ...a process by which things (and activities) come to be evaluated primarily in terms of their exchange value, in a context of trade, thereby becoming goods (and services); developed exchange systems in which the exchange value of things (and activities) is stated in terms of prices from a market.

A dictionary defines 'commodity' as 'article of trade, esp. product as opp. to service' (The Oxford Handy Dictionary, 1991). The process of commodification thus implies that the definitive distinction between goods and services is blurred. Travel as a commodity is called a product, just like a bottle of shampoo. Services become more and more like goods, the articles of trade that are inseparable parts of the package purchased as a commodity. Services are objectified; they are more or less separated from the personal level of being something done by one person for another. Instead, the people involved in the services are just the means to provide what has been paid for.

This development is simultaneous with the general commercialisation of relations between people; money begins to be required for services that used to be provided free (Dogan, 1989, p. 218). The traditional local value systems based on moral values are replaced by the global value system based on money. This was noted by the UNESCO conference in 'The Effects of Tourism on Socio-Cultural Values' in 1976: '...tourism somehow manages to codify human and cultural relations, hospitality, etc., as a number of cash-generating activities...' (UNESCO, 1976, p. 84). Since the travel industry makes profits only when it offers something that can be priced and charged for, it is natural that it plays an important role in this development. It is also worth noticing that commerce and money are languages that are understood everywhere; it makes interaction between people possible even if there is little other common ground between them. Tourism is a breeding ground for commercialisation of human relations because it relies heavily on *instrumental* interaction. The interaction is primarily just a means to consummate the commercial contract of travel; we interact with the people who are necessary parts of the infrastructure that delivers the goods and services we have purchased. We deal more and more with institutions, individuals who actually provide the service are just more or less incidental representatives of them. For example, we do not talk to waiters primarily because we are interested in them, but to receive the service we want from the institution they represent (and for which we pay).

Tourist Discourse and Tourist Space   The travel industry profits best by surrounding travellers with its goods and services. Starting a journey means entering into this tourist space. The essence of it is 'encapsulation' that includes e.g. mode of transport, accommodation, tourist attractions, and the associated time-frames that tend to create an apparent lack of time (Weightman, 1987, p. 231). Travelling by airplane, being fetched from the airport by a resort bus, spending time on resort grounds, attending a sightseeing tour in an air-conditioned bus and eventually, going home by airplane are common examples of how the tourist space both metaphorically and literally encapsulates tourists. They have material and cultural frames inside the touristic infrastructure, within which they largely experience the trip. The infrastructure surrounding travellers tries to present itself as the means to experience the Other, but actually embodies and represents the cultural practices and values the travellers have become used to at home. The visitors can feel secure and avoid the confusion that results from not knowing how to act in situations where the cultural rules of behaviour differ from those of home. Hottola (1999, p. 127) calls this tourist space a metaworld, from which the tourist can safely explore the Other.

In addition to encapsulation, Weightman (1987, p. 231) mentions directedness and outsideness as the consequent properties of being inside the tourist space. She uses the example of tourism in India: 'Directedness' means the tendency of tours to be heading towards northern India and to the cities, where the most famous attractions are located. The directedness also manifests itself in overt emphasis on the past. These tours are past orientated; the attractions shown are from the past and contemporary Indian life is largely ignored. 'Outsideness' constitutes of just looking at the places, not being a part of them. A lot of this is a direct consequence of the encapsulation. Being encapsulated from the environment means insulation from it and thus necessarily outsideness. It is thus doubtful whether the separate concepts of outsideness and encapsulation are needed; the former always follows the latter. Minca (2000) writes about 'Bali Syndrome', the formation of tourist space that creates spatial segregation between the tourists and the locals (Ibid. p. 393). According to him, the reason for this segregation is the process in which the local colour is used in a global touristic context to create an appealing destination. These intentions work only if the tourists are sheltered from the adverse effects that tourism itself has brought (e.g. touts, conmen).

Cohen's use of the term environmental bubble (1972) only implicitly includes the cultural environment of the tourist discourse that is equally part of it. Nevertheless, it is a central character of tourist space. As the tourist space encapsulates and protects us from many of the physical realities of our destination, we are also insulated from many of its socio-cultural realities. Of course, this is perfectly natural, since in a strange environment we are bound to interpret what we see and experience through our own socio-cultural stock of knowledge. The existing conventions of the tourist discourse as part of that stock provide us with ready-made interpretations of the local realities. Therefore those conventions further enhance our socio-cultural insulation by providing interpretations that are imposed on the Other, rather than arise from it. The tourist discourse is essentially a Western discourse. It is entrenched by guides, maps, guidebooks, general conventions about where to go and what to do, and so on. Many of these are, if not created, at least used by the travel industry.

When tourists are inside the obvious tourist space, the material frames confine them to their roles as tourists. The material frames also direct the mental ones; inside the touristic infrastructure our cultural experiences largely draw from the conventions of the tourist discourse. The flow of experiences is channelled through the material frames the touristic infrastructure provides.

Choice of Destination   In the pursuit of profits, the travel industry tries to control as much as possible of the process, in which their clients are separated from their money in the course of their holiday (Turner and Ash, 1975, p. 107). Consequently travel agencies have a tendency to sell packages that contain a variety of pre-arranged facilities and programme. An ultimate example of this is Club Med, which sells all-inclusive packages; all the money needed after purchasing the trip is for souvenirs and extra drinks. The competition in the travel industry means that the array of different packages and options in them is wide. However, if anything outside that array is desired, it is likely to be more expensive because the agent's resources and connections have primarily been channelled to serve the delivery of those items included in the array. We have seen that the Finnish conventional tourists escaping the winter put much emphasis on the cost effectiveness of the trip. It is highly unlikely that they would choose anything not included into that array. Their method of selecting a holiday by browsing through newspaper travel advertisement sections also supports this. Thus, where escaping tourists want (or are made to think they want) to go, is directed by the existing affordable options available in travel agencies. The art of the travel business lies in the delicate process in which the potential tourists are led to believe that they can travel wherever they want, but then to choose a particular *product* from the travel agent's array.

Of course there are also people who want to get to particular destinations. However, the mechanisms by which a particular place becomes the desired destination are often based on a quite commonly shared stock of markers, so that those places are available in the travel agents' array. In other words, few people want to travel to places where the travel industry has not yet established itself. A consequence is that whether the travellers have chosen their destination by themselves, or have merely been content with special offers the travel agents have, in any case they are likely to be placed in a tourist space.

As the escape component of backpackers' desire to travel is not necessarily strong, they are usually more conscious of and insistent on the destination to which they want to travel. But the choice of the destination is again based on the stock of markers they are familiar with, which means that the destinations have in most cases been established in the repertoire of the travel industry. Furthermore, often the backpackers' destination is defined quite non-specifically, in general terms only - e.g. Pacific or Southeast Asia. This leaves a lot of options for finer details over which the itinerary suggested by the travel agent can have influence. The backpackers do not purchase any ready packages from the travel agents, but they still have to book their tickets from them. Thus the standard air routes and arrangements between different airlines routes direct the backpackers' way. It is usual to buy an around the world ticket with several predetermined stopovers because these tickets are cheaper compared to one-way or return tickets. If the backpackers deviate from these routes where cheaper deals are available, it indicates strong commitment to get to a particular destination. It appeared that all of the backpackers I met who did not have one of these round tickets still travelled largely to the same places as the ones who did.

Accessibility in terms of cost is clearly an issue. Travel to places not frequently visited is expensive. Also the infrastructure that serves travellers in such places is not well developed; problems of where to stay and how to get around in such places are a tough challenge few are willing to take:

> If you want to get off the beaten track you have to go to the places where it is really hard to get transport or anything (Aron, 23).

The potential for freedom on travel is largely theoretical; the practical concerns severely limit it. The tourist discourse proves an existing, convenient and tempting answer to these practical concerns; it is easier and feels safer to rely on facilities that have the sanction of the tourist discourse. At the destination itself, the discourse is mediated by tourist maps, guidebooks and by other travellers. These act as markers of what is worth visiting. Backpackers almost invariably possess a guidebook (specially directed for backpackers), while the conventional tourists commonly use tourist maps provided by the local tourist industry. Getting information from other travellers is an approach common to both groups. Since the sources of information are quite uniform, many people end up seeing same places and doing the same things as the others:

> The impression you get of a country is based on those places where you have been, which are largely determined on the basis of experiences of other travellers (Sari, 28).

> I have been sightseeing the places that are mentioned in the 'Lonely Planet' as well as the places that other travellers have recommended, which are also mentioned in the LP (Inge, 30).

It is generally assumed that almost all places worth visiting are listed in those sources. In the case of guided travel the travel operator naturally selects the places visited, but again they are usually selected from the ones in the guidebooks and tourist maps. To find most travellers visiting the same places is evidence of how commonly shared the conventions of the tourist discourse are. The very same conventions appear to have varied ways in which they are mediated to the tourists. They may arise directly, as structures of the travel industry, or indirectly as the communicated experiences of other tourists. In any case they strongly direct the decisions of where to travel. This illustrates the institutionalised nature of travel as reach. We buy our reach from a travel agent, and once in the destination, reach where other tourists have done likewise.

Standardisation

> Tourism has a homogenizing influence and its effects everywhere seem to be the same - the destruction of the local and regional landscape that very often initiated the tourism, and its replacement by conventional tourist architecture and synthetic landscapes and pseudo-places. The landscapes of

tourism are typified by what Jackson has called 'other-directed architecture' - that is, architecture which is deliberately directed towards outsiders, spectators, passers-by, and above all consumers (Relph, 1976, p. 93).

In the following I want to illustrate some of the standardising processes that together with commodification create traveller's experience of place.

Airports Much of the physical touristic infrastructure is this kind of other-directed architecture. Airports are good examples; they are designed to facilitate efficient processing of the people who just pass through them. Their design is primarily functional. There are some airports which have been designed to be also representational (like the futuristic Charles de Gaulle in Paris, the display of excess wealth in Dubai, and 'traditionalist' Ngurah Rai in Denpasar), but the architecture of the majority of world's airports do not display any kind of local sense of place. Most of the airports are demonstrations of placelessness.

> If on arriving at Trude I had not read the city's name written in big letters, I would have thought I was landing at the same airport from which I had taken off (Calvino, 1974, p. 128).

Beginning the journey on an international airport places travellers firmly inside the tourist space. Entering an international airport in our home country means entering into a kind of liminal state where we are not quite home any more, but neither are we yet away. It marks the beginning of the transition from home to the destination. This 'liminal' state makes people in a certain sense quite equal. Everyone equipped with enough money (and most tourists have it after saving for the trip) can revel in the tax-free world of trendy products, which are representations of 'the good life'. Being able to buy those products is thus a symbol of participating in that kind of life. One can be a part of the universally acknowledged pleasurable image of those products. We can transform ourselves from the usual Jones into a successful jetsetter. It is an attempt to reach beyond the familiar everyday roles. Here the tourist discourse includes myths from the more general discourse of consumerism. These myths are presented as integral part of the touristic infrastructure, as duty-free shopping. In this way the airports pay tribute to the market economy by being an ultimate culmination of consumerism. While MacCannell (1976, p. 13) saw sightseeing as somehow resembling the structures of traveller's society, I would say the same about the world of international airports: their prevailing standard demonstrates the power of money. They are an exaggerated caricature of capitalism and they sum up the image-propelled consumerism inherent in tourism. The world of tax-free luxury products is a stage for individual reach for the images the advertising has created, not unlike the travel itself. By buying the tax-free luxury products we thus participate in a Barthesian myth in an institutionalised way.

Air Travel   In the airplane the travellers are even more literally in a tourist space or in an environmental bubble. Standardised conventions about what to do and what to expect are uniform in any international flight. We eat, drink, watch movies, listen to music, buy some more tax-free items and read newspapers and magazines. Also the sense of movement is not based on the change of the landscape opening before our eyes, rather on the knowledge of the movement. The Finnish participants said that the rituals at the airport heighten that knowledge. The anticipation of the trip translates into a strong feeling, all the preparations for the trip pointed to this very moment of going. Although the plane trip itself does not often provide much opportunity to see how the landscape changes, the experience of flying may be novelty in itself.

> The feeling of travelling is strong in an airplane; it is not often that you find yourselves above the clouds. It is so exceptional that the feeling of going is strong (Kaapo, 27).

On the other hand, the same people admitted that the sense of movement in an airplane is somewhat surreal. The anticipation of the trip may indeed create a sense of travelling, but the excitement it produces can also make us quite oblivious to the actual process of changing place.[1]

> In an airplane there is the anticipation of what the trip will be like. It is a bit like after a few beers when you prepare yourself for a night out. In fact, I may indeed have taken a few (Minna, 28).

Flying above the clouds or the sea severely restricts the possibilities of enjoying the changing landscape. Thus the attention is mainly directed to the things inside the plane and what is outside the plane is of little importance before arriving somewhere.

---

[1] Fear of flying probably has the same effect.

Flying over the sea does not offer interesting landscapes. You concentrate more on browsing through the tax-free catalogues and watching movies (Markus, 25).

Someone thought he saw Paris, but no one really cared (Arvo, 26).

In the airplane the travellers are totally encapsulated from the outside environment and the main task is to make the time pass. In some planes it is possible to follow the route of the plane in a map that indicates the current location and route travelled. But the knowledge of the location does not change the realities inside the plane. While it may be interesting to think what life would be like ten thousand meters below on the ground, it may not be easy. Vivid imagination may help, but once we have finished our meal and are served the second round of coffee and brandy, the image of a peasant on his fields becomes at least vague. Ruskin, an artist, was already complaining at the beginning of the era of railways that 'going by railroad I do not consider as travelling at all; it is merely being "sent" to a place, and very little different from becoming a parcel' (Boorstin, 1972, p. 87; Relph, 1981, p. 180; Culler, 1981, p. 130). Thus we can say, like Boorstin (1972, p. 94), that the movement happens not so much in space as in time. It does not matter whether we travel from Helsinki to Moscow or from Sydney to Nadi, the plane trip is always similar. Thus the airplane is as placeless as anything can be.

Florida is now 500 marks closer (an advertisement in *Helsingin Sanomat*, Jan 6, 1994, p. A13).

In travel the key to distance is accessibility; mere physical nearness or remoteness does not determine effective distance. Thus Paramaribo in Surinam is further away from Sydney than London is, even though the absolute distance from Sydney to London is longer. Access to Paramaribo is complicated by many changes of airplanes and associated high cost of a ticket. Travel in space turns into travel in time and measuring the distance in hours and money.

In a peculiar way, the airplane travel becomes detached from our existential space. It is as if the concept (existential space) was suspended for the time of the travel. The space and distance the airplane covers is now *lived as* behavioural space. The experience of plane travel can be very similar to a literary effect described by Lutwak (1984, pp. 37-38):

Journeys from one place to another do not adequately involve either motion or place if there is no attempt to suggest the sensation of body movement and the perception of and interaction with surroundings. The considerable travelling in *Don Quixote* and *Tom Jones,* for example, furnishes occasions to experience new predicaments in the plot, not new places; the heroes are moved around, but with little sense of motion.

The airplane takes us from home to away without letting us to be involved with the realms in between. The plane trip is a path through which the reach to distant places is channelled. The physical organisation of places in our existential space is thus comparable to the networks of airline routes. Route hubs are centres and routes are paths that connect different centres through domains. The way the world and places are organized between the point of our departure and destination remain on the level of 'geography'. We do not have the possibility of being personally involved with those domains. Thus air travel creates a fragmented view of the relations between different places. Removal from the chance to experience first hand the gradual changes in landscapes, peoples, and their cultures leaves one extremely susceptible to 'indoctrination' by whoever who wants to present the Other in a certain manner (and profits from doing so).

Arriving at the Destination On arrival at the destination we find ourselves once again on a standardised airport that does not necessarily tell us much about the place. From a Finn's point of view the most important first impression on arrival is likely to be the difference between the climate of Finland and the one of the destination. Sometimes the arrival is so filled with excitement about the trivialities associated with organising oneself or tiredness from the trip that conscious evaluation of the place gets postponed.

Usually the first sign of being away is heat. On the airport you did not feel that you were in Turkey yet because the airport was so similar to any other [airport] and the weather was not different [from that of home]. My mind was occupied in worrying that all my luggage would come along (Minna, 28).

In the plane I had filled myself up [with beer] and then we were supposedly in such a hurry [at the airport] that there was no time to go to the loo. So I was unable to see anything during that first sightseeing tour because I had to struggle against wetting my pants (Martti, 30).

So there can be various reasons why the arrival does not yet force us to pay attention to the presence-at-hand we may have wanted to experience. Some of the above or a comparable reason may cause our state of mind to resemble Seamon's 'obliviousness'. These examples are probably personal experiences that we sometimes share, but more often we do pay attention to the differences we can pick. Different language, different looking people, and new smells may expose the unfamiliarity of the place, even if it is still obscured by the familiar structures of the tourist space. Thus it is probably more usual to experience what Seamon called 'noticing'.

The conventional tourists are usually taken from the airport to their hotel by car, minibus, or bus. The concept of tourist space becomes very tangible. Also on our trip to Turkey this was the first contact with the Otherness of the destination:

> The chaotic traffic and different buildings were the first contact with strangeness; we weren't in Europe any more (Minna 28).

While the tourists absorb the impressions of what they see outside, the guide or some other representative of the travel agent explains the practical procedures or general facts. In this way the tourists receive an at least apparently authoritative dose of the tourist discourse. Sometimes this is ceremonially symbolised by some kind of a rite in which the tourists are 'initiated' to the discourse. The welcoming act of a drink, receiving a Lei, or partaking in a Kava ceremony in the tourist establishment is a ritual where the initiation is done. Such a feature is often carefully picked from the local culture and its purpose is apparently to make the tourists feel welcome and important. But it also enforces the power of the existing tourist discourse to dominate the tourists' mental framework. The tourists are made to appear in their own eyes as participants in the local culture while in fact, they participate in the tourist discourse about that culture (Taylor, 2001).

The backpackers' situation is different. For them the airport may feel like the last frontier of familiarity. By stepping outside they think they leave the safe realm of tourist space they are familiar with and enter the Other. In some ways, as one of the subjects of Murray's (1990, p. 140) study put it: 'arriving overseas is like the first day in the school'. No more do the travellers know exactly what to do and what to expect. In many places they are also welcomed by a noisy and eager mob of touts. Since the backpackers have not booked accommodation in advance, all the touts want to take them to their place. At this stage the information received from travel guidebooks and other travellers gives them the framework of what to expect. Although the backpackers apparently leave the tourist space behind, they counter the lack of it with stronger reliance on the pieces of the tourist discourse that is within their grasp, like guidebooks, and by other travellers. These translate most of the things encountered into forms that make sense.

Accommodation   In accommodation the standardisation of facilities is pronounced. Like international airports, international hotels everywhere in the world are similar in the ways they operate, for the same reasons. The needs of a traveller (accommodation) and the needs of travel industry (profits) are neatly combined in hotel business.[2] Naturally the consequence is that the business is standardised in the sense that its structure is everywhere the same; to provide services (which often are a part of a commodity of the trip) the traveller pays for.

> 'Why do you only take pictures in hotel rooms and airports?'
> 'Everything else I remember.' (Jarmusch, 1989: Mystery Train)

The architecture of international hotels can be extremely varied. There can be huge multi-storey buildings that are totally out of scale and style of the local features, or tastefully built resorts using local styles and materials, taking great care to create as much local atmosphere as possible. However, when several travel brochures about various places and hotels are compared, it appears that no matter how different those places and the hotels look, the actual rooms are very much alike.

Hotel rooms are all designed to same purpose and directed towards tourists who want comforts. Thus hotel rooms comply with Western standards of comfort. Again, local colour is added with decorations and some designs, but the basic idea to provide all necessary comforts like a good bed, tiled bathroom, and a sufficient amount of privacy still remains. The local colour makes travellers feel that they are involved with the Other, and 'away' instead of home, but still with all the homely conveniences and even more. Boorstin (1972, p. 99) goes so far as to suggest that 'the self-conscious effort to provide local atmosphere is itself thoroughly American'. Also Conrad Hilton himself declared that 'Each of our hotels is a little

---

[2] While in the case of international hotels, the needs of the local people can be ignored.

America' (Ibid.; Turner and Ash, 1975, p. 146). The 'local colour' appears in the architecture (not the case in Hiltons) or in decorating.

Despite the 'local colour', the structure of the establishments is always the same, Western concept of a hotel, where everyone's roles and what is expected are clearly defined. Thus a hotel or resort is not only a tourist establishment, it is also a representation of the power structures between the Western tourist discourse (and thus Western culture and economy in general) and the local culture. The underlying structures that govern the functioning of such establishments are profoundly Western, whereas the 'local colour' plays a subservient, merely decorative role, and is spatially located outside. This happens at least in the places where tourism is an important industry. This power structure unconsciously sustains the (Eurocentric) perception in which the Western market economy is self-evidently justified as the basis for interaction with other people(s). The local features are essentially merely components in an idealised Western image of the exotic Other. Thus the international hotels are part of tourist space; they mediate the world of the Other to our world. Hottola (1999, p. 132) claims that hotels are used as metaspaces, from which the tourists can safely explore the otherness around. Hotels are places in which the tourist can exert control over the circumstances, unlike in the potentially hostile domain of the Other. Therefore, contrary to what Harkin (1995, p. 651) suggests, I do not think that they provide a meta-perspective on the cultures, because they are so thoroughly part of the Western domain.

The Western framework of hotel is important in forming the tourists' image of a place. Already travel advertising suggests that the most important features of the destinations are their hotels and resorts. Mostly it even seems that compared to the importance of hotel, the place itself is somehow of second-hand importance. When I asked an elderly Finnish Australian couple what they thought of Bangkok, they told me that they had a very nice five star hotel next to the river with a wonderful views over the city. That was the essence of Bangkok for them. Some conventional tourists are so completely enveloped by the tourist space that it can replace the place itself as a main source of experiences. Such travel creates incidental outsideness towards the place visited; the place becomes quite incidental for the experiences there. On the other hand, the experience of the contrast between the familiar touristic infrastructure and the Other outside may in itself provide exciting. This can be seen as a central aspect in some tourism to places which represent radically different Other. Within the discourse of East African tourism Bruner and Kirshenblatt-Gimblett (1994, p. 440) find 'the assurance that the wild will be experienced under the most civilized of circumstances and their surreal juxtaposition enjoyed in its own right'.

> The area was fenced off, there were lots of activities and personnel to organise them... It tried to be an international place, the local culture did not show anywhere and they spoke German... [They had] an international kitchen, something for almost every nationality that was visiting and copious quantities of food, several smorgasbords... They cleaned every place all the time (Markus, 25).

The couple spent two weeks in a resort on a Caribbean island and told that only once did they leave the resort for a shopping excursion, as the resort was in the 'middle of nowhere'. The excursion was to a marketplace a couple of hours boat trip away and the place was filled with other tourists. The couple said that while their purpose on the trip was solely to relax and take it easy (it was a postponed honeymoon), they would still have desired more contact with some other local realities apart from their resort. The resort was developed to the extent that the only local people they saw there were the personnel. Everything was made to satisfy the standards that the tourists had got used to.

The couple also found the contrast between the poor local peasants they saw on the way to the resort and the gluttony-promoting abundance of buffet tables in the resort disturbing. This is a demonstration of how important it is to have the right balance between experiencing novelty, and the security of the tourist space. We feel most confident to explore the environment around us when the amount of novelty is moderate; too little novelty stupefies and too much of it makes one insecure (Lee and Crompton, 1992, p. 733; Hottola, 1999, p. 115). The tourists need to feel an appropriate amount of what Seamon (1979, p. 118) called 'at homeness', which enables them to encounter and discover new things without having to divert any attention to the feelings of insecurity. The tourist space is thus the element that provides the necessary security; within it, the experience of novelty is controlled. Seeing extreme poverty may thus appear too confronting because there is no way to control that experience other than get away from seeing it. In the resort far from those local realities, the poverty as an evidence of the neo-colonial power structures is easier to forget. On the other hand, too much tourist space and too little novelty is not good either:

What is so great about going to some Palmas and ordering meatballs and Lapin Kulta [a Finnish beer]? (Martti, 29).

Staying in a hotel and being away from home may be enough novelty for a while. When that starts to become more and more ready-to-hand, surfaces the need for new stimuli. The spontaneous excursions are tourists' personal efforts to answer this need.

The original idea of backpacking was to stay in close contact with the local people. This was achieved by staying in cheap accommodation that was provided by the local people for mainly domestic travellers. But as the number of backpackers increased, so did the amount of budget accommodation. In places frequently visited by the backpackers, their commercial potential was soon discovered, first by the locals and later by the outside investors; new developments mushroomed. As a result, there is now a well-developed infrastructure catering for the backpackers in these places. Instead of being places where interaction with the locals is spontaneous, hotels used by the backpackers are now places where the travellers meet each other.

Bali is a good example of a popular destination where the traditional 'losmen' (family owned small 'hostels') with intimate settings and rustic Spartan facilities have given way to budget hostels with Western-style toilets, showers and tiling. While they are still relatively cheap, they have been built to meet the Western expectations. Thus the accommodation for backpackers tends to become a part of their tourist space. Equally significantly, the hostels are important meeting places for the backpackers, who share information and thus contribute to and pass on the tourist discourse. This works through narratives of other travellers, advice from the staff, information on notice boards, and arrangement of excursions, for example. The accommodation also directs the backpackers to the places where it is available and thus helps to standardise the routes taken.

From the initial desire to stay and mingle with the local people, backpacking has developed into a special kind of tourism with its own infrastructure and own kind of tourist discourse. There are, of course, some backpackers who still keep exploring places where not many other travellers have been before, and who place few demands on those places. But the mainstream of the backpackers (represented by my sample) clearly induces the creation of a special backpacker infrastructure. They visit places mentioned in their guidebooks, and the guidebooks mention the places where there is some sort of accommodation (and if the guidebook mentions as worth visiting a place where there is no accommodation, the demand for it will soon activate some sort of development). While the backpacker discourse is in some respects opposed to the conventional tourist discourse, in other ways these discourses nevertheless quite closely resemble each other and share a lot of elements. Backpacker discourse provides Western interpretations of places in the same way as the conventional tourist discourse, albeit from a different perspective.

The accommodation somehow converts some visitors' desire to reach for the Other peoples and their cultures into a social reach for one's own kind of people. Observing backpackers gives the impression that the reach for the former can be quite shallow and it is satisfied just by travel to a place where the locals are 'quaint'. Once there the interest is largely directed to the other backpackers,[3] if they share a common language. Accommodating visitors in the same quarters also encourages social interaction among them and tends to discourage the social interaction between the visitors and the locals. The presence of other travellers who share the same situation makes it possible to quickly swap between the Other and relative familiarity. It can provide comfort from the strangeness of the Other. A balance between at-homeness and novelty is thus unconsciously sought. A result is that the tourist discourse, which is commonly shared between the visitors, remains the framework in reflecting on the experiences with others. An indication of this is that while chatting with other travellers, the local people are always referred as 'them' while the travellers themselves are 'we'. In other words, the local people are largely excluded outside the discourse.

Tourist Bus Travel In the bus the meaning of the tourist space is again tangible. We leave the familiar hotel ground in the comfort of an air-conditioned bus, watch the landscape and are taken from one sight to another. From within the bus we see local people on their daily activities and landscapes that appear through the window in a rapid procession. In this kind of bus travel everything encountered is primarily visual. This maintains the ontological difference between us and the Other; the Other remains a distant object (Graburn, 1977, p. 31; Tuan, 1982, p. 118; Karjalainen, 1986a, p. 91). The natural remoteness between the subject and object, the ontological distance between 'Us' and 'Them', becomes

---

[3] In fact, a survey conducted in a Backpacker Expo in Sydney revealed, that 'around 90% of backpackers said that they mixed almost exclusively with other backpackers' (*TNT for Backpackers Magazine*, 1996, Jan, p. 9).

accentuated by the presence of a tangible tourist space that exists in the shape of the tourist bus.

> You pass through numerous villages and rice fields and will no doubt be amazed and amused by many of the quaint customs and sights (Viva! Holidays Thailand, 1993/94, p. 28).

The cultural norms prevalent in the bus are securely familiar, unlike those outside in the cities and villages. The Other is introduced in a way that makes sense to travellers in the cultural context of the bus tour group. The local features are introduced as something to look at from the safe base of familiarity, conveniently and with little involvement (Smith, 1977, p. 54). Thus sightseeing provides us with a 'guided' understanding through the tourist discourse. In it peoples and their customs are 'quaint', and the very act of sightseeing allows the tourists to remain out of contact with them (see Pearce, 1982, p. 204; Boorstin, 1972, p. 99). Thus sightseeing emphasises outsideness.

> We did not have time to familiarise ourselves with the places (Kaapo, 27).

> Our schedule was so tight that it was bad both as a holiday and as a study trip... Instead of getting to know the country we just sat in the bus (Arvo, 26).

Touring Portugal by bus left my friends with the feeling that all they had done was sit in the bus to only occasionally unload themselves to see some sights. The local guide and the narratives of guidebooks imposed the sights and their importance on them; it did not arise from the personal interests of these tourists.

The tourist bus both directs the tourists to certain places and gives them the time frame for their experiences in those places. While the advantage of using the tourist bus is that it takes us to see the most remarkable sights that are considered as 'worth seeing', tight schedules and too many sights become counterproductive. There is certainly a limit to how much information and sights one can absorb in given time. These limits are regularly crossed on trips where emphasis has been put on seeing as much as possible in a shortest time. However, there seem to be striking variations between what different people consider as a tight schedule. A Finnish tourist was very happy with a trip on which he visited many sights in a relatively short time:

On the longer excursions we did not just hop out from the bus and back to go again. We had time to have ice cream and food, and the break always lasted from about a quarter to half an hour, even an hour (Erkki, 58).

It clearly depends on the intention of the travellers whether they are happy with just short bursts of sightseeing, or whether they want more time to spend in one place. Touring numerous sights is also easier if there is a base where it is possible to retire to digest all the things seen. In contrast, my friends travelled by bus all the time and only once stayed in one place more than one night. The shorter the stay in one place, the bigger portion of the time is spent inside the tourist space. These different requirements reflect the different extent of reach for the Other desired. If just a small amount of reach is required, it does not take long before an attraction or a place is incorporated into the existing stock of knowledge as an item of the tourist trip. Then we are ready and willing to move on to another place.

Places like Lanzarote are so small that you can see everything in them in one trip. There is thus no point in going there again (Kaapo, 27).

There are so many places I have not seen, so that I'd rather go somewhere new (Erkki, 58).

If I had money to travel, I'd go somewhere I have not seen yet (Satu, 28).

In the shallow framework of the tourist trip, the presence-at-hand of a place is soon exhausted. As soon as it is incorporated into the existing stock of knowledge, there is little in the place that addresses our intentions as tourists. The touristic encounter is felt to reveal us everything that is worth experiencing in the place. A new one is needed to provide the same impact of presence-at-hand.

Luxury buses await to whisk us off to the colour and glitter of earlier days. We thrill to the richly decorated apartments of women of the royal household. We will stroll across emerald-green lawns where peacocks strut. Through the train windows we see rows of Indians squatting, their bare brown buttocks facing us as they get on with their morning shit (Horne 1992, p. 140).

The routes of sightseeing tours are a part of the tourist space in the sense that they take the visitors to selected places. Places with something 'worth seeing' and places that have means of providing travellers with the services they need are selected. Naturally these usually coincide and thus places visited are often the ones where all tourists go. This aggravates the division between the tourist space and the 'real' place. The places visited are spectacles: magnificent natural wonders, historical monuments, or 'traditional' settings. Thus areas that do not meet these requirements are ignored; they remain insignificant domains of which the tourist discourse has little to say. In a way the discourse has its own centres of meaning to which its adoption directs the tourists. Those meanings are public meanings of the tourist discourse, but not the public - let alone private - meanings of the local people. The tourist bus takes us to these centres and the domains around them remain strange, and as such, maybe even intimidating.

A bus tour is an extreme example of the institutionalisation, and even devaluation of reach for the Other. The desire to see and experience the Other is acted out by participating in a sightseeing tour. There the control of what aspects of the Other are reached for, and how these aspects are presented, is solely in the hands of the provider of the tour. We buy the means of reach for the Other from a provider, who then provides not only the means, but also the content of reach.

Standardised Attractions and Meaning of Places The attractions travellers visit are largely standardised. Whatever the attraction, it has to be accessible to many tourists to be profitable for the travel industry. In practice, this often means building a road and a place to unload and load tourist buses, toilets, possible ticket selling facilities and so on. Often the vicinity of a popular attraction becomes like a market place once all kinds of souvenir vendors erect their stalls. For example in Bali, whether some hot springs or caves are visited, the first things found are car parks and souvenir stalls.

> Only a short distance beyond Peliatan, on the road to Pejeng and Gianyar, a car park on the north side of the road marks the site of Goa Gajah (Lonely Planet; Indonesia 1992, p. 384).

The standardisation sometimes diminishes the qualities of the attraction that originally turned it into an attraction (see Crystal, 1977, p. 122). On the other hand, from the visitors' perspective the standardisation makes an attraction appear as if it was directed to them; non-standardised features exist in their own right. In their presence the visitors may feel uneasy since those features ignore them and they themselves are meaningless from the perspective of the features. They do not fit in; they do not have any role whatsoever. This is especially evident when the attractions are the local people and their customs. If the features are presented as performances, the visitors know roughly what they are supposed to do and expect. But if the features are not organised into performances, then the visitors have to confront them without the security and predictability that organisation brings. The visitors can feel extremely uneasy if they do not know how to relate to what they see and what they are expected to do (see Hottola, 1999). An example is seeing poverty (not an attraction as such, but often unwittingly implied as part of the 'local colour'); for many it seems to be hard to come to terms with it. Sights as part of the commodity of travel address the travellers, because those sights are *for them*.

From the perspective of what our experience as tourists is going to be like, it is somewhat incidental whether we travel to a tropical island in the Pacific or the Caribbean. The actions through which the visitors experience the Other are likely to be somewhat similar everywhere; i.e. sightseeing, performances, familiarising ourselves with the local cuisine, sport activities, etc. Any differences are likely to arise mainly from the geographical and cultural differences the Other is supposed to represent. This reflects the difference between what I'd like to call *functional* and *representational* meanings of places (compare to Karjalainen, 1993b, pp. 32-33). Functional meanings arise from the things we do in the place. Thus these meanings are indirect derivatives from the conventions of the tourist discourse, which affect what we do there. For example, a backpacker interpreted the essence of a silent (at the time) beach resort:

The essence of [this] place is that there is not much to do (Inge, 30).

The perspective is unashamedly subjective, and illustrates how the intentions toward places define their identity. According to the tourist discourse about the place (guidebooks), the place was defined functionally (a nice beach resort). So the interviewee's consequent interpretation of the place arises from this function. The functional meanings of places for tourists tend to be quite uniform because of this natural tendency to interpret them through our perspective as visitors. This perspective is very similar everywhere, characterised by insulation, maybe even encapsulation, and directedness. As a result, different places are easily perceived to be similar everywhere:

[On our trip to Turkey] there was no place essentially different from any other (Martti, 28).

While the functional meanings are primarily private, the tourists largely share the situations in which these private meanings are constructed. Things that we as visitors do in a place, do not differ from the things other visitors do there. Thus there is often little difference between the private and public meanings of these places.

The representational meanings of places are often public meanings, shared by many. This arises directly from the tourist discourse's depiction of what places are supposed to represent (these public meanings are easiest to find from travel advertisements). It may be hard to discern much difference between what the tropical islands of Pacific and Caribbean represent in the tourist discourse. In these cases the representations may refer to the different cultural, racial, and historical backgrounds of the peoples. But in the tourist discourse they are both essentially reflections of our dreams of paradise. There can be private representational meanings in which a place represents something personally meaningful (like a personal memory of a friend associated with a place). However, the private representational meanings are mostly formed within the framework of public meanings.

Thus an underlying impact of the standardising effect of the travel industry is the decomposing of distinction between private and public meanings of places. This happens by providing circumstances in which the public meanings are likely to be internalised by tourists because of their similar situation in relation to place. In the same process the functional and representational meanings both become primarily public.

The tourist space is formed by standardising facilities, creating attractions and transforming them (Cohen, 1972, p. 170). Britton (1991, p. 455) writes in very similar terms: 'to transform travel and tourist experiences into commodities, they must be standardised and rendered amenable to capitalist production techniques'. Existing places, sights, and their features are marked to direct the tourists gaze to them. They are also integrated into a tourism development, and whole new features can be created.

The infrastructure, services, and to some degree the attractions are standardised so that they are easy to use and beneficial to the travel industry, i.e., it feels natural for tourists to pay for them. This more or less means that all destinations are presented to tourists in standardised forms as hotels, resorts, and sights, i.e. as goods and services. The touristic infrastructure everywhere is structured similarly to conform with the aim of providing investors with profits by offering the traveller goods and services to pay for. Writers with a critical attitude to mass tourism emphasise how this creates a paradox: while the primary motive to travel is to experience something different, the differences between places decrease as tourism increases and becomes institutionalised (Cohen, 1972, p. 172).

Guidebooks for Backpackers

Compared to the conventional tourists, the backpackers *apparently* leave the tourist space behind, or at least intend to do so. However, the apparent rejection of the touristic infrastructure does not have to mean the rejection of the conceptualisations that draw from the tourist discourse. This discourse is still mediated to the backpackers by the other travellers and by guidebooks. Those books introduce a whole world of backpacker-orientated low-budget travel infrastructure and translate local cultural practices into language that makes sense to backpackers. The books try consciously to avoid the tourist discourse of conventional tourism by emphasising the difference between 'tourists' and 'travellers'. They attempt quite sincerely to provide a 'grass roots level' description that would appreciate the local people's own perspectives. But they are still a Western tourist discourse, although differing in part from that of conventional tourism. The result is subtle communicative staging of the destination from an outsider's perspective. The staging effect is not intended, but unavoidable, when a Western discourse is used in describing non-Western places. The substance of the place is narrated in terms that are relevant for the backpackers. It is thus obvious that this discourse is bound to differ from the one a local person living in the place instead of visiting it, would produce.[4]

The development of budget accommodation is an important element in the institutionalisation of backpacking tourism. While such tourism was an enterprise of a few extroverts before the middle of the seventies, the launching of the first guidebooks for them in 1973 (Wheeler and Wheeler: 'Across Asia on the Cheap'; Bill Dalton: 'A Traveler's Notes: Indonesia') heralded a new era of growing interest in backpacking. These first guidebooks were little more than humble printouts; hand-collated, -trimmed

---

[4]   It is interesting to read guidebook descriptions of one's own home town. The shallowness of description soon becomes apparent.

and -stapled, with modest print runs.[5] The development from merely writing a guidebook to fully-fledged publishing companies (Lonely Planet, Moon Publications) whose guidebooks cover almost the entire world reflects the institutionalisation of backpacking.[6]

What started as an alternative type of travel, has developed into an industry. In the process it has established its own kind of tourist discourse that contains some of the elements it initially criticised. For example:

> Instead of being tourists, some people fall in a 'traveller treadmill' where you do and see all the things that are supposed to be done and seen - as tourists (Tina, 24).

Tourists going to the same places, seeing the same sights and doing the same things, and being separated from the local people, are the things that backpacking was meant to avoid. While there are some individual backpackers who still do avoid these things, as a whole the backpacking discourse largely incorporates them. It is a paradox that the guidebooks which were born from the desire to facilitate the sense of discovery for many, are the main agents in directing the backpackers to do all the same things as many others. Backpacking, once a revolutionary alternative to the discourse of conventional tourism, has largely approached the latter.

On my travels as a backpacker I have always had a guidebook and I have met very few others that have been travelling without one. All but one the backpackers I interviewed had a Lonely Planet guidebook. The one exception had a Moon Publications' Handbook. The guidebooks of these two companies dominating the backpacker market (at least the English speaking one) are very similar in every respect (also the other popular backpacker guidebooks in German and French follow the same formula). The books introduce either a cluster of countries of some geographical area, or concentrate on a particular country or state. First they contain a 'facts about' section about the history, geography, climate, government, economy, people, religion and language of the area. Then there is the practical travel information like visas, documents, money, mail, accommodation, dangers and annoyances, food and drink, etc. This is

---

[5] 1500 and 800 respectively.

[6] A developed version of 'Across Asia on the Cheap' was published in 1975 as 'South-East Asia on a Shoestring', which at the moment (2001) is in its tenth edition. 'A Traveler's Notes: Indonesia' evolved into 'Indonesia Handbook'. Both of these have sold hundreds of thousands of copies.

followed by how to get there and how to move around sections. After that the discussion is organised according to smaller areas and individual places. Again, more detailed practical information is included, followed by recommendations on what to see and do, where to stay and eat.

In the 'facts about' section a compact description of the area in question is provided. If the travellers really read the section, they can indeed have quite a good general picture of the events and circumstances behind the present state of affairs of the destination. Sometimes even the local people are amazed about the knowledge some travellers seem to possess. Studying the background information of these guidebooks, we can achieve what Horne (1992, pp. 132-137) describes as 'intelligent superficiality'. While it does not make us in any sense insiders or experts of the destination, it is still better to know a little than nothing at all. However, not all travellers read the section, or remember what they have read. They focus their attention to the practical information available in the guidebooks. This information is often very detailed and is clearly based on actual experience.

This is the main reason for the popularity of these guidebooks; they provide security by providing culturally decoded information that creates order in the unfamiliar Other. For some people most of the desired reach has largely been accomplished once home is left behind. In an alien place the guidebook may be one of the only remnants of familiarity and few are willing to give that away. On the other hand, the guidebook facilitates the sense of independence. I was exhilarated, when on my first long trip abroad I could walk the streets of Singapore knowing that in such and such an address I could find cheap accommodation. I felt that with the help of a suitable guidebook any place would be within my reach. This effect is due to the detailed descriptions in the books and the impression that the writers have really experienced what they write about. They are not just listing facts and facilities, and their perspective is truly practical for a backpacker. One of my interviewees complained that the information they give is overly subjective, but generally it seems that the very subjectivity adds to the practical value of those books; it gives an experience to which others can relate their experiences. The places have been 'tested' by someone with somewhat similar intentional framework and found worth visiting. It is also possible to send hints and corrections to the publishers, so that the guidebooks are quite literally parts of the backpacker discourse.

Another reason for the popularity of the guidebooks is that they are important markers. They mark the places of importance by naming and touristtouristdescribing them. The guidebooks also represent youth and adventure of which many want to have a share by participating in the 'collection' of the places marked by the guidebooks. The phenomenon is similar to buying trendy brand-products; the consumer wants to participate in the favourable image by possessing a representation of it. A further merit for someone who seeks for status by visiting places mentioned in these guidebooks is the convenience of transmitting the significance of the trip just by pointing to the markers of the 'collected' places.

The popularity of these books means that they direct the experiences of great many backpackers. Thus it is inevitable that many experiences are structured around the frames created by the guidebooks. They are thus catalysts in creating and sustaining the tourist space for them. Comparing different editions of the same guidebook illustrates this process, which connects to the institutionalisation and expansion of backpacking tourism. According to Lonely Planet's 'South-East Asia on a Shoestring' from 1977 (2nd edition), there are fourteen places in Bali where it is possible to find backpacker accommodation. In the 1994 edition (8th) the number of such places is 34 (Figure 7.1). Also the number of accommodation possibilities in any one place has increased immensely. For example, Kuta, the most touristic place in Bali, had over a hundred places where backpackers could stay in 1977 (South-East Asia on a Shoestring, 1977, p. 63), whereas in 1994 the number was expressed as 'hundreds' (South-East Asia on a Shoestring, 1994, p. 213).

An aspect in this development is that as places become institutionalised as parts of this backpacker discourse, they undergo drastic changes. By directing backpackers to the same places these guidebooks are effectively participating in the changing of these places. An example of this is the development in the village of Candidasa in eastern Bali:

In 1983 Candidasa was just a quiet little fishing village. Two years later a dozen losmen and half a dozen restaurants had sprung up and suddenly it was *the* new beach place in Bali. Now it's shoulder to shoulder

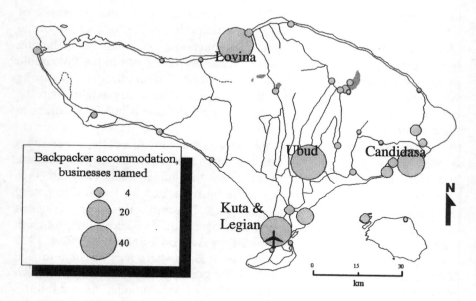

Figure 7.1   Backpacker accommodation in Bali 1994

Graduated symbols indicate the number of the places mentioned in the guidebook by name. Especially in Kuta & Legian, Ubud and Lovina, the list is far from comprehensive. There are hundreds of places in Kuta alone. The map corresponds well with the interviewees' accounts on their destinations in Bali.

Source: South-East Asia on a Shoestring, 8th ed. (1994).

development and suffering all the Kuta-style problems (Lonely Planet; Indonesia 1992, p. 420).[7]

In this way the exploratory backpacking which tries to avoid the established tourist 'traps' may eventually lead to the arrival of conventional tourism to the destination. Thus as the interest materialises as large-scale tourism, the original features that initiated the interest vanish. Eventually the backpackers are a part of what they wanted to avoid.

---

[7] For earlier accounts of Candidasa, see *Indonesia Handbook*. 1985. pp. 378-379 and *Indonesia; a travel survival kit*. 1986. (1st edit.) pp. 360-361. An interesting parallel from the past is provided by Helms (1988, p. 56): 'Egyptian desert fathers with their gaunt, unkempt, "spectacularly holy" appearances and reputations for spiritual wisdom, were soon "discovered" as tourist attractions for pilgrim tourists, who travelled great distances to admire, seek advice, or even become disciples themselves, and the monks' lonely cells took on the appearances of well furnished consulting rooms.'

The influence of the guidebooks is so strong that most backpackers, who want to experience novelty through seeing a culturally remote, 'traditional' place, try to achieve this in the places mentioned in the guidebooks rather than in the places not mentioned there. Despite the huge volume of tourism in Bali, there are lots of remote villages with novelty in this sense, but few tourists ever go there because those places are not mentioned in guidebooks. It seems as if the possibility of visiting and staying in such a place never occurred because people are preoccupied in their pursuit of the places mentioned in the guidebooks. This illustrates the power of the guidebooks as markers; the visitors ignore places unmarked by them. It would also require extra effort in finding accommodation and negotiating in an alien cultural environment without much knowledge of what to expect. The visitors would not have a convenient role there, neither control over the circumstances.

The vast majority of the backpackers are content to restrict their search for authenticity to the institutionalised destinations. The ones that do have the affirmation of the (backpackers') tourist discourse that they are to be considered 'traditional'. And more importantly, which have accommodation and other services directed to backpackers. Thus the remote Balinese villages are being left alone while ferries carry loads of tourists to the neighbouring island of Lombok which has the image of being 'like Bali twenty years ago' (an unrecorded comment from an Australian honeymooner). It is an idea of the tourist discourse that Bali is touristic and that if you want something 'unspoiled', you have to go to Lombok, or to some other less touristic places. Most visitors thus adhere to these ideas, like the following backpacker:

> If you want to see real Indonesians you do not come to touristic places like Bali, [here] you just pass through remote villages but you never stay there (Lis, 22).

Cohen (1982, p. 209) recorded a similar phenomenon. He observed that the very same backpackers, who took jungle trips to see well-preserved cultures in northern Thailand, stayed inside the backpackers' resort areas just lying on the beach and interacting with the other travellers in southern Thailand. The guidebooks tell these travellers that 'authenticity' can be found on those hill tribe treks and the southern beaches are for relaxation. The North is authentic and the South spoiled. As the travel industry has institutionalised the means of reach, the reach for novelty as authenticity is claimed (by the travel industry) to mean a trip to that kind of a destination.

While it is marketed as 'unspoiled', it has already elements of touristic infrastructure, the very prerequisite for marketing.

There is still another very important reason why only the places mentioned in the guidebooks are commonly visited. In such places the role of the visitors is clearly defined. It feels secure to know that our needs and expectations will most likely be met. For many people there is enough reach in the fact that they are backpacking away from home. Thus there is no desire to throw oneself into unnecessary confusion (Hottola, 1999, p. 110) that undefined roles in places with no touristic infrastructure can cause. Arriving in a place where we have no established ways to act, makes us completely dependent on how well communication with the locals works and how willing they are to take the role of hosts. We will have no immediate escape route to the tourist space. In such a situation novelty and reach is easily conceived to be too much to be desired. It is notable however, that when these kinds of irregularities happen spontaneously, they are likely to be the most remembered and appreciated occasions. This is understandable; they are the situations where we become strongly involved with the Other in a very first-hand way. Initially the guidebooks for backpackers were published to facilitate travelling in domains where these unmediated first-hand contacts would become possible (i.e. stay and eat in the cheap places that are geared mainly for local and domestic use and which the conventional tourists avoid). With the institutionalisation and the inevitable standardisation of backpacking those contacts differ little from the contacts between the conventional tourists and the locals. There is now the backpackers' tourist discourse and the appropriate tourist space (even if less conspicuous than the one of conventional tourists'), and the kind of travel the guidebooks originally advocated remains a pursuit of a minority of travellers with adventurous[8] minds.

The narratives of backpackers' guidebooks implicitly support the idea that by avoiding the infrastructure of the conventional tourists, travellers can experience the Other first hand. Of course, this is possible, but the practices of most backpackers (indeed, of all in my interview sample) do not support this. They tend to stay within the infrastructure of the backpacker tourism and direct their attention primarily towards the fellow travellers. These two aspects of their behaviour are not likely to foster first hand spontaneous relations with the locals. In this sense, the

---

[8] Here it can be seen how hard it is to use the term 'adventure' without its commercial connotations. If travel advertising is to be believed, every traveller is an adventurer.

backpacker discourse's claim for deeper authenticity (compared to the conventional tourists) of the contact with the Other tends to be an illusion. One could say that the institutionalisation of backpacking tourism and its consequent approach to conventional tourism is another example of a 'revolution' that was watered down as it became established.[9] In a way it closely resembles the Kuhnian cycle of paradigms. The main differences are that here the new paradigm starts to resemble the old one and that the old paradigm never loses its prominence.

Tour Guides as Middlemen

Now the attention is turned from guidebooks to tour guides. Cohen (1985, p. 10) divides the tour guides' roles in four principal components:

Table 7.1   Components of the roles of tour guides (according to Cohen 1985)

	Outer-directed (beyond group)	Inner-directed (within group)
Leadership sphere	Instrumental	Social
Mediatory sphere	Interactionary	Communicative

The instrumental component is based on the original function of guides as 'leading the way'. They decide the direction, facilitate access to the domains otherwise thought to be inaccessible and control the travellers in order to retain safe and effective conduct of the tour. The social component involves being a cohesive and morale boosting force for the touring group. The interactionary component means that the guides are middlemen between the visitors and the locals, sights and facilities. This consists of two main elements: representation and organization. Finally the communicative component, which is considered as the most central role of the guides, is the actual presentation of the Other to the visitors. This involves selecting what is presented, giving information about it,

---

[9] I participated in the 21st anniversary celebrations of the Lonely Planet publishing company in November 1994, and indeed, this institutionalisation of a 'revolution' was clearly visible. The vast majority of the guests were well-heeled middle-aged people. Much time seemed to have passed since they had been the messengers of the new 'anti-discourse' on the 1970s.

interpretation of it and possibly even fabrication. For the purpose of this work the mediatory sphere of guides' roles is more interesting, particularly representation and the communicative components.

Representation in the interactionary component of the guides' roles means that the guides on one hand integrate the visitors into the visited setting, and on the other insulate them from it. Thus the guides represent the setting to the visitors, and the visitors to the setting. In practice it is probably hard to distinguish this *representation* from *communication*, because the former is mediated through the latter, especially from the visitors' perspective (the perspective which is interesting in this work). The guides standardise the place and its features into terms familiar to the visitors (see Duncan, 1978, p. 276). This is done by selecting suitable features to show, giving information that can be comprehended, interpreting strangeness through the familiarising effect of the touristic infrastructure, and if need arises, even fabricating 'truths'. All these techniques belong to the communicative component of the guides' role; the guide represents the place to the visitors by communicating it to them.

We had guides so we did not miss anything (Erkki, 58).

In mediating between the alien place and the tourists, the guides have a great power in selecting what is shown to the latter, and equally importantly, what isn't. Naturally the selection is influenced by what the guides expect the tourists want to see and hear or what they themselves (or their authorities) want to convey. Irrespective of politics and authorities, a lot of this is adopted from the tourist discourse and the guide's understanding of what to select from it for different visitors.

Not only are the places shown selected, also the information given about them is highly selective. It is an interesting paradox that while tourists like Erkki above seem to exaggerate the ability of the guides to provide deep insights, at the same time they are aware of the guides' power to manipulate what they reveal:

The local guide has so much influence [on what you get to know], depending on whether he/she wants to reveal only the touristic view, or if he/she also gives the whole picture of the people. So many sights are just glittering surface (Erkki, 58).

This is an astonishing combination of understanding the partiality of what the guides can convey, while still believing in their ability to 'reveal the whole picture of the people', if they so wish. The guides' role as information distributors is commonly perceived to be the most important role they have. In many cases it is easy to impress the visitors - who mostly have little knowledge of the places visited - with knowledge of dates, events and interesting oddities (from the visitors' perspective) of the culture. I noticed that the above respondent seemingly enjoyed demonstrating his knowledge of some of the dates and events that occurred in Carthage, a place he knew nothing about before he visited it on a guided tour. It is as if such knowledge of places would give the person some power and prestige (compare Helms, 1988, p. 13). The conventions of the tourist discourse are the framework in which the information is easy to place. As a part of the visitors' stock of knowledge the framework can accommodate even the kind of information that otherwise would mean little to them. Thus the above respondent was happy with the information he got about Carthage. Although from his perspective it may have been only meaningless and isolated historical information with little connection to his perception of the world history, it still made sense to adopt it as a part of the tourist discourse that presents this knowledge as valuable. Thus he may have got the feeling of power through his new knowledge; involvement with some important aspect of the history of the civilization.

The guides' role is to mediate the tourist discourse, maintain the tourist space, and control the experience of novelty so that it does not become overwhelmingly strong. On the other hand they have to present enough novelty to facilitate the feeling of excitement and discovery. Here the skills of the guides become crucial; they have to be able to estimate how much and what kind of information gives the visitors that feeling. A failure to do so means that the group just becomes bored:

> The whole day was bus touring in Lisbon in a constant hurry, the guide explained all the time… You can listen to the guide for a while but not for long (Arvo, 26).

> We had that piss-headed guide who only narrated legends of the Greek mythology (Martti, 29).

For these people the smooth integration of the guide's narration to the conventions of the tourist discourse was not enough to justify interest to the narration. There was little that made the narrative relevant to them. My interpretation is that the object of reach of the students was not so much the sights and their touristic interpretation, but the personal indulgence into the experience of being on the road, away from the normal everyday routines. Thus the role of the tour guide was extremely difficult; there would hardly have been a way to reach the groups' intentions in trying to interpret the sights. This was especially clear in the evening, since the young guide of the group in Portugal was invited to spend time with the students. Her company was appreciated and enjoyed as a local person, as opposed to the touristic stories she was obliged to tell as a guide. This was meaningful in relation to the students' interests; they did not have to deal with the formal tourist discourse. Now they could live up their reach by interacting with a local person, a student just like them. The public meanings of the tourist discourse were replaced by personal meanings arising from the personal involvement with the Other.

The tour guides' roles as leaders also affect the tourist's experience of place. Because of the language problems, Scandinavian tour operators usually have Scandinavian guides in the destinations (Hanefors and Larsson, 1993, p. 29). For the same reason their role often seems to concentrate more on taking care of the practical arrangements of the tourists than actually knowing a lot about the place. The guides are responsible for the smooth conduct of the tours and they have to take care that pre-arranged events like arriving for a dinner happen in time. Thus the existence of the guides sometimes makes the visitors seem more helpless, stupid and passive than they actually are (Pearce, 1982, p. 215).

> In principle you are interested in the destination country, but in practice you just get bored listening the guide. When you think of it, a cultural holiday feels more appealing than a beach holiday but in practice you end up being bored while you follow the guide like a herd of cows (Satu, 28).

This woman clearly implies that the guides take away all the spontaneity of the encounter with the possibly interesting aspects of the destination. At the same time the sense of discovery vanishes even though the guide's narration possibly reveals something you would have wanted to know anyway:

> If you are yourself responsible for getting something from the trip, then the genuine interest in knowing arises. Anything too prepared is not interesting (Satu, 28).

Guides' narrations cease to be interesting because they restrict the experience of an aspect of reach, which often is the very aim of the trip.

There is a desire to know, but that desire has to be satisfied as a consequence of one's personal effort to reach for the knowledge, instead of it being imposed on us. The standard narratives of the guides are seen as an intrusion to our right to find out by ourselves. They are an insult against our desire to be considered individuals, not just cows in a herd.

The interactionary role of tour guides in its organisational meaning can be seen as a sustainer of the tourist space. The communicative and representative roles mostly involve mediation of the tourist discourse. These people are an additional filter in the tourist's experience of place.

Food for Visitors

Foreign food eaten on travel is one of the best examples of standardisation. People have to eat, no matter where they are from or where they travel. However, what to eat and how to do it varies a lot in different cultures. Food and customs concerning how to eat it have a big role in traveller's experience of being away from home. According to Moeran (1983, p. 97) 'food is a means by which the Japanese are invited to experience "being abroad"'. Because of the universal importance of food to all people this naturally applies to all peoples.

> Food is an important part of a culture, and it is extremely interesting to familiarise yourself with foreign foods (Sari, 28).

Sampling local food is one of the possibilities to get personally involved with the Other culture. It is even possible to adopt some of the Other by bringing home recipes. The involvement literally materialises; our reach is satisfied while we eat.

Since eating is an activity that all travellers surely do, the associated industries naturally try to make the best out of it. Travellers are offered what they want.

> ...there is plenty of variety and plenty of spice in Balinese food. But of course, you will have no difficulty in finding western-style food (Garuda Indonesia and Cathay Pacific, 1992, Hong Kong with Bali).

Here the travellers are lured with exotic foods, but simultaneously assured that in case they do not like them, there are always safe alternatives. Travellers are mainly offered either 'standard' food found everywhere in the world, or local food that has been modified to suit the tourist's taste. Hence, for example in Bali I ate Italian pizzas, Mexican tacos, Austrian Wienerschnizels and Swedish köttbullar. Naturally it is possible to eat McDonald's hamburgers there, as well as in Istanbul and Apia. Some of these foods are internationally well known, but if a destination is well established as a destination of people from a certain country, the food of that country may be well presented in the destination. Thus finding Finnish meatballs in the Canary Islands or Cyprus does not present any problems, neither does finding Australian beer and Vegemite-sandwiches in Bali.

Standardized food creates confidence among travellers who know that if they do not want to be at the mercy of strange food that might cause all kinds of troubles, they do not have to. Standard food is clearly a part of the tourist space, to which one can retreat if the exposure to foreign food starts to become too overwhelming. Cohen (1989, p. 56) noted how trekkers to tribal villages were in a 'mini-environmental bubble', since they were 'not ordinarily offered tribal food, and it is doubtful (...) that many would enjoy it or even be willing to eat it'. It is obvious that unless you have got used to eating something, it may taste not only utterly strange, but also totally inedible. It is easy to agree with Cohen's observation after personal experiences of boiled lamb, unprepared raw fish straight from the sea, and crumbed fish heads. Some local foods may be culturally inedible, even revolting. While some exotic foods like, for example snake, dog, worms, and the brain of a live ape may have great novelty value, few Westerners are willing to try all of them. The reach involved often proves to be too much. The repulsiveness of such foods is not necessarily connected to their actual taste, but to culturally rooted conceptions of what can be eaten (see Harris, 1986). A delicacy for one may be revolting to another:

> We were frequently invited by our Chinese hosts to banquets. At one of them, we were informed that we were to be feasted with the best food in China. Later we found that the main dishes had been snake soup and dog meat. I was revolted (Wei and Crompton and Reid 1989, p. 329).

An aspect that sometimes gets over-emphasized by travellers is the safeness of food. Many of them avoid eating certain dishes in a fear that they might ingest harmful bacteria. In extreme cases one may not eat anything that is not known to be absolutely safe. I have personally witnessed a person bringing her own food to our ten day trip to Turkey, and rather starving than eating local food that she felt was suspicious. Usually the avoidance does not go quite that far. A common form of protection from unclean food is to eat standard food in well-known restaurant chains like McDonald's. Most of my backpacker respondents avoided salads, unboiled water and food from street vendors, but otherwise were happy to sample local food. An interviewee was surprised to hear that I ate from the street vendors:

> You eat their food?! That is where I draw the line; I don't eat from them (Sigrid, 21).

Drawing the line somewhere obviously creates a feeling of control. No matter how perceived the actual effects of such line drawing are, the feeling of doing something to prevent oneself from getting harmed is essential. Drawing the line somewhere is a part of the tourist discourse. Staying within such lines is thus part of the visitors' tourist space. There is a direct link here to Hottola's (1999, pp. 127–139) concept of metaworld, into which travellers escape the overt confusion the Otherness causes. Hottola writes about this metaworld in terms of metaspaces (Ibid., p. 132). However, I would like to expand the term out of pure spatiality. Thus I would like to call eating familiar food as a metaworld. It clearly is escape from the confusion the Otherness causes. It is not a space, but it is an act in which a confused mind can dwell to recover from the confusion and to gain an experience of control. Of course, space is often involved, if the eating takes place in a restaurant.

This kind of safe food is typically transformed local or standardised global food, or food from the visitors' own culture. Thus a Finnish conventional tourist preferred to eat Finnish food while in the Canary Islands:

> You have to get proper tucker to be able to keep going (Erkki, 58; an unrecorded comment).

Implicitly his perception of foreign food is that it is less wholesome than the food he has got used to at home. Eating familiar food makes him feel at home so that he can be ready to encounter the Other on other spheres which for him are less critical in maintaining the ability to act.

Many of the limits for food and hygiene the visitors set are thus psychological. In Ubud, Bali, there is a night-market in the centre of the town.[10] It operates in the evenings (when it is dark) and it is immensely popular among the backpackers. At the daytime the site is the marketplace of the town. When all the stalls are packed away for the night, a caterpillar pushes the remaining garbage to the bushes behind the place and the food stalls are erected. I doubt whether any visitor would be willing to eat at the place if it was not veiled by the darkness. But the food is cheap and good, and the stench of rotting garbage rarely reaches beyond the stalls closest to the edge, which are almost exclusively occupied by the locals. Despite my obvious disgust, I also ate there a couple of times because the presence of other travellers makes the food appear reasonably safe. It is also mentioned in the guidebook. Because of the continued popularity of the night-market it can be assumed that not too many people have become sick after eating there. Indeed, I did not and I had not heard of anyone who had. It is thus obvious that despite the appalling (to a Westerner) setting the food is quite safe to eat.

Even so, the popularity of the place among the visitors seems to be contradictory to their desire to avoid potentially hazardous food. But as was seen above, that desire is actualised in defining certain limits within which one perceives to be safe (i.e. avoiding unboiled water, salads, food from street vendors). Thus eating in a place that is mentioned in the guidebooks and occupied by other backpackers is perceived to be on the safe side of the limits set. Another possible perspective to the contradiction is that somehow this very act of eating at Ubud night-market has developed into an institutionalised deviation from the usual constraints of being sensible. It is institutionalised because it is sanctioned by the guidebooks and because it is still safe. It is deviant because despite the fact that not too many people have got sick, it does not comply with Western standards of what is hygienic. Thus it can be seen as a symbolic declaration of independence from the constraints of one's own culture. Partaking in a collective defiance of what is seen as sensible, the travellers affiliate with the idea of independence. This is done as a contrast to dependence on one's own society's rules and conventions that have been implemented upon one since childhood. It seems paradoxical that the independence is declared in a collective act, but in such act the personal sense of the power of the declaration is emphasised by the presence of other like-minded people. The group is needed in order to have a concrete feeling of affiliation into

---

[10] This was in May 1993. The market did not exist when I visited the place in March 1996.

something as contrast to merely breaking free. Having our meal under a kerosene lamp far away from home, in a place we - according to our usual cultural constraints - should not eat, and sharing the experience with others who in many ways are like us, provides a strong sense of both independence and belonging: independence from the constraints of everyday, and belonging to a fellowship of independent people; being involved with the idea of freedom. And, of course, the food is so good that it is genuinely enjoyed.

Eating is such a universally shared phenomenon that in the absence of mutually shared language, eating the same food can be used to display at least some sense of understanding and togetherness. In this way eating the local foods can be a way to lessen the distance to the Other people. The opposite may happen, if the food offered is bad. As food is such a basic need, the experience of the place is partly coloured through the experience of food. If the food is considered as a threat to one's health, it tends to give negative shadows to the experience of the place at whole. The place may be seen as threatening, as a domain of danger that can be avoided by staying within the tourist space that appears as safe food. But the food can also be used to express the personal involvement with the Other and the freedom to do as we decide by ourselves.

Modification of local food is done in the restaurants that cater mostly to foreign travellers. The modification creates standard 'local food'. If a restaurant wants to prosper, it is not a wise policy to serve food that travellers are not able to eat. Some of the local foods are so spicy hot that unaccustomed eaters may just burn their mouths. In most cases modification amounts putting less spices in the food served. However, modification occurs more generally in the selection of foods that are served to travellers. Their impression about the local food may have been stereotyped already by the stories of other travellers, travel advertising, and by the ethnic restaurants they may have visited in their own countries. Naturally the selection of foods presented in such restaurants, as well as in the ones in the destination, is biased so that only the most appealing foods are accepted. Thus, when eating in a Chinese restaurant we do not eat fish heads in a soup but sweet and sour pork. When it comes to selection of food offered for tourist consumption, tourists are unusually carnivorous; few peoples eat as much meat as the menus in the destinations suggest. The 'visitor food' is often so expensive that local people cannot afford to prepare it every day; after all, it is food for feasts. If I think about Finnish cuisine as it is presented to visitors, it tends to be the food that I myself eat mainly on big family occasions and festivities. 'Traditional cuisine' thus frequently refers to the food that people eat at feasts and is quite distinct from the traditional food those people eat every day. Consequently, 'Chinese food' for Chinese is different from 'Chinese food' for tourists.

In terms of reach, a new kind of food is a way to reach for the new domains. Once again it appears that the industries involved in providing that reach attempt to smooth the passage into previously unknown domains by providing standardised food. The reach is institutionalised into conventions of where and what to eat. Although eating the destination's ethnic foods may in principle lessen the distance between the visitors and the locals, the actual effect can be even reverse. The situation is the same as when the tourists are greeted with ceremonies traditionally reserved for important visitors; by according a special treatment, they are effectively separated from the everyday domains of the people. In a similar manner, eating local food that for the locals is reserved mainly for big events may, in fact, underline the difference in statuses of the visitors and the locals. This difference becomes even more pronounced, if the cuisine eaten is totally different, as sometimes is the case:

> Thailand offers a wide range of international cuisine. Hotels and resorts are equipped with first class restaurants of international standard (Swingaway; Thailand 1993, p. 5).

In these cases the reach seems to be directed towards the domains of international cuisine rather than towards the everyday diet of the local people. This is not to say that eating in places like McDonald's or Pizza Hut necessarily separates visitors from the locals; indeed, many local people eat in these places. But such practices from the visitors are symptomatic of the need to retain a certain amount of security amid the Other. It is not reaching in any sense; rather, it expresses the need to balance the experience of the Other with something familiar from home.

The standardisation and modification of food is thus an intentional effort on the part of the travel industry (including the local restaurants) to accommodate the visitors' need for security. Being able to choose food that is not utterly strange (and possibly even unpleasant), gives the travellers a sense of control over how much they immerse themselves into the Other. This allows them a way to balance between the amount of home and reach they want to experience.

Travel as a Standardised Path of Existential Space

Standardising makes mass tourism possible and provides the travel industry with the biggest profits. As an institutionalised form of reach, travel is a standardised path in our existential space. Travel in the domains and centres of the level of 'geography' is made possible and easy by the travel industry. Our need to balance home and reach has become a battleground of industries that profit from providing apparently efficient ways of reaching. In the process of becoming institutionalised, reach forms convention-filled discourses within which reaching is considered worthwhile. This does not apply to travel only; every aspect of reach is subjected to the lures of various industries with promises of more and better reach. Overt institutionalisation of reach means that it loses some elements for which it is desired. The answer from the industries lies in inventing more and more adventurous ways to reach. In travel this can mean new 'unspoilt' destinations or special kind of adventurous activities like abseiling and bungey-jumping. Another possibility for the traveller would be to attempt to reach with as little help from the travel industry as possible. This was originally the idea of backpacking. The problem is that as many people start to do so, it soon becomes institutionalised and develops its own standard discourse. It is no wonder that the Kuhnian idea of paradigmatic cycles springs to mind. Creation and observation of certain standards creates ideas opposed to those standards, and in time these ideas themselves form into new standards in turn.

Transformation and Creation of Attractions: Staging

Services, facilities, attractions, and places are standardised by the travel industry. They are also transformed, and sometimes even created from nothing. Standardising is itself a form of transformation. Similarly, when a new tourist attraction is created, it is done according to certain standards. While standardisation is primarily an element in making travel a commodity, transforming involves alteration of the actual attractions to aid this commodification. The attractions are transformed from what they naturally or culturally are, to a form that is judged by the travel industry to have more appeal to tourists, or which is more readily usable in the industry of tourism.

Cohen (1989) uses the term 'staging' in a similar context as transforming in his earlier work (1972). Staging, probably more than transforming, expresses the process that intentionally transforms a feature into an attraction, into the object of gaze. Staging means that something is transformed so that it can be presented to spectators. Staging is thus one form of transformation, but not only that; staging can involve purposeful fabrication and 'garnishing' of reality to make it more appealing for visitors. There are good examples of this in heritage tourism for example (Brett, 1996; Richards, 1996).

Staging can be divided into substantive and communicative staging (Cohen, 1989, p. 33). Substantive staging involves actual changes in the features that are staged, distinguished from pure communicative staging where the features can be left intact but their interpretation and information about them are altered.

As an example of communicative staging Cohen uses hill tribe trekking in Thailand, where backpackers are sold trips to see remote hill tribes whose culture has supposedly remained 'unspoiled'. Because the motives of those backpackers are to experience novelty as authenticity, the tour companies make great efforts to emphasise that everything is authentic. Backpackers are provided with a local guide whose origins (despite the fact that their links to the local tribes are often superficial) 'is one of the principal means of communicative staging in the hill tribe tourism' (Cohen, 1989, p. 53). To sell a trip that provides the novelty of authenticity, the companies have to walk a tight-rope between making 'the trek itself appear as a spontaneous adventure' and providing the trekkers with a 'mini-environmental bubble' (Ibid., p. 39). Obviously those companies have managed to do this very well, since it appears that among backpackers these treks are a popular thing to do; of all the backpackers I interviewed who had visited Thailand, everyone had taken part to these trips. The trips have become institutionalised. Similar, but maybe a little less strenuous trips are also marketed to conventional tourists, who can have their adventure by riding an elephant or using a four wheel drive.

Communicative staging does not necessarily involve any substantive staging. Albers and James (1988, p. 153) provide examples of both types of staging. They explain the homogenising effect of ethnic tourism in which 'the features of an area and its people are stereotyped according to some dominant cultural model':

On one hand, only the most unusual or picturesque ethnic groups in an area are featured in regional tourist productions...

This is communicative staging in the form of telling just one part of a story that is considered the most appealing.

On the other hand, regional tourism can manufacture its own 'generic' ethnic imagery, and present it in the context of special tourist attractions where local groups perform dances and/or exhibit their craftswork (Ibid.).

This is combined communicative and substantive staging in which a 'pseudoethnography' is created. It is filled with Barthesian myths of the tourist discourse, which typically are supposed to point to 'authenticity'. Attractions are then set up to confirm the images (of 'authenticity', for example) that the pseudoethnography has evoked. Papson (1981, p. 225) mentions how this process alters reality (see also Taylor, 2001):

...government and private enterprise not only re-define social reality but also re-create it to fit (...) definitions. This process is both interactive and dialectical. To the extent that this process takes place, the category of everyday life is annihilated.

Thus the normal everyday life of people in an area is hidden away 'behind the scenes' because watching everyday life does not often provide tourists with anything specifically spectacular. Adoption of the tourist discourse that the advertising promotes makes the tourists expect a spectacle, because the discourse is saturated by lively stereotypes. The action that is visible to the visitors has to be compatible with these stereotypes. We are shown the aspects of the culture that are easily converted into commodities that usually appear as various performances. These aspects are representations of the Other.[11] In this way the tourist discourse and its myths largely define the 'realities' of the tourist space. These 'realities' could be called 'tourism realism' (Bruner and Kirshenblatt-Gimblett, 1994, p. 449). Thus the tourist space in which the

---

[11] Also nature can represent the Other; for example, the gorillas of Zaire represent wilderness. Tourists have become eager to observe these beasts in their natural habitat, so efforts are made to accustom more gorillas to the presence of people, so as to handle more tourists. The representation of wilderness has been domesticated so that the tourists can enjoy it. The tourists have become part of the gorillas' habitat. The result is more or less staged wilderness (Bruner and Kirshenblatt-Gimblett, 1994, pp. 438-439).

tourism realism mostly takes place is a 'virtual world' (ibid.). Although the 'tourism realism' is often obsessed with authenticity, it creates authenticity only within the discourse in which it operates, within this world of its own virtuality. In other words, the discourse gives the statement of authenticity, and if we take the narrative of the discourse as granted and as reality, the experience is authentic for us. Consequently we can err in taking 'tourism realism' for 'reality', and forget that the world of tourism realism is largely a mythical space. However, authentic or not, experiences themselves are always lived and thus 'real', authentic.

At worst, culture within the tourist space is perceived only as something that can be performed. This draws from the fact that to be able to market intangible cultural products, they have to be turned into tangible representations. Pretes (1995, p. 13) uses the example of the village of Santa Claus: 'Santa Claus and his village become simultaneously commodity, spectacle, and representation: Christmas is now available in a consumable form'. In a similar manner, the intangible phenomenon of culture has to be made tangible; it transforms to performances, handcrafts and cuisine. Tourists themselves sometimes adopt this view according to which culture would be something tangible, as if it had nothing to do with the normal everyday lives of people:

> [In the Canary Islands] too much tourism has largely eroded the culture away (Erkki, 58).

> There are great beaches in southern Thailand but there is more culture here in Bali (Torsten, 21).

These comments imply the view that if the local people do not wear their national costumes or perform 'traditional' rites so that the tourists can see, they have lost their culture. In the absence of spectacular rituals and 'traditional' performances there is little that addresses the tourists within their conception of what is culture. Furthermore, it does not count as 'culture' of the Other, if we see a Christian baptism of a child, for example, because we can see that at home. Instead, initiation rites of a tribal people for example, are suitably exotic to represent the Other, and because they have little meaning for us, they can be transformed to meet the requirements of a tourist performance.

The 'culture' of the tourist discourse is thus merely a display of the most 'showy' or staged aspects of it. The aspects can be, if not irrelevant, at least marginal in the course of usual everyday life of the people themselves.

The displayed aspects of the culture are often decontextualised; they are taken from their original contexts and transformed into a display or a performance (Albers and James, 1988, p. 153):

> *Decontextualization* is closely related to homogenization, and it involves a process whereby ethnic subjects appear in settings that lack some concrete lived-in, historical referent. ...the true history of a people is often derailed in the highly abstract and generalized language of 'cultural heritage' and 'cultural tradition'. Not uncommonly, this language reduces people to the crafts they make, the dances they perform, or the exotic costumes they wear.

The idea of culture as something tangible that can be pointed at (like a performance, ritual, costumes, and cuisine), is deeply embedded into the tourist discourse. This is the 'culture' the tourists have become accustomed seeing. Here is a conventional tourist's description of his experience of Berber-culture:

> You find this Berber-culture in both Morocco and Tunisia. You go to a feast where you eat and then the dancing and all the other performances in the arena start (Erkki, 58).

The description is based on his experience of the culture in a so-called 'Berber night', which obviously was a standard part of the tourist programme in Tunisia. Of course everyone understands that performances like that are staged. But still the touristic stereotypes of peoples and their cultures are in some degree reinforced by the performances because they are what the tourists see and witness with their own eyes. The experience clearly confirms the prior exotic images. This way of introducing a 'culture' as a theme night is optimal from the perspective of travel industry. It is relatively easy to arrange, it can be transformed into a spectacle, and it can be sold as a commodity. The suitable features of the culture of a people are decontextualised and presented as a show. Not surprisingly, decontextualisation can also be found in travel brochures:

> The Fijians have many *traditional* ceremonies which can be *experienced* at most of the *hotels, resorts* and *cruises*. The Meke - *authentic traditional* song and dance, where legends, love stories and historical events of the islands are told by song and gesture. The Magiti - a Fijian feast, prepared in a 'lovo' or underground oven. Yagona ceremony - the drinking of Yagona (Kava), made from the root of the pepper plant, is a common ceremonial

and social *custom* at such occasions as births, deaths and marriages and to welcome *important* visitors. Fire walking - perhaps one of the most *spectacular* sights in Fiji. Fijians, it is said, were first given the gift of fire walking on the island of Beqa (Qantas Jetabout Holidays, Fiji 1993/94, p. 4, emphasis added).

The example clearly illustrates the points made above. The customs that are easily convertible into commodities are transformed. They are displayed for the visitors in the form of shows, sights and entertainment. When visitors witness a ritual, it is more often than not specially staged for them. The transformation may well involve only the context; the rituals previously performed in the honour of an important visitor, are now being performed for tourists who pay for it. Naturally most tourists see the irony of this and take all the attention they get as a game that they came to play on their vacation. A decontextualised attraction, in this case a reproduction, is accepted as long as it is a good one, an 'authentic reproduction' (Bruner, 1991, p. 240). The critical factor is thus *perceived authenticity*. This applies also to a staged performance; a poor performance that does not match with the tourists' expectations of what is supposed to be authentic, is bound to leave the tourists with the feeling of being cheated. So did this conventional tourist who went to see Turkish belly dancing:

> Maybe I expected a dusky, sentimental cellar where you just about smoke opium pipes and an attractive lady would dance beautifully in the dimness. But as I remember, the woman wasn't attractive, neither did she dance beautifully, and the place was extremely gloomy (Satu, 28).

Obviousness of Staging

So far I have described transformation on the basis of what has been transformed; the messages about the attraction (communicative staging), or the attraction itself (substantive staging). Another perspective on the subject is the obviousness of the staging. The communicative staging often has strong effects on people who may have little background knowledge about the place they are going to visit. It may even be that the rosy expressions of the travel brochure are practically the only pieces of information the travellers have about their destination. Thus it is vital in forming their expectations and consequently, affecting their experience of the place. This is even more remarkable since most people realise that the expressions in travel brochures are purposefully created to lure them to purchase a trip to the destination, yet they are still successfully persuaded to do so. Although people may well see the commercial nature of these narratives, with little background knowledge they absorb at least a part of it. Naturally some - even commercially biased - information is better than no information. Even with some background information, the persuasion of communicative staging can still be effective; we want to be convinced that travel indeed contains highlights that are change from the usual everyday life.

MacCannell (1976, p. 93), using Goffman's theory of 'front' and 'back', raises the question of authenticity in the situations where visitors think that what they see is authentic while it actually is staged. 'Front' is what is shown to the visitor, and 'back' is a 'backstage' area that is not intended for the visitor to see. To satisfy visitors' desire to experience authenticity by seeing 'backstage' situations the travel industry arranges apparent possibilities to do this. What eventually happens is that the visitor is shown another 'front', staged as 'backstage'. Initially it may have been a real backstage, but in the process of becoming an attraction it has transformed into another 'front'. MacCannell (1976, p. 102) describes this even as a 'lie contained in the touristic experience', that 'presents itself as a truthful revelation, as the vehicle that carries the onlooker behind false fronts into reality'.

These front and back areas appear in both communicative and substantive staging. Substantive staging is usually more obvious in the sense that it is easier to realise that what we encounter is more or less staged, but not always. In practice this difficulty often manifests itself in situations in which photography opportunities are provided, as in the following example:

> Meo women appeared to go about their daily chores in front of their houses, like embroidering, batiking... In fact, however, they were usually dressed up in 'typical' colourful costumes, ready to be photographed (Cohen and Nir and Almagor, 1992, p. 228).

Locals often perceive how tourists would like to see them and stage themselves accordingly (Ibid., p. 227), as this is likely to provide them with more tourist dollars than not staging themselves. With little prior knowledge of the destination, the visitors have very little opportunity to confirm or dispute the authenticity of the features they see. Most of their knowledge is likely to be based on the commercial promotional material, which tries to present and mark the features of the destination as 'authentic'. Words like 'primitive', 'traditional', 'unspoiled', 'untouched', 'unexplored', etc. are used to achieve this. In this way the promotional material presents the substantively staged as authentic. Thus it is no wonder that substantive staging can be hard to expose; it may be the only 'reality' of the place the tourists know. This is tourism realism in which authenticity can be irrelevant from the point of view of the tourist's experience. If we perceive something as authentic, then it is authentic for us. Then again, if we earnestly seek authenticity, but are only able to experience staged authenticity that we can expose, frustration and cynicism arise. But a staged display of the culture of the Other can also be revealing and mind-opening, not to mention entertaining. In many ways better than no display at all.

In the backpacker discourse, the authenticity of what is encountered is highly valued. This means that many backpackers are eager to get to the backstage, to meet the 'real' people.

> We met *real* Sumatran people in a little village. We took a jungle trek there and they were so nice. They do not get a lot of money from tourists, only a small amount from the guide and that's all (Denise, 22).

The perception of authenticity in the example is determined by how much money is involved. If not, or if very little, then the setting can be labelled as backstage and thus authentic. This reflects the ideal of innocent, 'unspoiled', places where money is not everything. In contrast, profit taking exposes staged, 'spoiled', settings; staging is perceived to occur only for profit.

Substantive staging happens often without any intention to hide the fact that it is staged. For example, no one denies that a native dance performed at a dinner in a hotel is staged specially for tourists. But still on the other hand, even realising that something is staged does not necessarily mean that one knows how authentic the staged performance itself is. A visitor does not usually possess enough knowledge for this:

> ...organizers of a major ceremony altered the normal course of the ritual to create for the several score foreign tourists a more dramatic and shorter spectacle (Crystal, 1977, p. 120).

> A Chambri initiation ceremony was timed to coordinate with the arrival of tourists, the language used was changed from Chambri to Pidgin English, the hazing part of the ceremony was made shorter, and, most important, the

Chambri found themselves playing to a new audience of very wealthy and powerful foreigners (Bruner, 1991, p. 244).

Substantive staging regularly provides visitors with spectacles that would be encountered only rarely, if the local way of living went on in its normal everyday order. Transforming for example rites or ceremonies so that they are sometimes performed solely to visitors at certain set times makes sure that visitors see something interesting (see Bruner and Kirshenblatt-Gimblett, 1994, p. 450). Also performing a rite to the 'three minute culture' visitors means that much has to be shortened, and dramatic phases enhanced to capture the visitors' interest for the duration of the whole performance. A highly idealistic backpacker criticised the tourists who, according to him, lacked the appreciation of 'real' authenticity:

> If they see somebody dancing a little bit then that's the culture for them. And they get tired of seeing a lot of it. It is nice but not if it lasts too long (Aron, 23).

Bali is famous for its pride in and commitment to authentic and high quality dance performances, not only for ceremonial purposes, but also for tourists. However, at least some sort of transformation is inevitable. In a dance that told a story from the Ramayana epic all the dialogues were in Balinese (as I, equipped with some touristic knowledge, could only guess). But in a scene where the monkey warrior Hanuman becomes seemingly charmed with Sita, he says to her in English: 'I love you'.[12] Naturally we, the tourists to whom the whole performance was directed, responded with a laugh to this wooing, but afterwards some expressed disgust about it.

The staging in these examples of Bruner and mine above appear very different at the first sight. Bruner's was performed in the native environment in the absence of a stage, restricted entry and ticket selling, whereas I had to buy a ticket to get entry to the weekly scheduled show, performed on a stage in a closed area. On the other hand, in Bruner's example the transformation goes much further, beyond mere translation of a single line. However, the basic structure of both of these examples is the

---

[12] According to South-East Asia on a Shoestring (1977, p. 57): 'In Balinese dancing, animals and clowns are allowed to improvise and they are usually extremely funny, a good Hanuman can create an unforgettable role'. Obviously the wooing arises from this tradition. Also the little monkeys in the performance woo the audience by mimicking the stealing monkeys in the nearby forest; all tourists in the audience who have seen the monkeys there, immediately recognise them.

same, performers are getting paid for staging a performance for tourists. Only the actual methods of ticket selling differ; Bruner's tourists bought the performance as a part of their sightseeing tour, whereas I bought my ticket from the door. Both performances were transformed, one by altering the contents and the other by arranging a special show and including a single translation to woo the audience. Also the presence of the tourists is itself a transformation.

Knowing all this still leaves much unexplained. Did those Chambri youngsters really get initiated in that modified initiation ceremony Bruner mentioned, or did the Chambri people arrange a real initiation ceremony for them afterwards, or had they already been initiated earlier? Was the dance I saw, performed as it would be done in the real ceremony in the temple? Maybe something else on the top of the obvious translation of a line mentioned had been changed, or perhaps the performance is a feature of the altogether new kind of Balinese culture that is presented to tourists as traditional. In any case we remain outsiders who cannot grasp all the meanings that cultural customs and rites may bear to the people themselves. This however, underlines the fact that from the tourists' perspective, only the perceived authenticity matters. Furthermore, most of the conventional tourists I interviewed, were not concerned with authenticity; they were seeking entertainment. A good staging may be enjoyable. An authentic ceremony could appear boring for tourists, who would not be able to share and take part in all symbolic meanings. Understanding of those symbolic meanings would be essential in order to appreciate the authenticity. As outsiders, few of us would probably be willing to spend hours in watching an initiation rite or eat exactly the same food as the natives.

From Staging to Reality

Substantive staging is often arranged to confirm the expectations evoked by the communicative staging. In communicative staging an exotic impression of a people may be given on the basis of some exotic ceremonies they may have. Then in the destination the infrastructure and programme for tourists is arranged so that tourists primarily see the local people through those very ceremonies. A good example is reported from Western Samoa:

> The three hotels offer fiafia [feast] nights every week where island dances and songs are performed but these are frequently geared to local expectations of what tourists want to see and hear, thus the Hawaiian Hula, the Tahitian Tamure or Cook Island and Maori dances and songs dominate

the performances and the real Samoan Siva is seldom performed (Meleisea and Meleisea, 1985, p. 44).

Our stereotypes of Polynesian dances are probably strongly influenced by glossy Hollywood films that have shown colourful images of Hawaiian Hula with its hip twisting movements. Samoan Siva is much more stationary and instead of displaying swinging of hip its emphasis is on charming movements of hands and arms. To Western tourists at least, Hula may be more visually spectacular, since there is more movement in it. It is obvious that as visitors believe that Hula is Polynesian, they are delighted to confirm their impressions of Polynesia. As Boorstin (1972, p. 109) has noted: 'the tourist's appetite for strangeness thus seems best satisfied when the pictures in his own mind are verified in some far country'.

When transformation of some features of the culture to meet the requirements of tourism has been going on for a long time, it may happen that these transformed features become increasingly important parts of the culture. Thus religion, rituals, arts and crafts of a people may experience a revival as the skills involved have to be sustained to remain competitive in the pursuit of tourist dollars. This is what has been happening in Bali for example (McCarthy, 1994). Some travellers who have extreme desire to experience novelty as authenticity are critical of this and condemn it as cultural prostitution:

> I think they keep and emphasise their religion just for the tourists (Aron, 23).

This visitor feels that he is being cheated; he detests the idea that he would be a victim of a collective fraud, initiated by international tourism and executed by the Balinese people. This illustrates the perception by the visitors that the place has become too commercialised; it is no more an authentic Other, but a staged one. In Bali the rich cultural heritage is transformed into an attraction by adapting it into the tourist discourse. The result is a 'new' culture that evolves around tourism. However, a part of the tourist discourse is the illusion that some cultures have remained unchanged for centuries or that the change occurring now is somehow spoiling the authenticity of those cultures.

Cultures, of course, have always changed as a result from invasions, movement of people and diffusion of ideas. At present the underlying force causing changes is the spreading of the Western-style market economy throughout the world. Given the market-orientated nature of this economy, the transformation of some cultural features into forms that facilitate their marketing is a natural part of that change. From this perspective a change is inevitable and natural, and to suggest that the change would produce something unauthentic unlike the previous changes during history is at least problematic. The limit between what is authentic and what is staged becomes blurred because now staging becomes a part of the culture. This reflects the unequal distribution of power in the tourist discourse; authenticity is something the tourist industry and the tourists define (Oakes, 1992). This is one of the paradoxes of the tourist discourse; while it emphasises authenticity as something untouched or unspoilt, it simultaneously attributes the loss of those qualities to tourism that it promotes.

An important aspect of the tourist discourse is its tendency to seek and value nostalgia:

> Insight's Eastern Mediterranean takes you behind the veil of history to the very dawn of civilisation. You'll journey to lands where mighty empires rose and fell, visit the tombs and temples of the Pharaohs and marvel at their exquisite treasures. Gaze in awe at the majestic pyramids and wonder at the human endeavour that built them (Singapore Airlines, Insight 1994: Egypt, Israel, Greece, Turkey, Jordan, Kenya, p. 3).

Places are not allowed to present themselves as they are, instead, they are made into representations of past; golden eras of colonialism, great empires, or tribal innocence. Past is emphasised because it is easier to invest past eras, of which we have no first-hand experience, with the qualities that correspond our dreams.[13] Like distant domains on the level of 'geography' in the spatial dimension, similarly in the temporal dimension the past is a good entity on which to project our dreams. It can be done without the interference of the immediate experience that tends to cut the wings of imagination. The tourist space is partly created for this kind of imagination, which is directed and even controlled by the tourist industry. Furthermore, it is easier to stage the past than the present. Visitors are shown splendid colonial estates, glorious palaces and tribal rituals, while

---

[13] Even clearer example is the future, because we cannot have even vicarious knowledge of it. It is a domain where speculation and imagination can roam freely. However, it is not easy for the travel industry to use, because it involves total creation of attractions and requires huge amounts of capital. An example is the Epcot Centre in Disney World. But in the virtual world of computer games this is not a problem.

the present everyday life is typically ignored, except when it is turned into a spectacle by staging and otherwise transforming it. In Bali the past and the present have been integrated by adopting elements from the past into the everyday life of the present. The result is a culture that seems to have spectacles as everyday occurrences. Cultural evolution together with the highly tourist-orientated economy of Bali has produced a culture that values and maintains the features that keep its economy going. It provides the tourists with the spectacles they want to experience, but it puzzles the perceptive visitors who become unable to distinguish between staged and authentic. Thus they become unsure of the extent of their reach and feel frustrated.

Complete Staging

Above I have described some processes in which preceding communicative staging shapes the substantive staging of features of places. Now I will deal with the opposite, which takes place when communicative staging is used to create a story for already existing substantive staging. The clearest example of this is when an attraction is created from the beginning (e.g. countless adventure and theme parks like Disneyland or Santa Claus Village). This means that the attraction as a whole is completely, not only substantively staged. The whole attraction is created right from the beginning to correspond with dreams and utopias the tourists are perceived to have. Communicative staging is needed to reinforce the connection between those dreams and the sight. This is an ideal world of the tourist discourse where novelty is encountered as spectacles (and paid for). Thus those completely staged settings are often 'not merely copies or replicas of real-life situations but copies that are presented as disclosing more about the real thing than the real thing itself discloses' (MacCannell, 1976, p. 102). This is achieved by deliberate planning that ensures that the setting corresponds to the dreams that make tourists seek for their fulfilment. We all know that the real everyday life, 'the real thing', does not always do that. It has this unfortunate property of presenting unwanted mundane situations that are often utterly boring or sometimes even devastatingly tragic. But the synthetic utopia frees us from these constraints of our everyday life; as Eco writes: 'Disneyland tells us that faked nature corresponds much more to our daydream demands' than reality (cited in Urry, 1990, p. 146).

These kinds of settings are synthetic or pseudo places that, according to Relph (1976, p. 118), are 'manifestations of placelessness', 'other-directed' components of 'placeless geography'. Their 'staged placeness' addresses the dreams and fantasies, or stereotypical impressions of some other exotic places, but not the actual environment within which they are situated. There is a *perceived* bond between everyday places and mundane reality, while places in the domain of the Other are associated with fantasy. Thus, in order to be associated with fantasy, a setting must be 'other-directed'. The bond mentioned is more perceived than actual, as it is possible to attach wild fantasies to everyday places as well as mundane reality to Other places. However, to do the former requires some effort of imagination and it can be more enjoyable to let readily provided settings carry one away. The other-directedness of a setting does it, fantasylands 'appear to be to some extent utopias made real which provide guaranteed excitement, amusement, or interest, while eliminating the effort and change of travel or imagination' (Ibid., p. 97). Here the experience is quite similar to watching a movie; the place in which we are is irrelevant. It is the narration that we participate in, not the actual surroundings here and now that is relevant. These placeless settings address the visitors because they are specially created for them. We do not have to ponder about the meaning of cultural peculiarities or be worried about how to act in strange situations. Neither do we have that feeling of inferiority that sometimes arises when life seems to be indifferent to us. This time we are the centre of all the attention and we can feel confident as the element of uncertainty has been taken away. All we have to do is to let the narratives associated with the setting carry us away to the domains of fantasy.

Disneyland is a well-known example about this kind of fantasyland and thus the phenomenon of creating completely staged attractions is called 'disneyfication' (Relph, 1976, p. 95). A personally observed example of this is the island of Sentosa in Singapore. Sentosa is located just off the Singapore harbour, and over the past decade it has undergone massive development. The result at present is an island with beaches, museums, golf courses, gardens, restaurants, underwater world, and so on. It is possible to visit Asian Village, a fenced area (admission fee) with clusters of buildings built in different styles from different parts of Asia with displays of arts and crafts, dances, songs, rituals and ceremonies. Within the area there is also Adventure Asia, an amusement park with a few rides:

The lair of the young Pirate Prince and his merry men, Adventure Asia is a land of *adventure*, promising *endless thrills* and *fun* for the entire family. *Experience* the Pirates' adventures as you hop from one ride to another (an Asian Village brochure, emphasis added).

As a whole the island is a place where almost everything (even the beaches) is artificially created and where most activities involve purchasing a ticket or buying classy items from numerous shops. A backpacker's guidebook describes the place as 'rather plastic, although very popular as a local weekend escape' (South-East Asia on a Shoestring, 1992, p. 701). Thus the island as a whole is an example of a place that refers to the Other in the sense of fantasy, to something else but itself. It is also possible to find single features of the island that in themselves are examples of the other-directedness. The feature I am going to use here is the 'Ruined City', the faked ruins of an alleged ancient settlement, located on the Waterfront Promenade. It is by no means among the major attractions of the island and its location is quite inferior. However, as its size allows one to comprehend the attraction in a short period of time and its artificiality shines through the whole setting, it makes an excellent example.

The Ruined City has been built to display a few of the features an ancient city may have had. In an area of maybe 20x50 meters there is a broken bridge, a gate, a hypostyle hall and a two headed idol, all made of straight-cut granite, with elegant electric lighting fitted in the pavements and building stones. The idea of the Ruined City is that by directing visitors' imagination, the place can be filled with the mystery of past events. This is attempted by using signs that tell about the features. The pseudohistory told in those signs has been specially created for children, to evoke their vivid imagination by directing their thought in certain ways. The next four quotations are the actual texts in those signs.

The Broken Bridge
The original main entry, across the stone moat by the wood and granite bridge is broken, apparently by huge force, indicating attack and possible destruction by explosives (Chinese pirates perhaps).

The bridge reaches two meters over a 'drain' that extends just a few meters on each side of the bridge. Practically, the 'drain' starts from nowhere and leads to nowhere. The fake nature of the construction is apparent to any adult, but maybe not so for children.

The Main Gate

This is a strange mixture of Persian and Indian styles and is decorated by patterns of unknown origin. Heiroglyphics [sic] adorn the gate and paving, and so far no one has been able to decipher these. The strange mythical 'eye' -motiff [sic] can first be seen here.

Everything is stereotyped to resemble the image that we have about the patterns archaeologists find. The 'heiroglyphics' are not too unintelligible to allow visitor to try to work out their meaning. The 'mythical eye' evokes mystical connotations as it is commonly perceived to represent the presence of a spiritual being.

The Hypostyle Hall

Typical of ancient Persian architecture but executed in an individual style with capitals unlike those of almost any known culture. It is likely that these supported a timber roof, but most of the columns are broken, leaving only evidence that the whole settlement may have been destroyed by bombardment.

Recurring references to spectacular confrontation add excitement and provide imagination with fantasies of wild destruction.

The Two Headed Idol

This strangely shaped idol is unlike any other, and its origins are completely unknown. The snake feature indicates some Hindu influence but that is speculation. The viewing window was undoubtedly a spyhole and it has been reconstructed as such. It is possible however that this idol was an ancient form of guillotine, where the hapless victim's head was pushed through the hole from behind to be neatly severed by the executioner's blade.

Again the pseudo-style of Singaporean constructors has been explained as style from 'unknown origin', causing one to ponder about the origins of the impulses. Dramatic assumptions about the fates of ancient victims give an additional dimension to the imagined life of the inhabitants.

The setting plays with basic semiotic connotations with which most people are familiar from popular history and archaeology. The texts in the signs evoke wild images of what has happened, but these images have nothing to do with this actual location in Sentosa. There is not the slightest hint about the history of the real inhabitants of the island who may, indeed, have had violent encounters with pirates. Instead, the reference is made only to the realms of fantasy. Thus the place is totally Other-directed, the Other being fantasy. Here the preceding substantive staging (building the site) actually needs communicative staging to give it a context. The 'ruins' themselves, owing to their fake and out of place nature, do not refer to anything. The signs that give the reference complete the gap that the features without a reference might otherwise cause. In other words, the 'ruins' would not mean anything without something explaining what one is supposed to think about them.

This is what MacCannell (1976, p. 113) called 'marker involvement'; markers are needed to make the sight appear to have any significance. In many cases the completely staged attraction in itself is not as exciting as the communicative staging makes us to believe. The role of communicative staging, especially in advertising, is to convince us that the setting answers to our needs. Staging attractions and creating new ones then attempt to deliver what is promised, with varying degree of success (and will).

Here we can distinguish different degrees of staging: communicative, substantive, and complete. Communicative staging narrates the place or its features so that the potential travellers become interested in it, or/and establish a framework in which relate experiences there. Substantive staging involves transformation of places and their features so as to make them interesting to tourists and suitable for their consumption. In complete staging tourist attractions are created artificially. It is staging in the sense that such attractions are usually representations of dreams. They are stages on which we can project our own dreams. These dreams we have either internalised from the media, or then they are our own (but commonly shared) dreams that are utilised in travel advertising and the travel industry and processed into the completely staged attractions. If the complete staging works well, we have the illusion that we can live our dreams in the attractions.

In many cases the staging of attractions does not matter from the perspective of providing the visitors with a change from their everyday lives. The attractions are experienced (at least initially) as present-at-hand. Staging actually enhances the presence-at-hand of the things experienced. This happens because in staging many things are turned into spectacles, which seldom are encountered in the usual everyday life. However, earlier I have noted that experiencing the Other from a tourist space diminishes the presence-at-hand of the Other, and makes everything encountered ready-to-hand by incorporating it into a part of that space. This appears contradictory, but on closer analysis it is not; two different movements between readiness-to-hand and presence-at-hand have to be distinguished. When the tourist space diminishes the presence-at-hand, it operates on our perception of the Other. It makes the Other look as if it was a readily understandable feature within the structure of the tourist trip, i.e. an attraction to enjoy. The opposite turn from ready-to-hand to presence-at-hand takes place in our experience. Our experiences are made present-at-hand in a way that does not normally happen in our everyday environment; they are exceptional. Our attention is directed towards the experience, not towards the Other. In other words: *our experiences are present-at-hand* because they differ from our everyday experiences, but we perceive *the representations of the Other as ready-to-hand* as part of the commodity of travel.

Staging and Presentation of Space

As long as we are visitors, places tend to present themselves in a framework that is more or less infiltrated by staging. The consequent tourist discourse creates a staged sense of insideness; the visitors may feel behavioural insiders through being familiarised with the place as it is presented in the tourist discourse. Because of the myths involved in the discourse, the place becomes almost representational (as opposed to presentational). In this way the tourist space created by the travel industry, and the adoption of the tourism realism, can make the place, or at least the experience of it, Other-directed. The Other to which the experiences in the place are directed, often draws from something else than the very place itself. The Other represents the ideas, ideals and fantasies that are common stock of many members of the visitors' cultural group. Thus the tourist's experience of the place is often a reflection of our own world. The tourism realism adopted from the tourist discourse provides us with a way to project our world onto the place visited.

8 Sightseeing

Sightseeing as Ritual

Attractions are an important form of presence-at-hand and novelty that are sought during travel. The conventional tourists in particular want to experience presence-at-hand as attractions rather than as a confusion caused by the Other. Attractions can be a piece of rock, amusement park, complex cultural rituals, man-made, or natural, but according to Pretes (1995, p. 4), the most important division is created by whether the attractions have served some original function before they became recognised as attractions. Despite the huge differences in their actual appearances, the common denominator for all attractions is that they are on display; they are marked and marketed as representations of ideas, ideals, and fantasies. Thus they are an institutionalised part of the tourist discourse. They are there to be gazed at or entered, whether a landscape of natural beauty, or a theme park.

Attractions as Representations

For MacCannell (1976, p. 13), experiencing attractions (sightseeing) is an attempt to reconstruct the fragmented world by emphasizing how 'elements dislodged from their original natural, historical and cultural contexts fit together with other such displaced or modernized things and people'. This means that decontextualised attractions are brought into a new framework of tourist discourse and reconstructed into a whole within it. The attractions make sense as representations to gaze at. The determination of what the attractions are representations of, is an essential component of the tourist discourse.

Like a place, an attraction often signifies a larger entity, whose qualities are perceived in connection with the attraction. As we articulate the world, it is not done by considering all the elements it contains, but selectively picking features that we use as reference points. Like places, attractions are also such points. We use them by attaching the images we possess about the place or region to that attraction (and vice versa); it is considerably easier to grasp the attraction than try to comprehend the whole place, culture, or whatever the attraction represents. In this way, the attractions are woven in the conceptual framework that articulates the world and gives shape to it in our mind. As a representation, an attraction is an element of some Barthesian myth. Thus an attraction is more than a physical object or visible phenomenon; it is a signifier of a concept or idea. The attractions are not only objects; they are also constituted as signs (Urry, 1990, pp. 128-129). Hence, while watching the Eiffel Tower we do not only see a metal structure of remarkable height, but also our images of Paris and France materialized. This is probably why for many people, thinking about France or Paris also instinctively elicits the mental vision of the Eiffel Tower, even to the extent that it may be just about the only thing a person knows about Paris. This was illustrated when a friend of mine told his grandmother that he went to Paris and the grandma replied: 'To Paris, ain't that where the Eihvel [sic] Tower is?'. Also in the movies and cartoons a scenery that contains a well-known attraction often indicates location. The audience knows that the characters are in Paris when they see the Eiffel Tower. By browsing through travel brochures it also seems that the Eiffel Tower = France (e.g. Qantas, France 1994 [picture in the cover]; Explore Holidays 1994, Explore Europe [picture in the contents p. 3, illustrating the column devoted to France]).

Markers Point to the Attraction

While an attraction as a sign symbolises something, like an ideal or national identity, it is also the object of a lot of marking itself. The fame of the attraction and its meaning is mediated through markers, which can be 'on-site' or 'off-site' (MacCannell, 1976, p. 111). In fact, the existence of markers makes an attraction. For example, the attraction itself may be a humble stone in a glass display box. Thus its attractiveness can hardly be explained by its properties as a stone. Instead, the markers that explain that the stone is from the moon make it an attraction (Ibid., p. 113). The same theme appeared when a tourist described his feelings about the ruins of Ephesus:

> It could be any ruin or statue as such, but that is not the point. Ephesus is so well known a place that once you start thinking about it you soon wonder: 'Wow, what was it like at its heyday!' There must have been lots of things going on there (Martti, 29).

In most cases the significance of the remnants of the city is not in the ruins themselves, but in the knowledge of the bygone eras and events to which the ruins point. It is also important that those eras and events are generally acknowledged to have a lot of significance in history. Our appreciation of the ruins of Ephesus is probably greatly increased by the knowledge of the important role it played in the early days of Christianity, and by the fact that its heyday was during the era of Greek and Roman hegemony; the era associated with great importance for the Western civilisation. Of course Ephesus is well preserved and quite spectacular on its own right. But knowledge of its history gives the experience of the place a powerful dimension which would not be there if we could not relate our set of markers to that information. The information together with the markers heightens the justification of why the attraction is supposed to be admired and seen.

The mere existence of markers of a certain attraction tends to glorify that attraction, no matter whether they are purely informative and 'objective' or not. The fact that references to the attraction appear in various contexts naturally makes us perceive that it has a certain importance. Encountering these markers all the time is kind of social indoctrination that defines what is supposed to be considered as an attraction. The result is that some attractions are famous because they are famous. The present fame of the attraction may have little to do with the original conditions that initiated the fame. According to Horne 'the fame of the object becomes its meaning' (cited in Urry, 1990, p. 129). The attraction like the Eiffel Tower explains itself because it is so famous and hence rich with attached meanings. A sufficient answer to the question 'what is this tower?' is that it is *the* Eiffel Tower.

An important form of social indoctrination is transmitted through media. It brings us pictures and images that alter our opinion of what is worth seeing (Sontag, 1977, p. 3). Repeated involvement with the markers eventually leads to the formation of an image through which one mentally places oneself in the site of the attraction. In Western countries we are influenced by quite homogeneous social indoctrination since the multinational media we deal with are relatively unanimous about what is important. We are largely offered the same explanations about the same things. There is thus a strong agreement about what is famous:

> I've never been to America. (...) Perhaps people who want to go to America are told the story... on the place or on the boat, and then they go and hide somewhere and come back later and spin yarns about cowboys and skyscrapers, about Niagara Falls and the Mississippi, about New York and San Fransisco. In any case they all tell the same story, and tell of the things which they knew about before the journey; and that's very suspicious, you'll admit (Bichsel, 1971, p. 30).

Connecting Markers with the Attraction

While in Paris, we do not see 'Paris' as a whole; we see just some elements of it: the Eiffel Tower, Louvre, Sacre Coeur, Montmartre, etc. Each of these attractions is an element in a set called 'Paris'; each of them is a symbolic marker of it (MacCannell, 1976, p. 111). From the tourist's point of view, we must see at least one of these attractions, otherwise our experience of Paris may be incomplete in the sense that we have not seen a proper feature that marks Paris; we could as well have been in another French city. The focal point in the tourist's experience of the attraction is the very moment when we recognise it, ie. connect the markers with the actual sight. Here the information about the attraction gives way to the attraction itself (MacCannell, 1976, p. 121). Without seeing the attractions whose markers are familiar to us, we have not had this experience of recognition.

The recognition of an attraction is a unique experience; it only happens once and it lasts probably only for a fraction of a second. Despite this it is one of the most important experiences of travel, the one that the tourist has been looking forward to. It is the fulfilment of the 'I have always wanted to see...' -motivation. All the expectations evoked by the markers are suddenly compared to the actual attraction, resulting in anything between awe and disappointment. The wide range of possible feelings is due to the richness and variety of the references that the markers contain. The reference complex educed by all the markers of the attraction can be so complicated that now when the actual attraction is before our own eyes, our ability to relate to all of them may be stretched too far. Experiencing the attraction is no longer vicarious and mediated through the markers. It is immediate, it allows all circumstances present to affect on the outcome of the encounter so that they can leave the markers at least momentarily behind in their impact. This is why people who have had very similar expectations of the attraction may experience it in a different way. Seeing the Eiffel Tower for the first time on a warm and beautiful day in Paris spring probably leaves one with the impression that the image that the markers mediated was applicable and appropriate. Then again, when I saw the Tower for the first time, it was a dark, cold, windy and rainy December evening. My mind was occupied more with the uncomfortable feeling associated with the weather than with the admiration of the Tower of which I had thought so much in advance. With such an attitude, the Tower was a high and windy metal structure far away from my hotel, rather than the symbol of France. In a very similar manner John Steinbeck describes his feelings in a comparable situation:

> Curious how a place unvisited can take such hold on a mind so that the very name sets up a ringing. To me such a place was Fargo, North Dakota. (...) If you take a map of United States and fold it in the middle, eastern edge against western, and crease it sharply, right in the crease will be Fargo. (...) Fargo to me is brother to the fabulous places of the earth, kin to those magically remote spots mentioned by Herodotus and Marco Polo and Mandeville. From my earliest memory, if it was a cold day, Fargo was the coldest place on the continent. If heat was the subject, then at that time papers listed Fargo as hotter than any place else, or wetter or drier, or deeper in snow. That's my impression, anyway. (...) I must admit that when I passed through Moorhead, Minnesota, and rattled across the Red River into Fargo on the other side, it was a golden autumn day, the town was as traffic-troubled, as neon-plastered, as cluttered and milling with activity as any other up-and-coming town of forty-six thousand souls. ...I drove through the town as usual, seeing little but the truck ahead of me and the Thunderbird in my rear-view window. It's bad to have one's myth shaken up like that. Would Samarkand or Cathay or Cipango have suffered the same fate if visited? (Steinbeck, 1962, p. 122).

Here we see the variety of forms in which markers can present themselves. For Steinbeck, just the very fact that on a map Fargo was on the line along which the map was folded marked the place with vivid images of extremes and mystery. The fold that generated the images, had very little to do with Fargo, so the fold was not really a marker of Fargo in itself. But the fold inspired Steinbeck's imagination to create the purely imaginative markers of his own. These were at least as powerful as any received marker.

The Eiffel Tower has so established a set of markers that even my personal expectations were readable from any guidebook. I, like anyone else, was expecting the Tower to be the symbol of France and Paris, but once there, my concern was more to keep warm than trying to contemplate the Tower and the Frenchness it symbolises. The elements to satisfy my expectations were there in principle, but the bad circumstances in the form of the weather made it impossible for them to be realised. I could not replace the markers with the actual sight because in my pre-experience image there was nor cold wind, neither rain and darkness. Of course I had no troubles recognizing the Tower, but it was not the kind of experience I had imagined. Steinbeck's images of Fargo were doomed to be wrecked mainly because they were mostly based on his imagination. As everybody knows, lived experience may be unkind to the imaginative expectations. There may be little that connects the *imaginative* markers to the *actual* attraction.

Our imaginatively coloured expectations have elements, which in the real encounter with the attraction do not always meet the actual lived experience. In imagination we can accord the attraction all kinds of properties because it has not yet been 'rationalised' by the actual experience. It still belongs to the domain of 'geography' in our existential space. If imagination contributes to the image we have of the attraction, we can make it what we want; it becomes a part of the geography of our dreams. This is why distant fields are greener; we can project our personal wishes on them freely without the restrictions of real life. Naturally, the more the experience of the attraction addresses those dreams, the more the visitor is satisfied with it. A good attraction does not fall short of the expectations evoked by its markers, but at the same time gives room for personal elements in those expectations also. Here public and private meanings of attractions interact and cohere. The commonly known and distributed markers mediate the public meanings on which the private, personal meanings develop. Before the experience both kinds of meanings are quite similar. The personal involvement has not yet created the private meanings that would differ from the public ones. But we do not normally ponder on this and so it feels that the attraction fulfils or frustrates our very *own* expectations. The consistency between the attraction and its markers thus affect our eventual experience of the attraction. The intensity and vivid quality of the markers do the same.

What happens, if the eventual experience of a destination is less glorious than the expectation of it?

> As a tourist you don't consider the attractions as any kinds of wonders, you just expect them to be there; they are self evident, although separated from the everyday of that place like a harem or a palace (Satu, 28).

> If I look at something just because it is the thing to do I just end up looking at it and thinking 'so what' (Inge, 30).

The travellers feel that they are made passive recipients of a narrative that contains the attractions as they are described within the tourist discourse, but which does not address them as individuals. As an important travel motivation for these particular persons was the reach for the Other, they detested the kind of institutional reach which was imposed on them and hindered their ability to reach by themselves. Thus the motive of seeking presence-at-hand in the form of attractions is partly thwarted by the structures that limit the possibilities of our personal input into the encounter with the attraction. The attraction was felt to address masses of tourists rather than these people themselves. It is natural that such feelings are especially strong if we consciously want to distinguish ourselves from the tourist masses.

Another remarkable factor in the experience of attractions is the touring programme in which they are incorporated. There are certainly limits to how much new information and how many new sensations one can encounter without getting bored. I was astonished to read the following travel advertisement, which marketed a packaged trip under a theme 'The Egypt of Pharaohs':

> We have managed to squeeze a huge number of unique historical attractions into nine days (Aurinkomatkojen lomaopas, talvikausi 1990/91, p. 119; my translation from Finnish).

Personally I found that I got enough of such attractions in about an hour at the ruins of Ephesus, despite the fact that they were indeed impressive. We get tired of the continuous exposure to attractions and after our saturation point is reached they are just routinely inspected without the feelings of excitement and novelty that were there when we started the sightseeing. This was easy to see from the comments of the people who had shared the trip to Turkey with me. In consecutive days we visited Ephesus, Pergamon and Troy. All people had clear memories of Ephesus, and some remembered reflecting on its historical significance. But even the experience of such attractions did not take away some more mundane matters, which in a short time started to overshadow the experience. The following is a comment from a person who is usually responsive and interested, but who was a victim of the combined effect of unpleasant circumstances and an overdose of information:

> It was *hot*... The heat, thirst and sweat made you pissed off, since you had to slavishly follow the guide and listen to her stories. More so since you had a hangover all the time (Minna, 28).

In Seamon's (1979) terms, noticing and heightened contact fade away and are replaced by watching, and even obliviousness. In a procession of attractions their novelty soon wears out. They become a normal part of the routine of travel in which sitting in a bus and unloading and loading it can feel as mundane as ever. The attractions lose their appeal as something present-at-hand and become just something ready-to-hand. When this happens the very motive for experiencing them disappears.

The same thing happens in a museum, which is packed with relics that are totally separated from their original contexts by placing them in showcases. Initially they may be interesting to study, they are still present-at-hand and constitute a novelty. However, after a while the curiosity gives away to boredom because the endless rows of items do not address the viewer. They just lie there passively. The distance between their markers (the narratives explaining the significance of the items) and their frigid form of existence behind the glass is often too vast to evoke imagination. The items become ready-to-hand, not in the possibly exciting context of their original significance, but in the context of being an overwhelming presentation of lifeless rows of old articles.

Our reactions to the next attractions on our trip, Pergamon and Troy, illustrate the point. Compared to Ephesus the latter are not nearly as physically impressive. In Troy a big wooden horse has been built near the entrance. Otherwise there would not be anything to connect the markers of Troy with what is left of the ruins. Nevertheless, all our interest had been exhausted by the time we arrived, and the impressions of Troy tended to be quite incidental to the attraction itself:

> I remember the big horse in the front. I also remember that it was extremely windy, and that the film inside my camera had got stuck (Minna, 28).

Procession of attractions or too long exposure to a single one lacks the dramaturgic dynamics that would keep us interested. The problem is that such display of attraction or attractions is too stagnant; it does not lead anywhere. In the beginning of the encounter the attraction provides enough impulse to arouse our interest. But as the experience continues, there is often little that would carry on the interest. Consequently impulses from other sources (often negative and incidental to the attraction) such as the feeling of physical discomfort, replace the initial impulse of the attraction. Before reaching that phase, the experience, in order to be one-sidedly pleasant, should be concluded. An alternative strategy would be a succession of increasingly stronger impulses from the attraction so that before the preceding impulse has totally lost its impact, there is a new, stronger one ahead. The impulse needed to maintain the same level of interest has to become successively stronger because it does not take long before the intensity of a given impulse soon becomes ready-to-hand. This is analogous to the use of narcotics; to get the same effect, one has to increase the dose or switch to stronger substances. But unlike the narcotic users, the tourists seldom have any control over the order of the impulses. That is largely determined by the physical location of the attractions and the touring programme.

Attractions' Quality as Totem and the Experience of Them as Initiation

Above I have discussed two types of reactions to attractions: those in which the prior images were more brilliant than the actual attraction, and those in which the eventual experience of the attraction was diluted by its predictability or the lack of responsiveness on the part of the visitor. It should not be overlooked, however, that most experiences of attractions are probably thoroughly enjoyed. There is the delight of connecting our stock of markers with the actual attractions and experiencing first hand involvement with them. Thus the significance of the attraction is tied to the personal experience and there is a sense of involvement with what the attraction represents.

Here we can see mutual resemblance between sightseeing and some religious practices (MacCannell, 1976, p. 2). MacCannell refers to Emile Durkheim's (1976, orig. 1915) study of totemism. An essential point in Durkheim's study is that the power of religion draws from society: in religion the cohesion and organisation of society gets its conceptual manifestation. This relationship works also the other way around; religion acts as explanatory, cohesive and sanctioning element in the social group. Religious myths explain the origins and justification of the prevailing social reality. Rules and sanctions based on the myths of origins help maintain the social order and common identity. All this culminates in the rituals that reinforce the power of the social group by celebrating the totem. Identifying with the common totem provides cohesion in the group that considers themselves as of the same being. In those rituals the people are in communion with their totem and share common feeling of belonging.

There is thus resemblance between the pilgrims' journey to acquire some of the blessing or virtue that is present in the holy destination and the tourist's desire to have a personal experience of an attraction. They both expect to have an experience of the Remarkable in another place that gives something new to their lives. There is also a close connection between totemism and sightseeing. Some features of totemism are adaptable in touristic situations where we gaze on an attraction. Before us there have been thousands of others doing the same, and we ourselves may be just some of the hundreds of people on the site right now. We partake in a ritual that draws its meaning from the history of the attraction that its markers highlight. They imply that the attraction is and has been the object of awe of many. The attraction is a totem; while it is not of the same entity as we, it still represents the idea with which we want to be involved. We may feel close to the history associated with the attraction and we may experience and even get a feeling of retaining some of the aura associated with it. Of course, this requires that the history of the attraction must have some personal meaning. This may happen, when the attraction represents some phases of the history of our own group, or when the knowledge of the history has had a significant role in our apprehension of the world. The ritual side of seeing an attraction is the feeling of belonging to something that is bigger than just the present moment: a communion with history. In the case of other than historical attractions, the communion occurs with the ideas that the attractions represent. Whatever kind of the attraction, the visitors participate in a collective ritual in which we connect our own set of markers and knowledge to the attraction 'already marked by others' (MacCannell, 1976, p. 137).

The desire to share an uplifting experience with others supports this. Many people have commented on how a great, elated experience of an attraction has been hard to contain within oneself while travelling alone. There is a genuine need to share the experience by confirming the mutual awe: 'Isn't it great!' This is a way to confirm and enhance the feeling of involvement with something that has some universally meaningful value. Sharing the mutual experience with someone else is the manifestation of that universality on the personal level. There clearly seems to be inconsistency in the desire to share the experience with a person on one hand, and often-reported intolerance towards the other tourists on the other. For some reason the presence of the masses, while a powerful marker and confirmation of the 'worthiness' of the attraction, are somehow felt to interfere with the personal communion with the idea(s) represented by it. The masses make the attraction appear more as a mere touristic attraction than as a representation of the ideas and ideals we accord to it. It is hard to maintain one's ideal perceptions of the attraction while the lived experience of it (i.e. the touristic humdrum dominating the scene) tends to deny all such idealism. The immediate existence of the attraction does not seem to support our idealised prior images. Thus the attraction becomes trivialised by the other tourists who, we think, do not appreciate it in a way they should do in our opinion. Thus we have to distinguish between our willingness to share the experience of the attraction with someone we have a personal relationship with (even if brief) and our dislike of sharing it with a big crowd.

The initiatory nature of experiencing attractions is closely connected to the totemism inherent in sightseeing. Before we have experienced an attraction we are without a share in it. Despite all the markers we are familiar with, our knowledge of and relation to the attraction will remain incomplete as long as we do not actually experience it through personal first-hand involvement. The change of the authority and status gained in the encounter with the attraction is not necessarily great but it is, nevertheless, meaningful to the visitors themselves and their acquaintances who haven't experienced the particular attraction. We have participated in a ritual, which is so institutionalised that it justifies our feelings of authority. Like a totem or a trendy and expensive brand-product, the communion with the attraction gives us the feeling of being a participant of the images they represent; we act out a Barthesian myth and in a small way our new status draws from possessing some of the ideas the attraction represents.

The main element in increasing our status in the initiation is the knowledge we gain. After seeing the attraction we have our own experience of it and thus we have more authority to speak about it than before. Often this kind of talk is expressed in terms of how the attraction compared to its markers:

> They were smaller than I expected (unrecorded comment of a friend of mine about the pyramids in Egypt).

Here it is advantageous if the markers are widely known so that the knowledge beyond them seems even more impressive. In other words, the better known the attraction is, the clearer the rise of status in the encounter with it. This becomes further enhanced, if the access to the attraction is complicated. This lures some tourists to choose destinations that are far away and which therefore have novelty value from the perspective of where the tourists live. Thus the knowledge gained attracts even more acclaim. Others who have not seen the attraction ask our opinion of it and generally, consider us some kind of an authority in relation to the matter. This is quite significant since we already know how important as markers the experiences of others are. The status is manifest in the appreciation of your experiences as a source of information about the attraction. This is especially noticeable among the backpackers who continuously consult others who have seen a particular attraction about its merits and drawbacks. The status thus appears as a flow of information of which the 'initiated' are a source.

Attractions That Aren't Yet Part of the Tourist Discourse

By definition, attractions always have their markers. They have been institutionalised into the tourist discourse and thus they are encountered in a predictable manner that is often directed by the travel industry. However, we often encounter features of places, which are not attractions specified by the tourist discourse, but which nevertheless so charm us that they could well be. The encounter is spontaneous in the sense that the attraction just either happens to be on our way, or we get a hint of it from a source which is not (yet) part of the tourist discourse. These features' charm arises from the situation in which they are discovered, without the influence of induced images about the particular features. In other words, they are related mainly through the immediate experience, which has not been directly affected by the conventions of the tourist discourse. Of course we have largely internalised these conventions, but they do not directly indicate the feature's place in the discourse; we have to do that placing for ourselves.

I can recall my delight when, after a couple of hours strenuous walking along a creek we found a waterfall that cascaded into a pool. In advance I had no idea that there was such a waterfall and thus the experience was a total surprise. As Tuan (1974, p. 94) rightly puts it, 'the most intense aesthetic experience of nature is likely to catch one by surprise'. In contrast, at one place we were told that there were three waterfalls along a road and that they would be nice and easy to see ('do')[1] by car. We got a ride and went from the waterfall to another, but the experience was nowhere near the intensity of the one we had when we accidentally found the waterfall.

The harder we have to push ourselves to achieve something, the better it feels once we achieve it. Already Boorstin (1972, p. 97) saw that this applies also to tourism. When we arrive at the attraction easily by car or bus and the attraction is clearly pointed to us, our experience of it is mainly visual. The visual and aesthetic nature of our appreciation separates

---

[1] Nowadays we are asked whether we have 'done' certain places or attractions. This unconsciously implies the simplistic, and perhaps, materialistic, view of them. It is as if we could somehow completely and exhaustively experience them. Once 'done', they do not need further attention; they become parts of our collection.

us from it (Tuan, 1974, p. 64) and underlines the ontological distance between the attraction and us. The attraction is merely seen instead of really lived. Markers pointing to the attraction, like a mention in a tour programme, car parks, souvenir vendors and busloads of tourists, take away the element of surprise. If we discover a waterfall by walking for a long time along the creek, pushing ourselves and not knowing that the waterfall will be there, the experience is considerably different from seeing it as a part of a sightseeing tour. Our *travailing* forces us, very concretely, to *live* the place, we feel it in every step we take, water reaching our knees and slippery stones demanding attention. Because of this the experience of the waterfall is not only aesthetic; the place and the fall is so thoroughly lived that one is literally immersed in it. We feel that we are intimately involved with the Other. Naturally the ontological distance remains, but otherwise the separation between us and the fall is lessened. The contact is deeper than just visual; our feeling of the moment is of that place. This kind of involvement is very personal and thus satisfying. It gives us the feeling that we are the actors instead of being a pawn of the travel industry, or any other external force. We personally gain the reach in a living first-hand experience, unlike the institutionalised means of reach that are sold to us as second-hand experiences. There is also the delight of experiencing something more than what was included in the prior image; the image was vague or it probably did not even exist. Consequently there were few or no expectations. The lack of induced prior image means that the potential experience is not limited by the conventions of the tourist discourse. The experience can freely assert itself according to the situation. Even when the impact of the experience starts to be felt as something ready-to-hand, it does not necessarily have to become boring. There will remain the delight of personal involvement with the Other. We have established a meaningful relationship with a foreign place *by ourselves*. The reach involved feels deeply personal, not mediated or induced from outside.

Attractions as sights and places are representations of the Other. To experience them means some degree of involvement to them. Because the attractions are representations, the experience of them is always placed within a discourse that deals with the particular type of representation. The availability of such tourist discourse witnesses the unity of the world of tourists; no matter how quaint or exotic the representation of the Other is, the available discourse can make it intelligible.

Travel Photography

Photography is one of the most usual things to do on travel. Many of us have probably been almost bored to death by friends showing their travel shots. Travel photography records, reflects and organises travel.

Photographs as Documentation

Documentation of our encounters with the Other is one of the most obvious aspects of travel photography. According to Adler (1989, p. 8), this is a reflection of the empiricist heritage of much modern tourism. Documenting justifies and even glorifies the trip. Like hunters, the travellers come back with prey, and returning without some could be shameful. Likewise, prestige may arise from the skilful capture of those images. Pictures confirm the involvement with the exotic or prestigious and thus indirectly with what they represent. Also, the existence of the photographs makes it possible to share some of the experience. Sometimes the tourist discourse gives an impression that certain attractions simply must be seen (MacCannell, 1976, p. 42; Veijola, 1987, p. 63; Ezensberger, cited in Jokinen and Veijola, 1990, p. 110). Photographing those attractions proves that this has been done. All of these meanings of taking photographs (acquiring prestige, sharing experience, proving the contact with the Other) are included in the idea of travel photography as documentation. Photographs document the reach pursued, whether that reach has involved strange cultures, uplifting attractions, inspirational landscapes, or social interaction within the travelling group. After the trip those documents partly justify it and give impression that something has been accomplished. Thus a couple, when they showed me their honeymoon pool-side and beach pictures, told me that:

> We took these because we figured that some pictures should be taken (Raili, 25).

This theme of photography as documenting emerges in other comments too:

> By photographing I like to document where I have been (Jim, 29).

> If I told this, they wouldn't believe me at home, but I have a picture to show, so they have to (Denise, 22).

If you don't take a picture of the thing like this you cannot tell anyone that you've been there [showing a picture of a mosque]. (...) You remember the attractions because you take pictures of them and attach explanations [to those pictures] so that you can tell others what it was like over there (Erkki, 58).

The pictures taken sustain and direct the personal memories, which would otherwise easily fade. But even more significantly, they are an important element of the account reported to others, who do not have the personal memory of that particular trip to rely on, they are dependent on the account and pictorial documentation of the traveller. A picture is a proof and illustration of the traveller's account.

Taking pictures is largely directed by some internalised conventions of how to do it and what to include (or exclude). Before we depart, we have already been exposed to countless pictures from various destinations. The most significant in this sense are the pictures we have seen in travel brochures and other advertising materials. Looking through people's travel photo albums suggests that this kind of social indoctrination on what is worth seeing and hence worth photographing, makes us to take pictures of the very same things as many before us. This is what is called a photographer's hermeneutic circle (Albers and James, 1988, p. 136; Urry, 1990, p. 138). It means that the more pictures there are of a certain feature, the more people take photographs of it. As seen in the context of attractions: something is famous because it is famous. Taking pictures further adds to the amount of markers of the feature, thus photography is a form of signification (Harkin, 1995, p. 657).

The mass produced travel pictures in media (mostly in advertising) are appealing, and we want to capture the same images ourselves. We want to have a share in those images and by taking pictures we can do so. Coming back from a vacation with pictures depicting the very same features seen in the travel advertisements, we prove and document that our vacation was similar to that promised in those advertisements (Urry, 1990, p. 138). We want to take beautiful pictures. While watching people's pictures we are constantly reminded by the photographer that what there is in the picture does not look as good as it really was. That is often the case, but even the need to say it indicates that we would like to create an impression that the scene was truly exhilarating. Pictures in the advertisements the travellers are trying to replicate are often the results of careful semiotic calculations (in the sense of creating Barthesian myths), which assure that the product sells. By taking the same pictures we do not have to be semioticians ourselves; the work has already been done. We can be assured that the pictures we take convey exactly the message we want, namely that our holiday was marvellous and that we now have a share in the pleasant images depicted in the advertisements. Most of us are happy to leave these semiotical contemplations to the professionals, but nevertheless at least unconsciously, apply similar semiotics to their own pictures. We become, knowingly or not, amateur semioticians (Urry, 1990, p. 138). Mostly this is, however, just imitating the settings and objects of those professionally made pictures. 'Here's x coming from the sea, here's y coming from the sea, here's x having his drink in the swimming pool of the hotel, here's y having her drink in the swimming pool of the hotel', and so on.

Thus 'documenting' a trip may, in fact, involve a depiction of a Barthesian myth. Rather than documenting ourselves having a drink on the poolside, we demonstrate that we had a good time. The pool and the drink are meant to signify good life, and then we create a myth by connecting our holiday with these significations. Thus a picture as a document is not merely a 'message without a code' (Barthes, 1977, p. 17). The picture works on several levels. There is the 'denoted message' (Ibid.): the obvious analogy with the reality (x having his drink on the hotel pool-side). But there is also a 'connoted message' (Ibid.) (or several of them), which needs interpretation. For that interpretation a code is needed and it is provided by our stock of knowledge. An important part of that stock relating to interpreting travel photographs is the amount of advertising we have been exposed to; it has educated us to instinctively do these semiotic interpretations, we have internalised them. Connoted message is thus how we (often unconsciously) interpret the picture: for example, 'they could afford this fancy hotel with swimming pool and the exotic drinks; they must really have had a good time'.

Thus, by documenting we also want to convey a message. From travel advertisements we have learned the common conventions of what the content and even the composition of that message should ideally be. Content means what there is in the picture, and composition how the content, the objects in the picture, are arranged in relation to each other (Albers and James, 1988, p. 139). Urry uses the terms selection, structuring and shaping of pictures in describing the methods of creating content and composition (Urry, 1990, p. 138). Selection results in the content of the picture, and how we structure and shape the content becomes the composition.

Selection is the most powerful and used of these methods; taking picture always involves the decision of what to include and what to omit.

By selectively including certain kind of items and excluding others, we can convey an image we like, similarly to a guide who can decide what to show and what to hide. Sometimes the difference between taking a picture of a paradise or a garbage dump is only a matter of turning the camera a few degrees. Also timing in taking pictures is important. What in the dusk seems picturesque and charming, may in daylight look merely shabby, ugly, or even disgusting. An interviewee explained how he always deliberately avoids power lines and other equally disturbing objects in his pictures because:

> ...they do not belong to the real [essence of what is been pictured] (Erkki, 58).

Here photography is used in redefining reality. Hence, the photographers have a lot of power; they can decide what kind of image people get from a place simply by selecting what they include in the picture, and when they take it.

In structuring the picture, we may frame it so that the relations between the objects have a certain degree of harmony and balance. For example, we may ask people to move to get some feature also in the picture, or we make the horizontal and vertical lines intersect according to the 'golden rule'.[2] When shaping, we may ask people to pose the way we want. That may also involve wearing special clothes and more generally, staging. Thus travel photography involves kind of *pictorial staging*; what the picture conveys, is not necessarily conveyed by the setting as such.

In our attempt to 'document' our encounter with the Other, we actually create representations of the Other and of our relation to it. Because photographs are easily considered as copies of reality, these *representations* pose *as presentations* of the places visited. Travel photography thus deceives, since it supposedly acts as documentation, but effectively stages a representation according to our intentions. Because our intentions arise from our situation as visitors, our pictures easily become representations of tourism realism and tourist space. In these representations attractions, spectacles, and travel companions are the centres of meaning.

---

[2] A visual ideal, according to which those lines, or the main object, should be placed in a picture.

The Contents of Pictures

Looking through tourists' travel photographs reveals that the content and composition of them are invariably adopted from the same conventions. In the vast majority of the pictures there are friends, relatives, fellow travellers, or oneself engaged in some touristic activity. The rest of the pictures depict mainly attractions and landscapes. The more 'touristic', i.e. institutionalised the trip is, the more the pictures taken follow this pattern. Our role as visitors often effectively prevents us from taking pictures that would reflect anything but our outsideness in relation to the local 'realities'. To be able to follow the people in their 'authentic' daily activities requires some degree of participation, maybe staying with the people. Whether we are conventional tourists or backpackers makes a difference to what kind of situations we are likely to be able to photograph:

> ...there was a marked difference in the staginess of the photos that the two groups [trekkers and tourists] took. Trekkers were usually observed taking snapshots of people in their natural settings and normal activities. (...) In sharp contrast, tourists on 'town tours' were invariably attracted to the ostentatiously staged photographic opportunities (Cohen and Nir and Almagor, 1992, pp. 227-228).

Among my backpacker interviewees there were only few people who had stayed with the local people and had possibilities of taking pictures of them. Most of my interviewees were not interested enough to get involved with the locals in order to take pictures of them. This indicates that the backpackers I interviewed were more institutionalised than the ones observed by Cohen, Nir and Almagor. This may have resulted from the fact that their backpackers were on a trekking tour in which the discourse of backpacking supposes active involvement with the locals. Instead, my interviewees were on a more touristic mode, enjoying the well-developed backpacker infrastructure of Bali. On a trekking tour they could have behaved just like the other backpackers observed.

However, this nevertheless reflects the institutionalisation of the backpacking tourism. Being a backpacker does not mean that one would necessarily encounter any more backstage situations than conventional tourists; it is considerably easier to pursue activities within the backpacker infrastructure than engage in personal (as opposed to instrumental) relations with the local people. Even the backpackers, who had desired to take pictures of people in their 'authentic' settings, complained how hard it was.

Apart from the technical point of view (modern cameras seem to be able to do everything by themselves) the difficulty lies in the feeling of intrusion. It seems that the travellers who are the most interested in capturing these backstage images are also the ones who are the most sensitive to the intrusion which that act may cause. Pointing the camera towards people without asking their permission is felt as if you were stealing or violating the pride and privacy of the people. Often these travellers are too shy to ask permission because of their fear of the real or perceived possibility of hostile reaction to such a request. Sometimes the technical problems are a part of the feeling of intrusion; if you are not equipped with a suitably powerful zoom lens, you may have to take the picture disturbingly close to the subject. It is also possible that such act, as well as asking permission, may take away the spontaneity of the situation. Spontaneity, after all, is one of the keys to the backstage.

All this naturally applies to the conventional tourists also. The main differences between the pictures taken by the group tourists and the backpackers are that the formers' pictures often depicted the travelling companions, while the latter's ones were more outward-oriented. Among the pictures of the backpackers there is also a better chance to find an occasional picture of a personified local person, instead of locals being just a part of the scene, or pictured as a role-bound stereotype. However, the first difference is often attributable to the fact that many of those backpackers were travelling alone, or at least not in a group. The second difference occurs only, when the backpacker in question is actively seeking more than a superficial contact with the locals, and most backpackers just don't seem to be doing it. There does not thus have to be a great deal of difference between the pictures of the two groups. In fact, most backpackers are orientated towards the other fellow backpackers rather than towards the local people, and consequently their pictures often show other travellers who they have befriended in hostels. There are thus more similarities than differences in the pictures both the conventional tourists and the backpackers take.

This is surprising when we pay attention to the backpacker discourse, which strongly emphasises that they can get much deeper insights into the places visited than conventional tourists. In the pictures of both groups it is a common feature that the occasional local person appears only in a small minority of the pictures. They are usually travel industry staff or vendors on the street. The dancers in the performance are there to be photographed and a street vendor stays still and looks exotic. The hotel-staff are friendly due to occupation. For a visitor it is easy to approach these people and take pictures of them. In these cases the possibility to photograph is institutionalised and does not have to involve entry or intrusion to backstage. However, this usually involves clear distinction between front and back, sometimes even to the extent that a backstage situation is staged, thus making it just another front.[3] If the visitors seek novelty in authenticity, this staged authenticity does not satisfy them (if the staging becomes exposed). In these situations the 'real' backstage setting may be strictly off-limits to the visitors. Thus their efforts in seeking 'authenticity' are likely to be frustrated.

Different interests of individual travellers are a contribution towards the few differences in people's photo albums. Thus a geography teacher takes pictures of volcanic landscapes in Lanzarote and a carpenter photographs carved mosque doors in Samarkand.

> I try to take pictures of [woodwork] details everywhere, some day I may try to do them myself (Erkki, 58, the carpenter).

These features may also have more general aesthetic value, but it is more likely that they are appreciated by visitors who are involved with such things in their everyday lives as well. This became very clear when I saw this carpenter's album. There were many pictures of various kinds of woodwork. For him those pictures have a lot of meaning and depth by the virtue of his appreciation of the methods and skills involved in making such things. For me those things in the pictures were no more than just nice doors, carvings, or whatever; they did not address me.

Although travel within the tourist space limits the possibilities of getting involved with the places visited, taking pictures can provide a way to do so. A special interest in something that has personal relevance both at home and in an alien place is a means to be involved with that place. It provides a theme that helps us to relate home and the Other. Photography in these situations is a means through which we can meaningfully act out that relation (from the tourist role it may not be possible to get involved with, for example, the local carpenters). Meaningful involvement with life at home through a special interest can thus translate into meaningful involvement with an alien place.

---

[3] For an example see Bruner and Kirshenblatt-Gimblett, 1994, pp. 450-453.

Photographs as Narratives

Photographs are narratives in at least two senses. First, they can be interpreted as narratives of the perspective and situation of the photographer (i.e. the power structures and discourses which direct what has been photographed and how it has been done). Second, as a collection of images from a trip they narrate the story of the trip. In the first meaning, the narration is formed largely unreflectively; we do not usually elaborate on the power structures our pictures may reflect, we just take them. Interpretations that find narratives of the tourist discourse or neo-colonial power structures from the pictures have mostly little to do with the intentions of the photographers, unless they have deliberately wanted to reflect these narratives or structures on the pictures. Of course, any unintentional reflection of such things can be the more revealing. In the second meaning of narrative here, the narration the pictures create is in reverse largely conscious. There is clear deliberation on the part of the photographers to convey a certain kind of narrative, for example, that our trip was fun. In these cases the photographers themselves provide the interpretation.

The situation in which we take a picture and our interpretation of the picture often involve some sort of staging. At the same time, our interpretation of what is going on is frequently based on the insufficient, stereotyped knowledge of places and the people. The Other places, people, their customs and artefacts are seen as mere attractions rather than as products of a real socio-cultural group. As a result, both the selection of the scenes and our narrative of what there is in the photograph is more a representation of our situation and knowledge as visitors, than a presentation of the place. The fact that we see natives performing a dance in the picture does not tell us anything about the context and meaning of that dance to the dancing people themselves (see Albers and James, 1988, p. 154). The photograph underlines what is visually recorded in the picture, but it effectively separates the object from all contexts but those that can be seen in it. Everything else, no matter how essential, is ignored. Thus we can create our own narrative of the picture that is consistent with its image but can be totally alien to the real context of the people in it. The picture starts to live a life of its own as a part of the tourist discourse, without much meaningful reference to the 'realities' of the places pictured. However, the narrative we construct for the picture or the narrative that the picture seems to be telling is real for us who have little other knowledge to complement it.

In this way our pictures and narratives both reflect the tourist discourse and contribute to it.

For this reason, the 'typical' travel photographs reinforce the prevalent economic structures present in much tourism, especially in tourism to developing countries. The narrative of such pictures tells that when the local people are where they belong they are typically in a subordinate role. They are not persons like us; they are just a part of the local colour, the background. In this sense the photographs may act as sustainers of cultural misunderstandings and even racism. They reflect the prevailing unbalance between the power of Western and most other cultures. As long as this structural unbalance exists, it is unlikely that any kind of education can create widely shared cultural understanding (Donovan, 1988, p. 182). As long as travel photographs depict non-personified locals, the pictures do not contribute towards less stubborn stereotypes of other peoples. Travel photographs may unwittingly act as a kind of propaganda; the Others are made faceless stereotypes who can be accorded whatever qualities we like.

We can draw distinction between pictures that we have taken without much involvement with the object of the picture, and the pictures that depict something to which we have a personal tie. The pictures of the former kind, which have been taken with a lot of detachment, are likely to evoke narratives that draw primarily from the conventions of the tourist discourse. There is little in the pictures that could evoke narratives that draw from the personal involvement. The meanings of the pictures are assembled from the ready-made conventions because there is so little meaning attached to the actual taking of the pictures. Often the only such meaning is the fact that they have been taken by ourselves. But we want to have something which documents our involvement with the Other, even though it is only that little; otherwise we could be content to just buy some postcards of the same objects. While those postcards are often prettier than our own pictures, they would not represent our first-hand involvement. They would not qualify as documents of our achievement in reaching.

In contrast to pictures with little personal involvement, there are pictures that are loaded with personal meanings. In most of the tourists' pictures those personal meanings are integrated with the public meanings derived from the conventions of the tourist discourse. This happens especially when the pictures depict familiar people (fellow travellers) or us and when their acts and settings incorporate the semiotic overtones discussed earlier (i.e. a Barthesian myth is expressed in some widely known form). Then there are pictures that get their meaning almost exclusively from the personal involvement with the object of the picture. It may be a place with which we were closely involved, a person we got to know, or a thing to which we can closely relate (like the stunningly carved door of a mosque for the carpenter). Here the personal involvement overrides the conventions of the tourist discourse. These are the pictures which are likely to promote new ideas, understanding and appreciation of Other places, instead of reinforcing the existing narratives of them.

Photography Organising the Contacts with the Other

From the travel pictures of a couple and from their account of their trip, it was possible to discern that their contact with the Other was primarily mediated through taking pictures. Their pictures mostly depicted beautiful buildings, landscapes, the travel partner, and undefined groups of local people, but no individual local people appeared as a personality with whom the couple would have had a personal relationship. They had had few contacts with the local people, and they had spent their days by walking around and taking beautiful pictures. That had given them a meaningful theme, around which the daily schedule had been conveniently organised. Without taking pictures they would have had to come up with another way to spend their time, which, because of their small budget, could have been difficult. The pictures they had taken were also used as justification of the trip; without them there would not have been so much to tell about. Taking the pictures was also a convenient alternative to engaging in activities in which a lot of effort would have needed to establish a rapport with the Other people.

Photography creates action that structures our contacts with the Other (Bruner and Kirshenblatt-Gimblett, 1994, p. 440). Surrounded by the Other we have a need to resort to some familiar framework that gives meaning to our actions. Photography helps us 'to take possession of space in which [we] are insecure' (Sontag, 1977, p. 9). In photographing our role feels clearly defined, thus reducing the feelings of insecurity and confusion. While taking pictures, we have a familiar frame of action in which we do not feel as lost as we would without doing it (Ibid., pp. 9-10; Urry, 1990, p. 138). Our relation to the strange environment is thus arranged according to familiar lines of conduct. Taking pictures gives the contacts a sense of purpose; the collection of images and search for a good picture. We do not have to remain passive lookers of an attraction, for example; we can actively try to turn it into a nice image. This gives us a sense of involvement which, no matter how shallow, nevertheless takes us a little closer to our aim to reach for the Other.

In taking a picture the distance between us and the thing photographed is simultaneously imposed and bridged (Sontag, 1977, p. 58). We want to have a share in the Other by taking pictures of it, but at the same time we remain outsiders as we do so. Taking pictures diverts our attention to the act of photographing itself and leaves us outside what is photographed. By taking the picture we reach for the Other, but the significance of that reach is often thwarted by its institutionalised nature. Taking pictures can thus distance us from the Other by reducing us to passive observers. Meaningful interaction can be replaced by photography (Albers and James, 1983, p. 128). In a strange environment it feels easier and safer to just observe than to participate. To take pictures of people (with a powerful zoom, if possible) is safer than approaching them. Photographing attractions is easier than studying their significance in various contexts, and taking pictures at the food market has more appeal than eating the food there.

Photography creates distance also in another way; it effectively turns the Other into objects (Bruner and Kirshenblatt-Gimblett, 1994, p. 455). At the very moment of picture taking the pictured is something viewed through the view-finder and eventually the result is a tangible picture, very much an object. Turning the Other into objects gives control and power over it. In some sense it is seizing at least a part of what is photographed (Sontag, 1977, p. 4; Urry, 1990, p. 138). The possibility of deciding what to include in the picture and whether to take it at all means that we have control over that particular part of the Other. We are in the position to judge whether particular things are worth taking picture. No matter what part of the Other we picture, it is at least momentarily reduced to an object of our command. In a way we cease to be irrelevant outsiders in relation to the place and became the commanders of the people and objects of that place. We become the creators of our narratives of the Other. Naturally this is also related to the point above; control reduces the insecurity felt in an alien environment.

Photography as an act that turns things photographed into objects, is a powerful way in which the presence-at-hand of the Other is turned into readiness-to-hand of the objects. The eventual picture is not a totality, which in its inexplicability could be even threatening. A nice picture of the Other may become a fetish. It is a representation of the Other in a way we have wanted and therefore it is a constant reminder of our ability to control and tame the Other. In this way photography tends to suggest our superiority in comparison to the Other. It is a component of the tourist discourse, from which it draws its influences and to which it contributes, thus creating a hermeneutic circle. Unfortunately, in developing countries it tends to sustain the existing unbalance between the status of Western(ised) visitors and the Other people.

9 The Encounter With the Other Culture

Culture Confusion

Culture shock is a term popularly used in describing the anxieties that arise from encountering a foreign culture. The term was originally introduced and defined by Oberg (1960, p. 177): 'Culture shock is precipitated by the anxiety that results from losing all our familiar signs and symbols of social intercourse'. Oberg also distinguished four different phases; fascination, hostility, lessening of tension and bi-culturalism (these named by Smalley, 1963, p. 53). The first phase is characterised by fascination and excitement about the new environment. Hostility develops when the visitor remains in the place for a longer time and has to come to terms with the 'real' local conditions of life. Initially minor troubles arising from the different ways of doing things can develop into deep frustration. Eventually the tension lessens and one starts to feel more at ease after learning more cues about how to act. Bi-culturalism occurs when the person has at least partly adapted and accepted the customs of the country and can initiate and maintain meaningful relationships with local people.

Until recently, the general pattern of this U-curve of adjustment hypothesis has remained essentially the same in all discussions since Oberg's paper. Some have suggested that the further difficulties and readjustment processes that are experienced after returning home after a long sojourn abroad should also be included in the picture, thus extending the U-curve into W-curve (Lundstedt, 1963; Gullahorn and Gullahorn, 1963). Some others have given slightly different names to the phenomenon, like 'culture fatigue' (Guthrie, 1966, p. 25) and 'role shock' (Byrnes, 1966, cited in Bochner, 1982, p. 17). Also various numbers of distinct phases have been proposed: Adler (1975) finds five phases, contact, disintegration, reintegration, autonomy and, finally, independence, while Argyle (1982, p. 63) suggests four phases which include one after returning home. Furnham (1984, p. 45) argues that despite the anecdotal nature of Oberg's paper, 'subsequent attempts to clarify the idea of culture shock have not been terribly helpful'.

The concept seems so complicated that, while accepted in general terms, it escapes efforts to accurately define it. According to Furnham and

Bochner (1982, p. 171) the limitation of the term 'lies in its simplistic theoretical foundation, its non-specific nature and its lack of clear implications for remedial action, i.e. how to reduce culture shock'. In particular, the non-specific nature of the concept makes it possible to use it to explain almost any difficulty arising from inter-cultural contact. Since everything can be 'explained' by it, it does not necessarily explain anything. Its use gives little guidance in, for example, who is most or least susceptible, how long the shocked state lasts and what form shock takes (Furnham, 1984, p. 46). This criticism of the vagueness of the culture shock-notion is largely based on its reluctance to lend itself for measurement. In qualitative study, however, *this* is not a problem.

To narrow down the meaning of the concept Furnham and Bochner (1982, p. 172) have noted that: 'the major, if not critical core of what has been labelled "culture shock" is the reaction of sojourners to problems encountered in their dealings with host members'. Culture shock is thus essentially a social phenomenon, referring to our relationships with, and perception of other peoples. Interaction between the visitors and the hosts is a social performance that easily fails when there are no shared cues of how to act. Thus 'failures and problems experienced by the sojourner need not be regarded as symptoms of some underlying pathology, but rather due to the lack of the necessary cultural skills and knowledge' (Ibid., p. 164). On these grounds Furnham and Bochner refer to learning the characteristics of an alien culture rather than adjusting to it.

The studies cited here are mainly concerned with the hardships of sojourners like overseas students, missionaries or employees who stay in their destinations even over some years. Tourists, however, mostly stay only a week or two, several weeks at most. Even backpackers, although they may stay on their travels for a long period of time, frequently change places. Therefore it is unreasonable to suggest that a formulation based on one sort of material can be applied to another without problems. The later phases of culture shock clearly have relevance only for few exceptional travellers. In the context of tourism, it is meaningless to talk about adaptation, for example.

While this is a big problem in applying the U-curve hypothesis on tourists, there is an even more serious one: The 'U-curve of adjustment hypothesis' simplifies the dynamics of emotion fluctuation; our emotions do not follow a clear, causal pattern. Also it does not allow for negative outcomes (i.e. what if there is no elation, a mere disappointment?). Hottola (1999, p. 109) has altogether questioned the applicability of the model on these bases:

...the traditional U-curve approach does not capture the variety and dynamics of individual responses to the Other culture experience. There are too many variables and too much variation to be captured in a linear model. Additionally, the traditional approach does not recognise the importance and centrality of confusion in the process but focuses on the shock, which is a minor and haphazard feature of the phenomenon. Contradictory emotions and negative oppositional developments are not recognised. What is more, the absence of the stages presented in the U-curve approach and the contradictory findings of the location of euphoria and hostility in the empirical results of the present study indicate an error in the stages approach itself. ...the special nature of touristic and other temporally limited Other culture experiences does not in general agree with the culture shock approach.

Hottola replaces the traditional U-curve hypothesis with his own dynamic model of culture confusion. The central idea is the simultaneous interplay of contradicting emotions during the process of learning to cope with the Other. This creates confusion, initially between euphoria and disillusionment, and on the later stages of the trip between adaptation and opposition. The confusion is a product of the inevitable cultural and sensory overload, that the contact with the Other causes. Travellers escape to metaworlds (in this work the term 'tourist space' has been used in the same meaning) to deal with the confusion. For Hottola, the term 'culture shock' implies just an extreme form of disillusionment.

Obviously, the new model is not less qualitative in its categories than the U-curve hypothesis. But it does explain the individual differences and sudden changes in feelings towards the Other much better than the latter.

According to Harkin (1995, p. 654), the cause of culture confusion[1] is not merely the lack of knowledge about the local conduct, but also the inability to relate the experiences of the Other to everyday life at home. There has to be a framework in which these new experiences can be related to life at home, otherwise there is no continuity between them. Without this continuity the element of reach would be impaired in travel, as reach implies the widening of one's horizons. Differing sets of experience without any connective framework would constitute a 'topological schizophrenia'. However, I think that Harkin underestimates the role of the tourist discourse in providing the needed connection.

Before getting familiar with Hottola's (1999) work, I used the phases of U-curve hypothesis in organising the discussion. Already then it was

---

[1] He does not mention culture confusion, but seems to imply the same thing.

obvious that the model had shortcomings, but I was not able to come up with an alternative. I wrote that the different phases of culture shock are not sharply separable. They are more like a continuum following the U-curve of adjustment, where new feelings and modes of experience gradually overlap. The elation does not suddenly turn into the irritation neither does the recovery overthrow the feelings of irritation at once. However, now I shall apply Hottola's dynamic model of culture confusion here, since its use does not call for so many reservations.

Hottola elaborates on the feelings of disillusionment, euphoria, opposition and adaptation. These feelings are not phases as much as our emotional responses to our encounters with the Other. Euphoria and disillusionment take place in the initial contact with the Other. From the sustained contact follow the feelings of opposition and adaptation. This opposition of positive and negative feelings remains through the contact and warrants the use of the term confusion. It may be, though, that few travellers stay in their destinations long enough to be able to either adapt or oppose. I'd say that adaptation is possible in relation to the circumstances of travel, rather than to the Other itself. Opposition in this context has less meaning, as one would rather go home than oppose the circumstances that, after all, are the traveller's own choosing. Thus culture confusion in travel primarily revolves around euphoria and disillusionment, and the need to balance this confusion by escaping to a metaworld: tourist space. Therefore I will organise the discussion around dealing with the feelings of euphoria and disillusionment. The meaning of tourist space has already been elaborated.

Euphoria

The vast majority of tourists experience euphoria because their stay is so short and they mainly stay inside the tourist space. Here the fact that I interviewed the conventional tourists after their trip and the backpackers while they were on their trip may cause too much emphasis on the conventional tourists' experience of euphoria. After the trip it is easy to forget the acutely felt disillusionment and concentrate on the pleasant side of it (dynamics of this are discussed in more detail in a later chapter). Nevertheless, euphoria is an important theme of travel; otherwise travel would not be so popular. A part of the tourist space is the fact that the tourists are usually affluent compared to the local people (especially when the destination is a developing country, not so much in places like North America, northern Europe or Japan). Thus the tourists are able to afford to stay in a hotel, a domain mostly beyond the reach of the locals by any other means than as employees. This affluence is a consequence of the difference between the standard of living in the visitors' home country and the host country, or if that difference is not remarkable, the visitors have at least been saving (or borrowing) money for the trip. Thus they are able to spend more than they would normally do at home.

Being at least temporarily affluent, and only temporarily at the destination means that they simply do not have to adapt in any real sense. In fact, since they have purchased the trip, the tourist industry has caused the destination to adapt to them. Marchand (1979, p. 257) expresses the view that tourists want to experience the contradiction between familiar and strange by living in fine hotels and with other fellow travellers: the contradiction 'appears between the lounge and the street; he has only to push the door open, or look through its glass panels, to feel uprooted' (see also Bruner and Kirshenblatt-Gimblett, 1994, p. 440). But at least equally importantly, we also want to feel secure by having a familiar base from where we can make controlled excursions into the surrounding Other. Here the contradiction is a by-product which, nevertheless, gives a new, different dimension to our experience; it allows us to appreciate on the one hand the security and comfort of familiarity and on the other hand the exotic, novel properties of the Other. Any shock experienced is likely to be aesthetic, culture shock cannot really even occur. Tourist space here is the metaworld that is our safe haven on the domain of the Other. The feeling of confusion can be esacaped and there is little chance that it could develop into a shock. In the brief time outside, the euphoria of everything new and exotic outshines most negative feelings.

A conventional tourist to former Soviet Union (Erkki, the carpenter, 58) gave me a long account of famous museums and ballets he had seen there. The enthusiastic account revealed that he had felt euphoria because of the possibility to personally participate in these symbols of Russia, prominently marked in the pre-trip information about the trip. Without the tourist space in which tourist groups in the former USSR were customarily placed, the tourist who spoke only Finnish, could not have had a similar feeling of involvement. The euphoria was thus result of the ability of the tourist space to fulfil the prior expectations evoked by advertising. Again though, the account was given after the trip, so that the elated impression is partly understandable from this detached perspective. In fact, the tourist confessed that he fell asleep in the ballet. But the euphoria was nevertheless there, the actual visit to the ballet was itself novelty sought; the actual programme performed did not matter.

A backpacker couple who were clearly irritated in Bali told me how their relatives who had visited Bali for only short time on organised tours had told how wonderful a place it was. The couple pointed out that their relatives were so protected from the less flattering sides of Balinese realities that:

> They could only see the beautiful things (Aron, 23 and Denise, 22).

The efficient tourist space and the short time period involved in a typical tourist trip can sustain euphoria even over some encounters with the less pleasant elements of the place. Thus a tourist can say that occasional harassment:

> ...doesn't affect the overall picture; the crooks are a minority which you find everywhere (Erkki, 58).

Of course, after the trip it is easy to understate the disillusionment acutely felt at the time of the encounters.

Resorting to the tourist space is a means to avoid the disillusionment. Duncan (1978, p. 272) writes about avoiding culture shock without elaborating on the meaning of the term, but it seems that he uses it in a sense that refers to disillusionment here. For Duncan, some of these means of avoidance are 'unconscious psychological mechanisms', while others 'are for sale in the market place'. The latter obviously refer to the tourist space that is sold to us as a part of the 'commodity' of travel. The 'unconscious psychological mechanisms' involve processes in which we interpret and translate what we encounter into concepts familiar to us, or altogether reject other views (Ibid., p. 275). The translation and interpretation mainly draw from the conventions of tourist discourse. As these conventions intend to present everything encountered as entertaining spectacles, it helps to maintain the euphoria. It also has a simplifying effect of translating the unfamiliar things encountered to easily understandable stereotypes. The 'tourism realism' thus created provides elation, since we are able to connect the markers of the Other to easily recognisable types and comprehend the narratives told about the Other. These narratives make sense in the light of our stock of knowledge. The part of the tourist discourse we have been exposed to is a part of this stock. It brings continuity between our experience of the Other and our experience of everyday.

However, the euphoria is not entirely a result of the comforts of the tourist space, nor of the tourist discourse, which helps to translate everything into familiar, understandable terms. Another backpacker couple were strongly disillusioned after a few weeks stay in Bali, explained how they:

> ...really enjoyed the first week or so that we were in Kuta. ...we had read about Bali already in advance and were really looking forward to familiarise ourselves with the culture (Roy, 30 and Mary, 28).

They were backpacking within a loosely organised tourist space and attempted to have contacts with the locals as much as possible. Of course, like most others, they largely relied on the tourist discourse (the backpackers' one) in a form of a guidebook to help them translate things into familiar categories. However, the most important element in their feeling of euphoria on that first week was the fact that they had been travelling already for two years, but only in Western countries (USA, New Zealand, Australia), and Bali was their first non-Western country. They said that after spending such a long time in Australia (working for a year) it was extremely nice to get on the road again and see something different. Thus that first week was a considerable change in their travel. To apply this more generally: travel as anti-structure or at least as change from everyday life is hence a source of euphoria. The very fact that the readiness-to-hand of the everyday environment has been replaced by the presence-of-handness of the Other is an important part in the actualisation of our travel motivations. The comforts of the tourist space may surpass the conveniences of our home or the relative simplicity of backpacking travel may provide welcome change from the commitments and responsibilities of our everyday life. Whether the trip facilitates being 'a peasant or a king for a day', in any case there is elation from the change. Even if the mode of travelling within a pronounced tourist space provides only a superficial change from life at home, and ensures that we have similar kinds of comforts, there is at least the contrast between the tourist space and the strangeness of the 'outside' to marvel at.

Sometimes the experience is so negative that there is little or no euphoria at all. The cause may be an illness or some other unfortunate circumstances that effectively flatten the mood and create disillusionment, even shock. Everyone is familiar with the stereotype of a tourist who complains all the time and who is impossible to satisfy. But in Bangkok I realised with my wife that we do not have to be like that stereotype to be able to feel disillusioned without being elated. Arriving in the middle of the night, finding ourselves cheated by the taxi driver, and having to resort to shabby accommodation in a tiny room with no windows, does not create a fruitful environment for a euphoric first contact with the Other (a travel agent would say that this is why it is advisable to make a booking in advance). I expected the disillusionment of that first negative impression to disappear with time but this never happened. According to Hottola (1999, p. 114), this is common among the tourists in India.

Disillusionment and Opposition

In the literature on culture shock (that I am familiar with) I have encountered no references to the feeling of insecurity as the first reaction to an alien place. I suppose this is due to the fact that these studies mainly deal with sojourners like students, missionaries, anthropologists and employees. It is fair to assume that people who end up in such situations are usually outer oriented and open-minded, and therefore their psychological qualities make them likely to feel euphoria on the first contact with the Other. To a lesser degree the same applies to the backpackers, who would not travel like that if they were too fearful. However, this is not always the case with some tourists, who may start to feel quite insecure once the home ground has been left behind. Especially people who travel to a strange country for the first time or are otherwise inexperienced travellers are prone to this. As these people tend to travel within the tourist space, their insecurity, even fear, concerns the durability of that space. The essential concern is how to manage in the strange, maybe even perceivedly hostile place, if there is no sufficient backing from the familiar elements of the tourist space. This feeling of insecurity is not disillusionment in the sense that the hostility of the Other would be in contrast to what the traveller expected. It is rather disillusionment of the fact that the Other is not completely controllable. A traveller from our bus trip to Turkey reported on a first-time tourist:

> She was totally upset because of the chaos [of the traffic] and dirtiness (Minna, 28).

On the same trip we also had a person who refused to eat the local food and was generally very nervous about leaving the bus or hotel, let alone the group, behind. The feeling of insecurity may override all other concerns so that the result is obliviousness (in Seamon's [1979] sense); one is incapable of relaxing and enjoying what is seen and experienced. The role of the travel industry here is to maintain tourist space so that when the tourists realise they can safely act within it, the initial insecurity dissolves and obliviousness can become replaced by watching and noticing. The tourist space is the metaworld that allows the escape from the confusion. The feeling of euphoria can occur only when this possibility exists. The extent of this kind of fear is of course dependent on the personality of the traveller.

Those tourists who stay in the destination only for a short time feel euphoric because of the change the destination and the travel itself offer. Possible moments of disillusionment are mainly brief and do not destroy the overall impression. In contrast to the conventional tourists, many of the backpackers who had been travelling for a long time and possibly stayed at a destination for extended periods of time were clearly disillusioned or in the state of opposition. Disillusionment is triggered because the initial presence-at-hand changes into readiness-to-hand. In other words, when newness and novelty diminish and are replaced by more mundane feelings. A longer period of stay in a place creates its own routines, which may even become just another kind of everyday. Any kind of negative aspect of the place is prone to have an irritating impact because there is no overwhelming positive presence-at-hand to capture our attention.

The very same person who admitted having enjoyed the first week in Kuta lamented at being harassed by vendors all the time:

> There is something wrong with this society... They just do not have any respect; they are arrogant, cheeky, disrespectful, uncourteous and very, very annoying... It is rude when sellers intrude while you are having your breakfast in a bar (Roy, 30).

This is indeed strong talk from a person who told that he and his girlfriend Mary had tried to learn a little bit of the culture and the language before they came to Bali in order to really appreciate the culture. It appeared that sickness and constant harassment, which he did not expect prior to trip, caused the disillusionment. There was a clear contrast between him and Mary, whose extent of disillusionment was much milder (she had not been sick) and seemed mostly to just reflect his frustration. Here came into play the rejection of the other peoples' ways; Roy was ready to conclude that the whole Balinese society was somehow crooked. Not because he was being deliberately ethnocentric, but because the circumstances were such that he found it hard to see anything but the negative. Another couple shared similar feelings. They felt that as foreigners they were easy to take advantage of:

> You cannot ask anything here, they always want to cheat you (Aron, 23).

They realised how that frustration affected their perception of the place:

> You start to see only the bad side... I did not want to think badly about these
> people but I cannot help it (Denise, 22).

Even the desire to understand does not prevent the disillusionment. It is an obvious reaction to blame the place for the negative personal feelings; it has to be bad because it makes you feel bad (Oberg, 1960, p. 177). Kelles (1984, p. 60) underlines the emotional nature of this disillusionment: It does not matter how much we know about the nature of it and its causes. Even if we have previous personal experiences of disillusionment, we still fall victims of it. No rational reasoning can relieve the anxiety.

The fact that we have little control over how people approach us, whether they respect our need for privacy, or whether we can judge if we are being cheated are the most important creators of the feeling of disillusionment. We can be harassed to the limit by persistent vendors and beggars. Their methods of getting our attention by loud voices and intrusive foisting often evoke feelings of irritation and even disgust towards such annoyances. No matter how much we try to see them as being just a different way of doing business, we do not like them because we feel intruded upon. We feel inconvenienced, because we are approached in a way that we are not used to. What to the other person may be just a normal way to approach potential customers can make us feel intruded on, embarrassed or even threatened. We may be outraged or embarrassed by an emotional display of extreme poverty by a dirty crippled beggar because it can hurt our conscience. It may feel like a form of extortion. We feel that our privacy has been violated, not only physically, but also psychologically, by making us so graphically conscious of our relative wealth.

Another similar concern I frequently encountered among the female travellers was continuous unwanted attention from the local males (see Hottola, 1999).

> They whistle after you all the time and they won't leave you alone (Sigrid,
> 21).

> The loss of privacy is the most tiring... One of the things I am looking
> forward to is to be able to walk down the street without being talked to
> (Inge, 30).

This harassment was felt more strongly when it occurred together with some other difficulties like illness, language problems and lack of cultural understanding. A woman who was suffering from diarrhoea and travelling alone complained that she was absolutely disgusted by Balinese men who were 'nothing but sleaze-bags' (an unrecorded comment). It was easy to see that her illness made her sentiment strong. However, this is always easy to say from the outside; no matter how much those feelings are exaggerated by other conditions, they are still very real for the person experiencing them. Some women said that they would not mind that kind of attention at home; however, the lack of ability to interpret and communicate others' real intentions make them feel insecure and even threatened while away. At home such attention is usually occasional, not constant, and they know the cultural code that directs the events. The constant attention ceases to be a novelty, and away from home the feeling (real or imagined) of being perceived as game for the local males can be pressing. A result is constant (and from the single woman's perspective, probably justified) suspicion of the motives of local people no matter how you are approached:

> They are really nice for you when they want to get something from you (Sigrid, 21).

Much of the disillusionment can be a consequence of the frustration arising from the loss of cultural confidence and control. You know neither how to act, nor what to expect. As we negotiate in the new environment, we may start to realise that our knowledge is not enough to deal with the situations we encounter. We become irksomely conscious of our social clumsiness; what we have learned at home does not necessarily apply here. Trivial hardships encountered even in the simplest activities, if still quite amusing in the beginning, start to become aggravating. This applies also to language skills:

> Problems with language and the misunderstandings they cause are funny, but just for a while (Inge, 30).

This is especially obvious if the travellers stay with the local people and are thus very much separated from the cultural spheres of what they have got used to. Again, the novelty of negotiating a new symbolic environment wears out and is replaced by frustration. What is merely interesting and funny when it is still present-at-hand can be frustrating and annoying when ready-to-hand. There is still continuity between the experience of the Other and the experience of everyday, but that continuity just emphasises what is perceived as the negative attributes of the Other.

Homesickness is one of the symptoms of the irritation phase. Of course it can be felt even without being disillusioned, but being disillusioned surely accentuates it and makes it felt often painfully acutely:

Homesickness comes when people are not nice (Denise, 22).

Such a feeling reveals that the new place does not provide the impulses that are needed to keep our positive attention fixed on this new place any more, as it does when euphoria prevails. Negative feelings apparently triggered by the alien place are contrasted with the pleasant images associated with home. What happens is a reversal of home and away; at home a reason to want to travel is the pleasant images a distant place is associated with, whereas home is the mundane location of everyday events. When disillusioned, the place originally distant has become everyday and the everyday at home is associated with pleasant images in turn. The locality of existence, the fact that we are always here and not elsewhere, means that we always have to more or less imagine what it would be like to be elsewhere. Although being here has the element of personal involvement and thus the potential for powerful experiences, it also bears the everydayness of our existence. As the euphoria wears out the everyday-side starts to be more and more prevalent. It is simply impossible to stay euphoric for extended periods of time anywhere, and exactly because the immediate experience here becomes characterised by everydayness, sooner or later we start to entertain pleasant images of being somewhere else. Now that we are away from home, it becomes the subject of our pleasant images. Because it is not within our immediate reach, it is possible to glorify its everydayness. However, for most of us, personal involvement with places (including home) is less glorious than it is in our dreams and images; imagination can afford to create unfounded fantasies. Homesickness is thus a reversal of the motivation to travel; negative here is contrasted with perceived good elsewhere (home).

During disillusionment all experienced inconveniences, even the smallest and harmless, accumulate into a big whole that oppresses the traveller. Harassment, illness, mosquitoes, cultural misunderstandings and language problems etc. all contribute to the negative attitude, which the cessation of euphoria makes possible. This accumulation can be made acute by an overdose of a particular mishap; being sick or robbed can take away any sense of humour, continuous harassment can push us over the limit.

Once we are disillusioned, the remedies are either to learn the right social conduct (Furnham and Bochner, 1982, p. 164), or to escape into tourist space. The former is advised in the context of sojourners, but the latter is applicable in travel. One's thoughts must be directed elsewhere to give room for healing. To get distance from the causes of disillusionment facilitates this. To operate smoothly in a society requires knowledge of its language, bodily expressions, cultural customs, religion, social and economic organization and history, to name a few. Especially the role of the language is crucial here. Knowing the language considerably speeds up the process of learning about the other features. Without the ability to communicate effectively with the local people we are always bound to remain outsiders, no matter how extensive our knowledge of the other features (indeed, even learning the language does not guarantee an insider position). Knowing the language and the possibilities it opens for meaningful interaction would provide additional dimensions for the experience of place. The place would not be just ready-to-hand in the collection of places 'done'; it could offer new discoveries, presence-at-hand in the form of deeper interaction. In other words, the place could stay longer as an interesting source of new knowledge and experiences. In these cases the inevitable irritation would be easier to take because there could still be novelty to be experienced and it would be possible to avoid a lot of misunderstandings.

Reflections on Personal Experience

Here I am going to introduce some extracts from my personal diary of my first big trip abroad. My friend and I stayed in Western Samoa for three and half months in the last quarter of 1988 as part of our seven and half months travel around the world. At the time we were young (both 22) students of geography and anthropology, eager to experience a 'well preserved culture'. Western Samoa was chosen to be our destination because we had read from a guidebook that the culture there was indeed well preserved and in our studies we had become familiar with Margaret Mead's account of Samoa (Coming of Age in Samoa, orig. 1928). Also the traditional image of Polynesia as a paradise lured us into our decision. While there, we kept diaries that vividly reveal the extent of culture confusion we experienced. It is easy to distinguish different emotions described above.

The stay started with the euphoria of finally being there and seeing some of the things that we had only read about but never really seen before:

> Mouths open we watched how people went along with their daily tasks in their fales [houses] and everyone could see them because there were no walls! Bare light bulbs made the fales look impressive in the darkness of the

night. There was a fridge in many of the houses and here and there were people watching tv. (...) Apia [the capital] looks beautiful. The main street is next to the sea and colonial buildings edge it. (...) The biggest wonder was how people at the marketplace just put their mats on the ground and slept there, in the middle of their wares (Personal diary 1988, my translation from Finnish).

Euphoria is clear; the attitude is enthusiastic and characterised by awe. Being able to recognise the features to which the markers we were familiar with pointed was great. Everywhere we sought confirmation of the paradise images we held. The first week we stayed in a hostel and spent our days walking on the streets and seeing sights, but we were looking forward to establishing friendship with some people and thus to gain more insight into the way of life. After that week we were invited to stay with a family and we happily accepted. However, it did not take long before the euphoria was gone. Being constantly surrounded by the people and customs we knew so little about really put strain on our nerves. The jovial attitude towards the strange culture was replaced by disillusionment:

I know I should understand that some things depend on the culture, but it's damn hard. Some things simply make me nuts: for example that the words have no meaning. It seems to be important that you speak nicely, but you don't have to mean anything. (...) Lots of promises but little action is the way here (Personal diary 1988, my translation from Finnish).

Despite the fact that I wanted to understand in principle, in practice I was not able to resist my anger and frustration. With the advantage of hindsight and the detachment it provides; the local way of pleasing in speech described in my diary was perfectly natural in that cultural environment and getting angry about it was unreasonable. But at the time the disillusionment was felt acutely; no reasoning could have lessened it.

During disillusionment we were also depressed. Primarily it manifested as miserable homesickness; all friends and relatives became more important than ever. Daily trips to the post office to check the mail were a habit and any mail from home dearly appreciated. We also spent plenty of time in the local library and made swimming trips to a pool in a river nearby. The post-office, the library and the pool were our metaworlds into which we escaped the constant presence of the Other people. They were not tourist space in the sense described in this book, because they were not part of touristic infrastructure.

Depression also occurred in a form of constant and exaggerated concern about our health (see also Oberg, 1960, p. 178; Smalley, 1963, p. 53). For example, certain bodily functions received much more attention than they normally would.[2] Not knowing the language made the irritation considerably worse. While some of our hosts were able to speak English, we were nevertheless unable to understand their mutual conversations. To be reduced to the level of a child again in terms of communication adversely effects on one's self esteem (see Smalley, 1963, p. 54). Since just about all I could say was 'my name is Jaakko, what is your name?' it is no wonder that the insight gained even in a period of months was not deep.

Despite the fact that we never learned the language, we learned a little of what to expect. The thought of going home also started to relieve the pressure. We started to hover between adaptation and opposition; our disillusionment lessened and sense of humour came back as the date of going home became closer (we had *decided* to stay the Christmas):

> Now we've started to get some clues about this system of nice talk and no action. Whenever these people speak about what is going to happen the next day, you better not to believe. Now that we understand it and are prepared, it feels like a funny game. After this trip we are going to have a good laugh at all of this (Personal diary 1988, my translation from Finnish).

Here the adaptation was greatly helped by the knowledge of getting back home soon. Without such knowledge, I do not think our views would have been so good-humoured. This is also a great example of how adaptation is helped by learning to anticipate the actions of the Other people and the outcomes of these actions. At this stage the confusion still describes the mixture of feelings well; adaptation in our case involved simultaneous opposition. By good-humoured opposition to the local habits we were able to laugh at them and thus adapt and keep ourselves sane.

The orderly organisation of the different emotions of culture confusion that I present here is of course simplification. It reflects the theoretical background of the U-curve hypothesis. This is not an accident, though. Despite Hottola's criticism about the rigid temporal order of definite stages, there is a kernel of truth in them. Especially the turn from presence-at-hand into ready-to-hand indicates that disillusionment tends to follow euphoria and not vice versa. Of course, the feelings do create a curious blend, thus creating confusion. In my diary there is evidence that

---

[2] There are numerous examples of this in my diary but in the name of decency I am not going to quote them here.

emotions do not follow a neat pattern. While we have already seen that towards the end of our stay we started to adapt a little bit, at the same time we were strongly disillusioned just before we left:

> Lot of our possessions have started to disappear lately. Harmonica, shirt, lavalava [waist-cloth], fans, comb, hairbrush, toothpaste and God knows what else we don't even know, has changed its owner or is in public use. The nasty feature in all this is that it has been done without asking for permission. Mappe is also over the limit and writes bitter remarks in his diary. Losing your privacy and this kind of pilfering really takes you to the edge. It's easy to understand the explorers of the past who totally lost their temper. I guess it's possible to appreciate the strange culture only when you read about it. When you start to lose your own clothes so that soon you'll be left with your bare essentials, you reach the limits of understanding at least when your last pants have gone (Personal diary 1988, my translation from Finnish).

My companion wrote in his own diary:

> It is impossible to know if all this is just friendly exchange based on a reciprocal relationship or whether these people are simply crooks (Personal diary of my friend 1988, my translation from Finnish).

Despite these later-day incidents the general pattern from euphoria through disillusionment to some kind of adaptation/opposition was visible. As the example of my visit to Bangkok and the experiences of backpackers to India suggest, the pattern does not always actualise. The pattern can still be used as a framework in trying to understand why. Thus my suggestion is, that while Hottola's dynamic model of culture confusion is accurate, it does not remove the idea that there is temporal dimension in likelihood in which the different emotions arise. Then again, Hottola does not even claim that it would; it is just too easy to forget amid all this criticism against the U-curve hypothesis.

Implications

It is now possible to add these emotions to the circle of travel introduced in Figure 6.1 (Figure 9.1). At the same time the shape of the circle becomes disturbed by the presence of the tourist space. Tourists explore the Other from the tourist space and the backpackers frequently escape into it to get a relief from the confusion the encounter with the Other causes. The feeling of insecurity that provides disillusionment can be lessened by providing a tourist space where the fearful travellers can feel secure and eventually encouraged enough to enjoy the Other, or at least the contradiction between the tourist space and the Other. In other words, the disillusionment has to be removed by providing necessary conditions for euphoria. From the perspective of the travel industry it is important that the euphoric state of the traveller is sustained through the traveller's experience. If the industry wants to have the tourists in the destination again, their impressions must have been pleasant. Furthermore, this is also necessary if the travellers are expected to promote the trip to others. This obviously means that the travellers must not have returned back home in the state of disillusionment. Therefore the tourist industry tries to control the travellers' experience as much as possible so that it can provide sources for euphoria. It tries to insulate them from too much uncontrolled contact with the local 'reality' outside the tourist space so that possible negative experiences lurking there would not trigger disillusionment (and of course, keeping the travellers within the tourist space channels the profits to its provider).

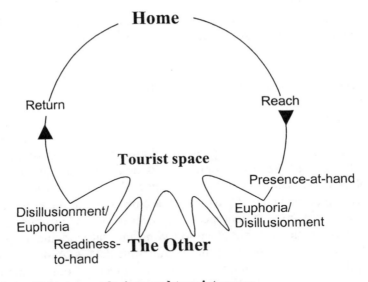

Figure 9.1 Culture confusion and tourist space

Figure 9.1 illustrates the conceptual dynamics of our balancing between home and reach in travel. Outward reach progresses through possible insecurity to euphoric enjoyment of the encounter with the Other. After a while, when the presence-at-hand of the Other diminishes, or even develops into readiness-to-hand, the disillusionment can easily set in and turn the reach into the willingness to return home. Escape to or remaining within tourist space fights back disillusionment.

Some backpackers do not have enough support of tourist space to keep them euphoric. Also the duration of their trip is usually so long that the euphoria experienced anywhere could be overshadowed by the eventual readiness-to-hand of the place, if the stay extends for too long. This is a part of why the backpackers continuously change place; to ward off boredom. Continuously changing places provide new sources of euphoria, as well as the change between being on the move and staying in a place. It is interesting that while the backpackers often stay on their trip for extended periods of time, they rarely spend time in just one place any more than the conventional mass tourists. Like these, some of the backpackers can have a list of attractions they want to 'do'. They may have stayed in Bali for four weeks but they can have been to dozen places there. It seems that by putting emphasis on maintaining the euphoria by the successive change of places, many of the backpackers get nothing but fleeting and shallow experiences of places. This is one reason why the difference between the backpackers' discourse that promotes deep insights into places and some of the backpackers' real conduct is so great.

Stereotyping and Contacts With the Other People

Stereotyping

The coherence and continuity of the domains of our existential space, especially at the level of 'geography', is achieved through typifications. Stereotypes are centres, which organise the world around them by representing certain characteristics that are perceived to be present in those particular domains. Stereotypes are necessary to arrange otherwise complicated realities; without simplifying and categorising the world, it would be a chaotic mass of infinitely numerous details. A stereotype is like a label that allows us to quickly assess the objects of our concern. It may help our survival and clarify otherwise uncertain situations (e.g. all sharks are dangerous, therefore I avoid all sharks). Stereotyping thus turns our sensory input and unorganised impressions into meaningful wholes (Steward and Powell and Chetwynd, 1979, p. 5).

Our prior images of the local people of our destination are usually stereotypes. These stereotypes are a natural part of our stock of knowledge, formed on the basis of our socio-cultural heritage and personal experience.

During the course of our life we accumulate information (and misinformation) about distant peoples and their ways of life from various sources. These include education, mass media and possibly the experiences of the others who have had contacts with the people in question. However, much of that information is often vicarious and as such it lacks the immediacy of the real experience. In the information process the small details fade away and in the end some of the most conspicuous attributes stand for the people about whom the information is acquired. This is a key aspect in the formation of stereotyped images (see Fridgen, 1984, p. 25; Evans-Pritchard, 1989, p. 98; Fakeye and Crompton, 1991, p. 10).

There is no lack of conspicuous attributes that are offered to the potential tourists to form their stereotyped impressions. Examples of stereotypes are easy to find in the way travel advertising depicts the local people of a destination. It is usual that they focus on the unique and exotic, thus distorting our impression of the people: 'study of photography of traditional people in magazines (...) reveals that exotic nature of such populations is typically emphasized - not a humanity the average Westerner can relate to' (Walle, 1993, p. 17; see also Albers and James, 1988, p. 137). Our stereotypes of the Other people are largely based on the Western discourse of the exotic Other.

This means that the established stereotypes have little chance to change, because they are rapidly turned into referential mental frameworks. The information we accumulate about other peoples becomes arranged around those stereotypes. As noted, travel advertising is an important contributor in this. From the travel brochures we can read how 'in the rural areas, Zulus follow an ancient, traditional lifestyle' (South Africa Travel Guide, [no date], p. 7). Bruner (1991, p. 240) writes that these narratives of the tourist discourse look very much like 'simplistic overgeneralizations', but that they still 'organize and give meaning to the touristic encounter'. He goes on to emphasise how the tourist discourse paints an exotic picture of the peoples and in doing so imprisons them inside a discourse which is totally alien to them, but which, nevertheless, has the power of representing them in whatever terms it wishes. From this follows that in the Other peoples the Westerners sometimes see only the reflection of their own stereotypes. Hanefors and Larsson (1993, p. 27) explain how promotional videos supplied by the travel agencies for prospective customers to view contribute to this: 'the tourist's stereotyped perceptions of any host population may be reinforced by the (...) message of the videos, which in turn creates increased likelihood of typical tourist behaviour'. Exploiting stereotypes is probably beneficial from a marketing perspective but at the same time it can have the side effect of institutionalising them (Walle, 1993, p. 17). Thus the stereotypes we hold of distant peoples tend to sustain and confirm themselves, because we are given information that is intentionally structured around those stereotypes.

Travel as Means to Bring Peoples in Contact   It is usual to say that travel adds to our understanding of other peoples. It is believed that travel eases negative prejudices and adds new dimensions to the stereotypes we hold by bringing us into contact with other peoples. This is based on the assumption that contact and interaction created by travel result in formation of meaningful personal relationships, in which the Others are apprehended not only through stereotypes, but also as individuals. However, there are several prerequisites for the interaction to be met before this happens. These are (Milman and Reichel and Pizam, 1990, p. 48; see also Pearce, 1982; p. 216; Gergen and Gergen, 1986, pp. 152-153; Amir and Ben-Ari, 1988):

1) Equal status
2) Intergroup cooperation in the pursuit of common goals
3) Intimate contact
4) Favourable social climate supporting the intergroup contact
5) The initial intergroup attitudes are not extremely negative

Unfortunately, in travel these requirements are seldom met, so that the result is the strengthening of already existing stereotypes. Sometimes the attitudes towards the hosts can even get worse (Pearce, 1982; Milman and Reichel and Pizam, 1990; Pizam and Jafari and Milman, 1991; Anastasopoulos, 1992). Anastasopoulos (1992, p. 641) concludes that tourism can indeed change attitudes, but by itself it 'neither leads to automatic prejudice reduction nor facilitates improvements in social relationships'. Tourism places visitors in a totally different position compared to the local people. The role of the tourist space in separating people is prominent here. Brewer (1984, p. 500) concludes his study of 'Tourism and Ethnic Stereotypes': 'Of most importance, this study indicates that not only is communication between native and tourist small, but also that native - tourist interactions themselves generate distortions of understanding'.

Despite the above, there is also a view that stereotypes are not necessarily rigid and fixed, but that they vary with 'intergroup relations, the context of judgement and the perspective of the perceiver' (Oakes and

Haslam and Turner, 1994, p. 211). However, travel does not necessarily facilitate this variation. The intergroup relations, the context of judgement and the perspective of the perceiver tend to be tied into the structures of travel. Therefore also the stereotypes tend to remain little changed, because the structures of travel are largely organised to confirm the stereotypes created or reinforced by the travel industry.

Stereotypes as Concepts of Definition and Expression The dialectic between our dreams and travel advertising creates and sustains stereotypes. On one hand we are offered stereotypes, on the other our own stereotypes are confirmed by the advertising material. It is thus no wonder that those stereotypes become an essential part of the terms in which the experience is both arranged and expressed. The stereotypes help us to define our relation to the other peoples and to arrange our experience of them (see Farrell, 1979, p. 125; Evans-Pritchard, 1989, p. 102). We have seen an example of how the stereotyped expressions of advertising become confirmed in the Far place, and how this confirmation can be reflected on the account of the trip. However, here is an interesting example of a situation in which the prior stereotypes have been reversed on the trip. It is a Finnish priest's account of his trip to Kenya:

> In Kenya I saw for the first time a country ruled by *blacks*, and in Nairobi a city ruled by them. Beforehand I imagined I would see a *primitive* nation and an undeveloped city. I was pleasantly surprised. I saw a completely *modern* big city with its wide streets, high-rises, hotels, banks, shops, schools; with all the buildings and offices you find in any of the world's big cities. I also had had prejudices about the *cleanliness* of Nairobi, but the cleanliness was, in fact, eye-catching (Rapeli, 1987, p. 148. My translation from Finnish, emphasis added).

This text must be understood in the context of Finland, which at the time was still characterised by monolithic culture with little day-to-day experience of the Other. In the stereotypes of the priest the element of unconscious construction has been strong. Thus when he personally encounters the 'reality' of the Other, which does not confirm his stereotypes, it is easy for him to change them. There has not been enough information that would have triggered the processes of negative memory bias (we remember the facts that support our stereotypes) and illusory correlation (we overestimate the information that confirms our stereotypes) (Gergen and Gergen 1986, pp. 146-147). The change in stereotypes is accentuated by the fact that as a priest the person is eager to see good in people(s) (this is evident from reading the book). The quotation also illustrates how polarised people's stereotypes are when they are based on shallow knowledge; the priest's stereotypes change from overly negative to overly positive. His euphoric visit to Kenya in a pronounced tourist space provided him with the experience that warranted the reversal of his stereotypes.

However, the important point in this citation is not how the stereotypes have changed, but how they direct the experience by providing the concepts through which the experience is seen. Language used not only shapes and *is* the *communicated* experience; it also tends to define the experience itself in some degree. Thus language is not only the expression of an experience, it is also a part and even sometimes the creator of it (Heikkinen, 1993, p. 9). The impressions of experiences may be vaguely arranged in our minds and the expressions we use about them bring some order to those experiences. Therefore, even though, and probably even because of the fact that the expressions may not exactly equal the impression, they may shape it. Also, it does not matter whether the experiences confirm the prior stereotypes or not, everything is still experienced in relation to those stereotypes. Our expression of the experiences draws from the stereotypes, thus making them a part of the framework in which we place our experience.

Separation and Distance from the Other People

Within the tourist discourse the Other people are presented in terms of some stereotyped characterisations. These characterisations are parts of Barthesian myths, in which the Other is made exotic. The stereotypes about people are important because our impression of the people characterises our experience of the place as a whole:

> It is not places that are important, it is the people that you meet and it's the people that make the places (Roy, 30).

> The difference between home and here are the people (Inge, 30).

Thus what the place is like for us tourists depends much on the stereotypes we use in defining the locals. Distance and separation are essential in stereotyping; without them the need to use stereotypes would be absent altogether. Physical *separation* is a consequence of the tourist space. There are some locals who work daily physically close to tourists, but in the context the interaction is largely regulated by the structures of the travel industry. This means that the interaction occurs in the course of the activities in which the visitors engage while they act out their role as a consumer within tourist space. The relationship between the visitors and the locals is thus fleeting. The local people provide the goods and services of that space, including performing to the visitors as the exotic Other. The subservient role of the locals creates *distance* between the two groups. Thus distance is *not only physical, but also existential*; differences in status, roles, and situation easily overwhelm any possible closeness, which could arise from universally shared common interests. The touristic infrastructure creates few situations in which the interaction would overcome the distance. This is accentuated by the fact that the distance itself is what constitutes the Other. Crossing the distance would annihilate the Other as it is presented by the tourist discourse.

Stereotypes Distancing the Other People The tourist discourse and its tendency to portray Other peoples as exotic relics to gaze at, or as parts of the commodity of travel, is capable of holding back meaningful personal contacts. The local people become seen as if they were on display and the result may be what Krippendorf (1987, p. 60) called a 'zoo syndrome'. As planes on which to project our dreams, the local people have little status of their own and therefore meaningful interpersonal contact is unlikely to occur. The asymmetry (Ap, 1992, p. 667) that characterises the relations between the visitors and the locals originates already from these layers of unrecognised bias. It carries on right through to all aspects of interaction. Thus paradoxically, the distance and separation between the visitors and the locals have their origins already in the very discourse within which the contact and reach for the Other are supposed to be happening.

The local people should represent authenticity, and if they don't, we lament that they have lost their cultural identity. This was reported by Albers and James (1988, p. 137): 'When tourists see Navajo working in places such as banks, hospitals, and mining operations, they are no longer identified as "real" American Indians'. Those people do not match with our understanding of what is authentic, the understanding which is created by our exposure to the tourist discourse. The 'authenticity' of Other peoples is characterised by exoticness; their 'Otherness' is strongly emphasised. Thus the contrast between the modern Western ways of life and, for example, the 'traditional' ways of the Other's has to be strong. The inevitable gaps in the knowledge are easy to fill with stereotypical projections of our own dreams. This is probably a reason why there is the concept of 'unspoilt', 'real' people; local people who apparently live as we do, working in banks, hospitals and factories, are not the Other, because we can relate to their everyday existence too well. It is not possible to project our dreams of the ideal Other on these people because their (relative) similarity to us renders such projections fruitless. Working within a Western type tourist economy is thus deemed to equal deviation from the 'traditional' ways of life. Tourists frequently express this idea:

> If you want to see real Indonesians you do not come to touristic place like Bali (Lis, 22).

Many travellers said it is maybe still possible to see the 'real' Bali somewhere in the local villages that are away from the beaten track. The Otherness of the people there is so fundamental that we can project our dreams of what is 'real Bali' on them without too much familiarity hindering the process. Hence 'real' becomes something *we* define, as in photography.

Our pre-experience impressions and stereotypes of peoples are based on the information we have accumulated from the media and other travellers. Especially the latter information derives from experiences, which have happened within the scripts of the tourist discourse. Consequently, these impressions and stereotypes tend to deal with the characteristics that are relevant from the perspective of the relations and interaction between the tourists and the locals. People are characterised for example in terms of friendliness-hostility, reliable-unreliable, clean-dirty etc., notably in similar terms to those in which employers might characterise their employees. By far the most expressed characterisation in my sample was made in terms of being friendly. Everyone used it in describing the peoples they had visited:

> Malaysians are not as friendly as Thais and Indonesians (Torsten, 21).

Comparisons between peoples are typically expressed as different degrees of these quite superficially defined characteristics. These characterisations are thus operational and normative; the local people are evaluated in terms of how well they fulfil their role as a part of the commodity of travel. Most locals encountered in various places remain consistently in these same roles in relation to the visitors (e.g. in the roles of staff in tourist establishments, vendors, performers and as 'local colour'). This gives the impression that the only difference between peoples is how well they act these roles. Thus from tourists' perspective the local people become performers. The terms used in describing people reflect the mostly operational value that the relations between tourists and the locals usually have. It is as if the tourists were employers who are primarily interested that their employees fulfil their tasks, and characterise them according to their performance in those tasks. From the point of view of the smooth running of the enterprise, the finer details of individual personalities do not need to matter. In this way people become performers on the stage of the tourist space, and their roles are scripted in the tourist discourse.

The apparent prevalence of stereotypes as expressed by my interviewees, draws probably partly from the relation between experience as it is lived and as it is communicated. There is often a considerable gap between how we feel and how we can express that feeling. When confronted with the need to express our feelings, we often use those stereotypical expressions that first spring into mind, and which we know other people can understand. It may well be that we haven't articulated what we are asked even for ourselves. Thus it is no wonder that we cannot articulate it to a sudden inquirer, especially if the person enquiring about those feelings has a tape recorder in operation in front of us (like I did when I was interviewing travellers). This may explain a little of why many visitors merely seem to desire confirmation of their travel industry-induced preconceptions (e.g. Boorstin, 1962, p. 109; Krippendorf, 1987, p. 33). Nevertheless, using these readily available expressions is not as innocent as it may seem; earlier I commented on how the language we use in expressing our experiences shapes and even creates them. Even if the stereotypical expressions are used as a matter of convenience, they still articulate experiences so that the stereotypes become integral parts of it.

Tourist Space Creating Separation and Distance The separation and distance between visitors and locals is largely created by the existence of tourist space. The character of that space encompasses such things as directedness and insulation, difference in economic status, language problems and cultural differences in the ways of thinking.

The distance and separation can appear as directedness and insulation of tourist space. Above, a backpacker described Malaysians as not being as friendly as Thais and Indonesians. However, it later became apparent that he had stayed a few weeks in both Thailand and Indonesia and visited relatively remote places where people are still interested in visitors. On the other hand, he had travelled through Malaysia in express buses, just to get from Thailand to Singapore, and had only stayed a few nights in Kuala Lumpur. It is obvious that people are friendlier in remote areas than in big cities. Yet unreflectively, he was ready to compare Malaysians as a people with the Thais and Indonesians, about whom he had much more experience. In Malaysia a part of the tourist space, namely the mode of transport he was using, brought him to places where he was constantly strongly enveloped by some aspects of the tourist space and where the interaction with the local people was especially limited by the roles operating in that space. Thus the stereotypical impression of a whole people can be directed by the tourist space. In this case, the effect was negative, since it was (maybe unfairly) compared with the positive experiences of relations with the local people in settings more favourable to meaningful personal interaction. The formality displayed by the locals in the interaction within the tourist space may thus be felt as a contrast to warm-hearted curiosity they may display in places where the role of the tourist space is smaller.

The difference in economic status creates distance and separation. The visitors' relation to their destination is fleeting. They are having their vacation, unlike the local people, who are tied to their normal tasks of the everyday life. According to Pearce (1982, p. 199) two qualities, which govern the relationships between the visitors and the locals arise. First, the visitors do not have to adapt to the local ways. The visitors expect the destination to respond to their requirements as they have purchased a commodity of which the destination is an important part. Second, they are affluent compared to most locals. Both of these qualities of a tourist trip are especially evident when the destination country is in the developing world and its culture is distinctively different from the one of the traveller. This can cause guilt among some of the visitors. The locals can rightly consider even the most worn-out looking backpackers rich. The relationship of those who are served (the visitors) with those who are servants (the locals) bears great resemblance to colonialism (see Farrell, 1979, p. 134; Krippendorf, 1987, p. 56). As a British backpacker on his bungalow verandah in Bali puts it:

> Just sitting here and having coffee brought to you makes you feel very white and very rich and guilty, it is like a new form of colonialism (John, 26).

A Finnish couple in a resort in Dominican Republic had quite similar feelings, when they noted how everything was made to meet the needs of the mostly European tourists (the resort was in German ownership). They told how the boss was all the time checking that the local employees kept the place spotlessly clean and was very angry with them if this was not done. For some sensitive and responsible visitors, the conspicuous difference in economic statuses and the structures it creates is disturbing.

To accord the visitors a special guest status is another way to use this economic status difference in distancing the visitors from the locals. This does not have to be limited only to conventional tourists. Also an occasional backpacker who stays in a local village may feel welcome and very much involved with the local life, but is in fact separated from the people by getting a VIP-treatment. Of course this is seldom a source of significant income for the locals, but their sense of social decency may compel them to treat the visitors well in order not to lose their own face. I experienced this with my travel companion in some villages in Fiji and Samoa; we tried to participate in the daily tasks of the people, but we were usually denied that possibility on the grounds that we were guests and thus not allowed to do any work. The guest status clearly closed us off from many usual everyday concerns of the people and accentuated the contrast between Us and Them.[3]

While the conventional tourists most likely enjoy their role as celebrated guests (irrespective of whether they realise that it is simply a part of the package they have paid for), the few backpackers who really want to have close contact with the local people find it frustrating. However, the institutionalisation of backpacking tourism means that these backpackers are a small minority. In my sample there were no travellers who desired to stay with the local people and deeply partake in their daily lives. There has to remain a certain degree of contrast between the visitors and the Other; this is in fact a part of the charm of travel. It allows us to retain some of our images of the Other without having to expose us to the realities of strong involvement which may prove fatal for those images. Staying with the locals may also be seen as partly interfering with some of the motives for travel. One of the important travel motives was to achieve personal development through the experience of freedom to do what one wishes; thus we confirm that we can control our lives. Staying with the locals drastically restricts that freedom and takes the control at least partially away.

For the wealthy Western visitors there are many apparent reasons to justify ethnocentrism. Tourist space works according to systems they have got used to, even in the middle of an alien culture. Likewise, everything can be translated into terms that readily make sense in the tourists' Western stock of knowledge. Because everything can apparently be managed without having to change their Western framework too much, it is easy to

---

[3] Here the perspective is from the locals' angle; we, the tourists, were Them and the locals themselves were Us.

conclude that the framework is superior. Not to mention the local level of material sophistication, which may leave a lot to be desired. The ethnocentrism displayed by both parties (although here I concentrate only on the visitors) heightens the tourists' distance from the locals. No education can ease the ethnocentric tendencies as long as the travellers' experiences seem to support them so strikingly. Cleanliness, for example, is one aspect that for many Westerners (especially Scandinavians) is an important indicator of the 'worthiness' of other peoples:

> When travelling, you learn to appreciate your home country, which is so tidy. Down south [means the Mediterranean, Canary Islands and Madeira from the perspective of Finland] they are not able to take care of tidiness because they haven't been taught that since childhood (An unrecorded comment of an elderly Finnish lady after her visit to Tunis).

> It has to be said that the eastern neighbour [Russia] does not know how to keep places clean; it is so dirty and they destroy the nature (Erkki, 58).

It is easy to see the contempt these two Finns felt for the people whose attitude to cleanliness is much more relaxed than their own. Here the presence-at-hand we encounter captures our attention in a negative sense and it is hard not to let that impression overshadow many other aspects of what we experience of the Other. This is just one example of the phenomenon that, when we evaluate other people(s), we are largely unable to depart from the values we have internalised ourselves. Furthermore, the difference in affluence in our favour often accentuates those features that stand out negatively as the attributes of the local people. Whatever the reasons behind the ethnocentrism, it effectively undermines any efforts to lessen the distance and separation between the people (see also Wei and Crompton and Reid, 1989, p. 324).

Tourism brings to the same location people whose culture and whole mode of thinking may be different. Difference in culture, subsequent differences in modes of thinking and the mutual inability to communicate, all contribute to the distance and separation between people. Together with the differences in status, goals and roles the result is that little meaningful dialogue is likely to take place (Krippendorf, 1987, p. 60). Language is the most obvious obstacle we often face in trying to communicate with the other peoples. Even if the language used appears to be the same, there may be cultural differences in how that language is supposed to be used. As an example I give the following episode I witnessed at the nightly food market in Ubud, Bali:

Visitor: 'Is this vegetarian food?' (pointing to an item in the menu)
Waiter: 'Yes' (with a broad smile)
Visitor: 'So there is no meat in it?'
Waiter: 'Yes' (with a hesitant smile)
Visitor: 'There is meat in it?'
Waiter: 'Yes' (with an embarrassed smile)

I do not think that episodes like this are uncommon. It appeared that the waiter could speak English sufficiently to be able to understand the questions, but was reluctant to use the word 'no'. Such cultural practise of using language makes little sense to the visitors who naturally react by deeming it weird and nonsensical. This obviously adds to the distance the visitors feel from the locals. But it is not only the spoken language that may differ; sometimes the cultural differences in body language and bodily expressions are a great source of misunderstandings (see Morris, 1967). The personal space required is a typical example of this. It may be hard for a Westerner to understand the habit of grown-up men walking hand in hand without any homosexual connotations.

Language problems can severely hinder communication with the locals and thus the threshold to seek more intimate relationships gets higher even if both parties would like to do so. A few common words hardly constitute the basis for a meaningful change of ideas and aspirations. Thus the lack of common language as such already creates distance and separation. Furthermore, the people who do not command foreign languages are less likely to choose anything but tightly organised travel, and are consequently restricted to a strong tourist space.[4] The lack of common language increases the chances that our possibly negative stereotypes become confirmed. If we are superior speakers of the language that is used as a means of communication, it is easy to get the impression that the others lack intelligence. In our group travel in Turkey we naturally understood that most of the local people might not have as good a command of the English language as we did, but we nevertheless made jokes about the expressions they used once we were by ourselves. It is inevitable that despite *knowing* the facts the *impression* of the unintelligent

---

[4] Naturally this is not so much a problem in English speaking countries, whose people are able to travel in most parts of the world and get themselves understood in their own language. However, there are very few countries where a Finn, for example, is able to do so.

Others is there. Expressing that impression, no matter if only as a joke, directs the experience.

Travel Companions Promoting Separation and Distance Travel in a cohesive group is likely to accentuate the distance and separation from the locals. Bruner (1991, p. 242) concludes from the literature:

> The tourists spend only a few days or weeks in any one locality and even then move so rapidly that there is little opportunity for sustained interaction with local people, that they do not speak the language, that through the infrastructure of the tourist industry they are protected from direct interaction with natives, and that most of their time is spent on the company of other tourists.

My own experiences of our trip to Turkey and what other informants told about a similar trip to Portugal clearly demonstrate this. As the tour groups consisted of fellow students, the cohesion between them was probably more pronounced than that of a typical tourist group. This had the effect that it was possible to enjoy the trip even if one was relatively indifferent towards the local people, who merely provided a stark contrast to Us.

Sharing a trip with familiar people, or at least people who are becoming familiar, diverts the attention to relationships and socialising within the group. These people share our situation and respond to us in the way we are familiar with. Social groups within the ranks of the visitors themselves form easily and naturally. Instead, getting familiar with the locals becomes unnecessary because the social relationships desired are there already, or are at least in the process of forming within the visitor group. It may even be that people travel for recreation more than to mingle with the locals, and are not necessarily at all interested in getting to know them. Moving around in a group also sets time limits, and the possibility to familiarise oneself with the local people even if the desire were there, is diminished. A typical one or two weeks period of a vacation trip, not to mention short stays in any one place, is hardly enough to reach over the distance and separation. The social dynamics within the travel group tend to gain precedence over the desire to seek new ones outside the group. Also the strict tourist space, often quite literally in the form of the tourist bus, clearly defines the boundary between Us and Them.

Travel companions' ability to increase the separation from the locals is not limited to travel in a group. Having even just one travel companion often reduces the need to make other contacts. The couple met earlier told me how Roy's illness affected their perception of an island they were visiting. For me it seemed that their common experience of Bali was a constant dialectic between his disillusionment and the experiences they had. Another respondent reflects on his travel to the Czech Republic with his de facto spouse:

> When you move about rapidly, just the two of you, you don't arrive in situations where you talk with the people (Olavi, 32).

A travel companion simply reduces the need for the formation of other relationships. The reach required becomes satisfied when the travellers are able to mutually contemplate their reactions and feelings about the Other. The Other is merely the presence-at-hand which creates the background for new experiences. These new experiences, in turn, are the focus of mutual interest, which then revolves around these experiences and not around the Other. Thus the experience of the Other with a travel companion can direct the reach towards new dimensions in the relationship with him or her, instead of the Other.[5]

Even when travelling alone, people frequently find it much easier to make contacts with other travellers than with the local people. Somewhat common cultural background, and shared situation creates a feeling of comradeship among travellers who refer to the local people using the word 'Them'. Reaching out to 'Them' requires thus much more effort than just socialising with people who share our situation and aspirations. Furthermore, sharing the same accommodation with other travellers provides a lot more time and many more situations for meaningful relationships to occur spontaneously. As a contrast to the comradeship felt with other travellers, the local people may be a source of distress.

> It is very hard to rely on anything in India, the people seemed to me quite unpredictable (Kathy, 28).

The contrast between Us who share somewhat similar aspirations and situation and Them becomes stark and easily makes us to seek conformity from the fellow travellers. Among Us we can retain our confidence and

---

[5] In the situation in which we do not get along with our travel companion(s), it could be assumed that the desire for interaction would be directed towards the Other. However, we have seen that in a group tour situation there are limited possibilities for this to happen. In the case of just one travelling companion, it is usual to split rather than continue travel together, if the disagreement cannot be solved in reasonable time. In Bali I met three solitary travellers who had started together with someone, but at some stage found that they could not travel with that person.

control because we know how to act and what to expect. We can have the sense of control and the ability to enjoy the contrast between Us and the Other from a comfortable base (social and material) of familiarity. This would not be the case if we tried to mix with Them. Insecurity, maybe even outright fear, could result from not being able to comprehend things using the socio-cultural frameworks we have internalised. The whole of our self could thus be questioned and put in jeopardy.

All the above suggests, that the main obstacles for the visitors in getting familiar with the local people are the other visitors and travel companions. The interaction with them is likely to sustain the tourist discourse from a one-sidedly visitors' perspective. Travel companions and other travellers provide a marked contrast to the Other, which is exactly the contrast the tourist discourse also emphasises. The travel companions provide social and material support in our attempt to face the Other (see Murphy, 2001). The fact that the support is there contributes to the phenomenon that the Other has little opportunity to 'speak' for itself, since it is primarily experienced through our relationship with our travel companion(s). Thus I suggest that travelling alone provides the best opportunity to get familiar with the Other. We could not compare the Other to our relationship with someone whose socio-cultural frameworks resembles or is similar to our own. Of course we would still have our own socio-cultural heritage, but there would be nobody to give it any support, therefore there would be a strong incentive to build a meaningful and working relation with the Other. Had Robinson Crusoe landed on an island that had a local population, he surely would have got familiar with the people (unless he had got mauled to death) since they would have been the only ones he could have mingled with.[6]

Contacts With the Other People

Despite all the distance and separation, there are naturally also contacts between the visitors and the locals. The contacts are shaped by direct (personal) and indirect (structural) factors (compare Pearce, 1982, p. 200). The direct factors involve our personal input into our relationships with the local people. The indirect factors are the structures of the tourist space,

---

[6] When he finally encountered the Other people, his world in that place had been established already; there was no room for others except in a role strictly defined by Robinson himself.

which largely create the frameworks in which the direct factors eventually occur.

By far the most important such framework is the economic one. The visitors are consumers and the locals are there to provide the goods and services the visitors need. The asymmetry of the relation can even get neo-colonialist forms. However, it has to be noted that criticism of the commercial base of the relations is not always justified; one should not forget that an important part of the interaction between people has always been commerce. Completely authentic and meaningful personal relations have been and can be formed while engaging in such relationships. But the relationships based on commerce become spoiled if the relationships themselves become commercialised, and/or if there is clear unbalance in the power relations of that commerce. Unfortunately, both of these elements are often present in tourism.

As a result, interaction between people takes place mostly in commercial situations where the visitor either buys something or uses the services of the travel industry. In these kind of situations there are certain generally accepted ways of behaving based on the clearly identifiable roles of the participants. It often happens that the participants interact more on the basis of their respective stereotyped roles than as individuals. McKean called these behavioural patterns 'narrow bands along which interaction takes place' (cited in Farrell, 1982, p. 231). Here the relationships are mainly staged, and the communication uses established paths, thus reinforcing the roles from which it is generated.

I purposefully use the terms of existential space here, as this is clearly a description of moving within the social dimension of existential space. The stereotyped roles are familiar centres with which we organise social space. Because the communicational paths we use are readily established between the stereotyped roles from which and to which we communicate, there is no need to open up new paths. There is little reach involved; the whole exercise revolves around the familiar stereotyped roles and thus is not likely to widen anyone's horizons. The relationship is staged because it involves acting out roles. The script of the roles originates from the tourist discourse (Bruner and Kirschenblatt-Gimblett, 1994, p. 467), rather than from within. In practice this means for example, that the bartender of the hotel is a friend of the visitor while working, but when his hours of work are finished he retreats from the 'stage' of interaction with the visitors into the local spheres where the visitors have little share.

In the context of language it is possible to apply Goffman's front and backstages again. Visitors and the locals use language as a stage. If there is a common language, it creates a 'front', a stage where the both parties perform the social exchange in mutually acceptable way (or at least try to do so). In doing so they use the established paths of communication. One's own language that the other party is not able to understand can then be used as a backstage. There the comments and ideas not intended for the other party can be expressed freely among one's own group. This situation often places English-speaking visitors who are not able to speak any other language in a slightly disadvantaged position because their own language is often the common language used. There is no language other than lowering their voice they can use as a backstage. A typical situation where the locals resort to this backstage is when the visitors realise that they are a laughing stock; from the expressions of people's faces they can see that they are the object of their laughter but naturally they can not understand what is it that causes the amusement. An example of the situation where the common language is a stage and visitors' own language a backstage is when the people invite backpackers to stay in their place. The backpackers may politely accept the invitation using the common language, but among themselves assess the reliability of their host using their own language.

Ambiguity and even frustration arises in some situations precisely because it is not always possible to distinguish between the front and back.

> We saw Balinese people in the small villages, they were really nice and said that they did not like Kuta because there were so many people from Java and Sumatra there, always wanting to sell something. But Balinese people are not like that. After a while however, they suggested that you buy something: 'Just look!' so you are forced to buy (Denise, 21).

Many backpacker respondents expressed the practical problem of how to recognise when friendliness displayed by a local person was genuine interest and when it was done only to sell something or to gain some other kind of advantage of them. Some had refused an offer to visit someone's home because they automatically supposed that they were simply trying to sell something. It is hard to conceive that whole-hearted friendliness and commercial interests would be displayed simultaneously which, however, sometimes is the case. Many of the backpacker visitors have an idealised picture of what constitutes genuine interaction with other peoples; it should not involve money. They forget (or do not realise) that commerce may also be another form of meaningful interaction.

Negative Commercial Contacts The distance and separation between the visitors and the locals was summarised by a backpacker who said about the Balinese:

> You seldom get to talk to them unless they want to sell you something (Tina, 24).

Whether the visitors are mass tourists or backpackers, most of their contacts with the locals are likely to be commercial. The visitors are either customers or they are pursued by the locals to become such. The distance is so great that this kind of contact, shaped around a commercial interest, is the most natural path through which the interaction can take place. The structure of travel simply does not allow for a large number of spontaneous situations in which contact without some commercial connotations could freely occur. However, a significant proportion of these contacts are experienced negatively:

> We visited the market place by boat. It was quite a tourist trap; we got tired of the continuous bargaining. It would have been an advantage if we hadn't looked so German or had been able to speak Spanish (Markus, 25).

> Those blackies tried to press all their wares on us and if you did not buy you got cursed (Kaapo, 27 explaining why he does not want to go to the Canary Islands any more).

> Continuous bargaining puts you off (Jim, 29).

> Every time someone says something to you they want to sell you something (Denise, 22).

I think this situation strongly draws from the difference in economic status which is so great, that from the locals' point of view the visitors are seen mainly just as a source of income. The visitors feel as they were considered as 'walking chequebooks' (Roy, 30), or 'walking purses' (Aron, 23). For the locals who perceive themselves as economically inferior, it is perfectly justifiable that any possibility to gain from the affluent visitors has to be used in the short time available. Thus the difference in economic status and the short time of the contact contribute to the vendors' enthusiasm to sell the visitor anything and if possible, even cheat.

This, in turn, is made easier by the distance and separation in other areas; there are no loyalties. Being in a different cultural and linguistical environment makes the visitor more susceptible to cheating. These things happen especially easily when the visitors have just arrived and do not yet know what to pay and expect. In Bali, I paid five times the normal price for a bottle of water in my first day. After finding out I laughed; this would be material for my PhD. As a newcomer, it is still easy to let the feeling of euphoria overpower any irritation such inconveniences may cause. However, if similar incidents keep occurring, they are likely to leave a permanent negative impression of the local people. Furthermore, the first impressions tend to be the most influential in image formation.

Among the most sensitive backpackers there was concern about the impact of unfriendliness on the way they themselves related to the local people. One complained that:

> Hassles with people demand you unwillingly be unresponsive (Kathy, 28).

Being forced to give up the possibly idealised expectations of the Other and having to behave in the manner they do not feel comfortable with is a double humiliation. The control of events is lost. The forcible intrusions on the tourists' personal space by the local vendors, for example, are consequences of the power structures that create the distance and separation. A local vendor begging the visitor to buy reflects the inequality of the two in terms of wealth. In these practical situations the visitors become painfully conscious of their personal involvement in these power structures. It shatters the visitors' belief that they could somehow overcome the distance. Suddenly they find themselves incapable of managing friendly relationships with the Other. The imaginary ideal Other does not actualise in the harsh contact with the 'real' one.

Even the less sensitive travellers may have quite similar experiences when the continuous harassment from persistent vendors impairs their ability to enjoy the Other.

> Mount Batur is impossible to climb without being followed by a cold drink seller and someone wanting to be your guide (Aron, 23).

The couple's attempt to gain an uplifting experience by strenuous walk and the magnificent views offered by nature was frustrated by the constant presence and insistence of sellers. The ideals associated with mountaintops disintegrated amid the annoyance. The couple's experience of ascending to the summit and reaching it was trivialised from an exhilarating experience to mundane struggle against ever-present vendors. They could as well have stayed in the worst tourist areas. Consequently the impression of the local people on the basis of these experiences is very negative. This tends to add further distance and separation, by making the visitors willing to avoid the locals:

> There are very few Indonesian people you want to talk to without wanting to buy things (Roy, 30).

> You just try to look into your book, and if you are lucky, maybe nobody will talk to you (Heidi, 22).

The original distance and separation has in this situation produced circumstances in which they accentuate themselves and bring a peculiar conflict in relation to the initial motives to travel. The distance and separation initially originate the desire to try to reach over them, but eventually they just make us to avoid the contact with the Other people. It appears that the novelty found is not the kind we were looking for. While being a continuous object of attention may be just a part of a new exciting experience of novelty in the beginning, the novelty soon wears out. The reach for the local people is transformed into reach for the fellow travellers and contempt for the locals.

Positive Commercial Contacts Naturally, the majority of commercial contacts are surely not negative, but because this is considered self-evident, these contacts are not so commonly reported. Acquiring accommodation, buying food and souvenirs, and possibly using public transportation are, in fact, means of bridging the distance and separation between the visitors and locals (for many tourists, the only means). We can interact meaningfully with the locals and be involved with at least some of their practices (see Boorstin, 1972, p. 92).

> We had decided to buy a lot of clothes since they were so cheap. It quite extensively occupied our minds... Well, the shopping was an experience [of the place] as such (Minna, 28).

> Bargaining is a means of adapting to their way of life and I quite enjoy it (Kathy, 28).

Continuous bargaining can put some visitors off, but it can also be a gratifying experience of immersing ourselves into a foreign culture. Learning to enjoy and partake of many aspects of different conduct of business gives a satisfying feeling of involvement. An aspect of this is that some travellers measure the success of their command of the local culture by what bargains they have managed to get. It is usual to compare prices paid with other travellers. Even if the ability to communicate in the situation of buying leaves something to be desired, the ways to overcome this (lingua franca, hand gestures) provide a humorous encounter that will be warmly remembered (if the visitor did not get cheated).

> We managed all right, a word in Russian, another in English and the rest by using our hands (Erkki, 58).

In this way shopping, for example, can satisfy many motivational needs the visitors have. It provides personal contact with the Other people and novelty in negotiating in their commercial practices. It confirms our ability to do so and thus gives a feeling of freedom and reinforces our self-esteem. Because of the structural separation and distance, the commercial contacts are largely the travellers' experience of the Other people. This is the case especially in conventional tourism, but also the institutionalised backpacking travel seems to restrict the most likely contacts with the locals to commerce.

Non-Commercial Contacts My interviewees generally agreed that non-commercial contacts with the locals were rare but often the most satisfying when they did occur. They are nice change to the situations where we are talked to only for the purpose of getting some monetary advantage of us. Here we actually overcome the separation, if not the distance between the local people and us. Language may often be an obstacle, but it nevertheless feels good to get at least a glimpse of backstage as a contrast to the touristic front. The absence of money in the relationship is seen to be the proof that the interest in you displayed by the locals is genuine.

> Getting to know those local boys was the most gratifying experience since you could see the places where the local people went. It was hard though, because their English wasn't very good; we did not understand even close to everything they were talking about (Satu, 28).

The satisfaction felt is not primarily the result of any deep insights, which do not necessarily follow from these, after all, quite superficial experiences. The satisfaction results from the realisation that we can make a personal contact with someone from the Other without any commercial connotations. However, few conventional tourists pursue, not to mention achieve such relations. Similar dynamics apply to these relations as in culture confusion in general. Initially there is strong euphoria caused by this contact with the Other, but soon, the novelty wears out as the problems of communication and the lack of common ground make anything but superficial interaction possible. The above quoted respondent complained that while the contact with the local boys was gratifying, it was also psychologically demanding because of the language difficulties; they eventually ran out of things to say. There is simply too little to carry mutual involvement beyond this quite superficial level. While there would be a lot of ground to reach for, the very fact of being so much apart makes that reaching hard. Even though the situation itself may be informal and spontaneous, the interaction still has to be channelled through the narrow paths on which all the parties concerned can feel themselves comfortable. In other words, with a complete stranger it is often hard to talk about anything but the most usual trivialities - even in your own language. While the separation is overcome, the distance remains. However, despite this, there is still likely to be feeling of great satisfaction because of the contact. It is personal contact with the Other, and even in its superficiality it provides a great contrast to the normally experienced separation. The reach involved has opened up new dimensions, maybe small, but nevertheless personally significant.

Even greater is the satisfaction of those who have managed to reach beyond the usual conventions of interaction between strangers. Apart form a shared means of communication, this requires a special personality with certain amount of courage to probe under the surface, from both the visitor and the local. Then the established paths can be left behind and it becomes possible to reach genuinely new dimensions. I personally experienced this at the Kuta beach in Bali, when I was approached by a local gay. Of course, for him the paths of interaction in his context were familiar, but for me they certainly were not. Despite preferring to refuse his proposition, I managed to discuss with him about what it was like to be a gay there. This was certainly something beyond the normal everyday trivialities for me and I was absolutely fascinated about the new dimensions I had encountered. For me the amount of reach involved was immense and rewarding. But as said, these contacts require that the persons involved share somewhat unreserved personalities and a common means of communication already from the beginning; the original distance has not been as great as the separation prior to contact suggests.

One further point emerges here; most locals that the visitors encounter possess an occupation, which lessens the physical separation between them and the visitors (hotel staff, vendors, etc.). Alternatively, they may have a personality that makes them more willing to approach the visitors, or they are marginal and want to seek support from the outside. This was the case when the Finnish girls spent time with the local boys in Istanbul; the boys they met were Kurdish and very eager to vent their perspective on life in Turkey. If there are local people who approach us, they tend to be extroverts who have had previous contacts with 'the outside'. Most of those who have approached me have been studying abroad or wanted to practice their English. This means that those people are seldom representative of the local people as a whole. Thus the 'usual' people the visitors meet may be similarly marginal in their relation to the local society.

There is thus slight resemblance between the visitors and these 'local' people who seek contact with them; both have some degree of outsideness in relation to the place.[7] While the visitors' outsideness is naturally more profound, these 'local's' outsideness is felt in relation to the mainstream society of the place. Thus it is possible for the visitors and these marginal locals to share a viewpoint of being 'Them'. Of course, for both groups being 'Them' appear from a very different perspective. A marginal 'local' person can be another visitor, although from another world than the tourist. These slight structural similarities in these perspectives do not mean that their contents would be even closely similar, the perspective of a marginal 'local' is just another Other to the visitor. This means that the perspective that is narrated to the visitors is often one of an outsider. It gives little room for the Other people of the place to 'speak' for themselves, and the Other we encounter is not necessarily the 'Us' of the very place.

Personal involvement that is based on the experiences shared with familiar travel companions can indeed be rewarding, but it is still bound to remain a reflection of our own ideas, which we impose on the Other place. Instead, if the personal experiences have taken place in intimate involvement with the local people, these experiences are genuinely of that place (or at least of some Other). In this way we have personal experience of the Other which is not only the plane for our own frameworks, but includes also a genuine input by the Other.

Distance and Separation as a Lure

The locals are important part of the Other, because the Otherness of the place is largely mediated to the visitors through them. Without the local people the Otherness of places would only embody as physical features.

---

[7] Some examples are Kurdish people in Istanbul, Javanese in Bali, Algerians in Paris, etc.

We can invest those features with the meanings of our own, or with those adopted from the narratives of the place, but our experience of its Otherness would nevertheless lack the potentially exciting meanings and myths associated with a 'quaint', or 'exotic' culture. The experience of the Other people confirms and consummates our encounter with the Other. In this light it is apparently peculiar that distance and separation nevertheless characterises much of these experiences.

On the closer analysis this is not as paradoxical as it first seems however. In some occasions in the discussion it appeared that the distance to the Other has to be maintained in order to preserve the contrast between the familiar and the Other. This is the contrast that lures visitors. Despite shallow familiarisation with the destination, we seem to exhaust its presence-at-hand that is perceivedly available through a touristic experience. We must then seek new places on consecutive trips to find similar pristine presence-at-hand for us again. Thus the distance and separation do not hinder our reaching, because in institutionalised travel that reach is satisfied in a mere experience of the contrast between familiar and the Other. There is no need to try to overcome the distance and separation, because the experience of these is, in fact, what we are after. Furthermore, they contribute to the possibility of creating exciting myths and fantasies about the Other. The creation of this geography of dreams would not be as readily possible without them.

Narratives of the Other thus created become parts of the tourist discourse which is then transmitted to others at home. Thus the biased and partial narratives derived from the distance and separation accumulate and become parts of the experiences of other visitors. We should not fall into the illusory belief that superficial contact can deepen our stereotyped images of Other peoples. Instead, we should recognise their presence and analyse their role in our thinking. In a shallow experience we do not necessarily learn a lot about other peoples. But we can learn how we relate to them and why.

10 Integrating the Experience of the Other and Home

After the Trip

In travel studies the link between the experience of normal everyday life and the experience of travel has been commonly emphasised (e.g. MacCannell, 1976; Cohen, 1979a). However, these qualitative studies mainly concentrate on the experience of the Other, rather than on the dynamics through which that experience changes the traveller's relationship with home, although home is a more central aspect of a person's life. This emphasis on the experience of the Other is likely to draw from the fact that most qualitative studies of travel experiences (e.g. in the *Annals of Tourism Research*) closely relate to anthropology and sociology. They study the interaction between people rather than the psychological processes within one person. There are quantitatively orientated studies, which do study the psychological processes of the traveller after travel, but these studies are mainly concerned with measuring the impact of the visit on the visitor's destination image (e.g. Echtner and Ritchie, 1991; Chon, 1991; Ross, 1991), or satisfaction with the trip as a product (e.g. Fakeye and Crompton, 1991; Clarke, 1992). Tourism is seen as 'consumer behaviour' (Ross, 1994, p. 10). The usefulness of such - essentially marketing - studies is limited in understanding travel experiences as having the potential to shape the traveller's life. There is thus room for new qualitative understanding of how, if at all, the experience of travel contributes to the definition of one's world-view and the consequent sense of place in society and in the world.

Travel as Release or as Detachment

Travel motivations relate to a need for change. Travel is thus reaching for new experiences that are perceived to be unattainable at home. The experience of *home* requires the balance of *reach*. Thus a central element in travel experience is how it has answered to our desire for reach. In travel this reach is ostensibly spatial, but the spatiality nevertheless encompasses the experiential aspect as well; the change of place allows a brief and maybe shallow but nevertheless welcome disengagement from daily life at home. Depending on the prominence of different motives for travel, this disengagement is experienced either as release or detachment. The prominence of escape motives provides release, whereas the prominence of search motives creates detachment. This distinction appears also in Cohen's (1979) modes of travel, in which his diversionary mode of travel describes travel as release and other modes have varying degrees of detachment.

Travel is experienced as release, especially when escape from alienation or mishaps is sought. The experiences away are directed towards deadening the feelings of everydayness associated with home; to temporarily wipe it out of our mind. Thus the creation of new perspectives on home is not emphasised. However, the dynamic of a particular trip is usually such that unless the traveller is totally passive and pathologically oblivious to anything but the angst felt, the initial experience of travel as mere release gives way at some stage to travel as, at least to some extent, soothing detachment. An example of this was the lady travelling in Bali after the death of her baby; she wanted to get away from the place that reminded her of him, as soon as possible. The travel was mere escape; the destination did not matter as long as it was far away and she could leave at once. After a while, however, the new place began to provide her with other things to occupy her mind. The soothing effect started to take place, if only a little. In this way even travel as primarily release may facilitate new perspectives on home. Thus travel as release and as detachment are not exclusive categories; generally the motive of escape from various mishaps is just one of the motives that initiate travel. It is not the overriding theme behind every experience while on travel. This was the case with some of the backpackers who had left a broken relationship behind and commented that it was one motive to travel, but by no means the only one.

In contrast to travel as release, detachment implies active, conscious disengagement from home. As a result, new perspectives on home arise. The new vantage point is used to re-evaluate the relationship with home; the relationship is invigorated. In this way travel is always related to the experience of home. A backpacker expressed this:

> Your home place is the comparison to everything you see... Your home place is part of you; you take home with you (Kathy, 28).

Because travel as release has little direction apart from being mere escape, home is bound to remain the dominant point of reference. Even - and maybe particularly - the unhappiest relationship with home lingers as the focus of the travellers' reluctant attention. In travel as detachment, home can become the centre of new meanings, which are discovered because of the new perspective. Also the existing meanings already associated with home may attain new clarity and significance:

> You learn to love your own country when you are travelling (Sigrid, 21).

Travel as Rite of Passage

Much of the discussion of this chapter reflects the interview material I have. The distinction between conventional tourists and backpackers is the most obvious such reflection. Another is the fact that I interviewed the conventional tourists after their trips, and the backpackers while they were still on the trip. Thus the former were in a better position to evaluate the meaning of the trips afterwards. Nevertheless, the interviews with the backpackers included much speculation on that meaning too, as many of the travellers approached the end of their trip at the time of the interview. I draw further experiential depth from my personal experiences as a backpacker, and from the profound changes these experiences caused in my life after the trip. There will thus be plenty of subjective bias in my analysis of travel as a rite of passage, for example, because my own experience strongly supports such characterisation. However, in many instances during my interviews I found exhilaration from the realisation that I could see many people living through very similar experiences.

One of the motives for travel was precisely to find new perspectives on familiar things, like home, or one's own life (search for self-development). These new perspectives are brought about by the experience of presence-at-hand of new things, and also by the presence-at-hand of the already familiar things that appear in a new light because of the detachment produced by the distance. Ideally, the monotonous readiness-to-hand of home is 'refreshed' through the 'revelations' gained while experiencing the Other and the presence-at-hand resulting from the detachment from home. This experience appears as a central element in travel as search for personal development. New perspectives gained on the trip may have a far-reaching effect on how we see our life at home and what we would like it to be like. As a result our whole attitude towards our life changes:

> When I get home my whole life is totally different... I am not the same person [as when I left] when I go home (Sigrid, 21).

> Afterwards probably the main thing to remember would be not so much a
> particular incident but an impression, the appreciation that you have had
> time to sort things in your life out (Tina, 24).

In the case of the backpackers this clearly emphasises the trip as a rite of
passage. Several themes of backpacking travel show this. In the case of
almost all the backpackers I interviewed, travel was a liminal (or liminoid)
period of time in the middle of distinct phases of life. As backpacking
travel typically requires a few months of time, it naturally creates a break in
the life at home. For this reason, it is commonly done after studies, before
finding a permanent job, or before a new job. The time on travel is used to
give ourselves time to contemplate on what we want from life and what
kind of job to seek, for example. Thus a backpacking trip is a distinct ritual
between our different statuses in our own societies. It contains precisely the
elements of ritual; the departure (separation), contact with the Other
(liminal period), and return home (reintegration).

A conventional tourist trip can also be a rite of passage ritual, albeit
to a lesser extent. Because of the initiatory character of having visited
certain places and sights, our status in the eyes of those who stayed home
changes. Our social standing increases because we have now been initiated
into the group of people who possess a piece of the ideas that places and
sights visited represent. The trip is thus a ritual in which this kind of
transformation of status takes place. For the backpackers some of this
transformation consists of the perception of the others that the traveller has
gained valuable life experience and thus personal development. For both
the backpackers and the conventional tourists the change of status often
means that other people consider them a kind of authority in the knowledge
of the place or sight visited. This authoritative standing manifests itself
when other people consult the travellers about the places the latter have
visited and the experiences they have had. The backpackers seemingly
enjoy being able to give advice about what is worth visiting to others who
have not yet visited a particular place, or when they can elaborate on the
meaning of their experiences in their lives. Similarly, the conventional
tourists can have increased social standing as authorities in what it is like to
experience a particular destination.

The trip can be a rite of passage ritual also in the eyes of the
travellers themselves. Such meaning arises from the fulfilment of a long
dream. The sense of accomplishment after completion of such a dream
may, for us personally, amount to some kind of coming of age. Many
backpackers expressed their satisfaction with the fact that at the moment,
on their travel, they are actually doing something they have been dreaming

of for a long time. The conventional tourists can have a similar sense of accomplishment when they have experienced places and sights they have been dreaming of seeing.

Another theme that emphasises travel as a rite of passage is the new perspective to our own home. On travel, we may open our eyes to pay attention to the things that are at home, and which we took for granted there. Our home place is suddenly not here; we can see it as a part of larger contexts, which from that home place itself are not so easily visible. This change of perspective is stronger, the more the Other and our experience of it differ from our home, and the longer period of time the trip takes. This is why backpackers frequently emphasise the change of perspective of home:

> Travelling makes you appreciate what you have at home (John, 26; also Sigrid, p. 243).

The conventional tourists I interviewed were less concerned about changing their perspective of home, but it was still a visible theme:

> [Travel] is change, [after that] you appreciate your home differently (Minna, 28).

Seeing our home from a new perspective requires considerable adjustment of the composition of our existential space. The comments cited here show that an aspect of this adjustment is a new clarity in our emotional ties with our home. The new perspective seems to increase our appreciation of home, but dissatisfaction can also appear, as I will discuss later.

While travel away from home can change our perspective of our home, it can also give us a new understanding of ourselves. To be removed from our familiar life-world forces us to react to new things on the basis of what we are, rather than on the basis of familiar, habitual response patterns we have established in our familiar environment. Of course, the adoption of the conventions of tourist discourse and tourist space provide us with ample opportunities to avoid action without a familiar framework, but at least sometimes we are still forced to cope without such support. Managing these situations forces us to define ourselves without much of the support we have in the familiar home. If we are successful, this increases our belief in ourselves. This is exactly the theme expressed or implied by many backpackers as the most important aspect of travel:

> I think the most important thing from this trip is the belief in yourself (Inge, 30).

This kind of travel is like Murray's (1990) vision quest, and clearly a rite of passage. Travel as a rite of passage provides us with a stronger identity; a clearer picture of who we are and ideas about what we want from our lives. Again, the experience of increase in self-confidence is more pronounced in the case of the backpackers, who are likely to experience longer periods and a greater degree of self-reliance on their travel than the conventional tourists. Thus at least four different themes of a rite of passage can be present in travel: it is a transitory experience from one social status to another, it can give a personal feeling of coming of age, it changes our relationship to our home, and it helps us to know ourselves.

Both backpacking and conventional tourism have a rite of passage character, although in the latter this character is often less pronounced. In my material this outcome is accentuated by the fact that the conventional tourism as represented in my sample is recreationally orientated, and not intended to provide deep insights to our own identity. However, an example of a situation in which a conventional tourism trip is even more clearly a rite of passage than a backpacking trip is a honeymoon trip; there is an obvious transition from one social status to another. Mostly though, while conventional tourism indeed has some characteristics of a rite of passage, backpacking travel is loaded with them. But since both can have them, it is useful to try to find out what it is in the individual travellers themselves, which makes their travel function as a transitory rite. Two such elements emerge: life situation and personality of the travellers.

At the crossroads of our lives, the changes in our social status require us to re-evaluate our identities. Hence the reach in what we do is directed towards defining it. If what we do as part of this reach is travel, it consequently has a lot to do with that re-evaluation. When young, we tend to have more of these changes in our lives, and therefore travel is a rite of passage mainly for the young. Furthermore, later in life our identity has been established to a great degree, so that the reach required, and therefore also the travel, does not need to be directed towards defining the identity. However, the critical factor is not the age but the changing life situations, which, admittedly, often depend on age. This is supported by the fact that there are always a few older backpackers, but more importantly, there are masses of young conventional tourists (like the ones I interviewed) who do not travel in order to define their identity (although I believe that many young conventional tourists do travel in order to do just that).

Not everyone who is living through a changing life situation travels. On the basis of the people I have met during my travels, I think that those who do (consciously or not) are often people who have the need to prove themselves to themselves time and again.[1] Irrespective of their age, these people consider travel as testing themselves. Their 'selves' have to be tested to prove that their identities are not founded 'on sand'. These people seem to have a strong identity already; few would probably be willing to test a weak one. The strong identity of these people does not mean an established identity. Consequently, the reach for identity remains. It is hard to understand (and is out of the scope of this work) why some people's identity becomes established while other people have a constant need to prove and test it. These latter people strive for perfection; they want to use the full potential of everything, including themselves, while the others are satisfied with less. This difference, nevertheless, appears as the difference between the extents of desired reach for the identity of each individual.

Roughly generalising, we could say that those with the desire for much reach tend to prefer a mode of travel in which the potential for reach is perceived to be greater, i.e. backpacking. The potential for these people's travel to be a rite of passage is great, as the very reason for travel has often to do with bolstering identity. People, who are happy with less reach are more content to remain largely enveloped by a tourist space. However, not all reach necessarily requires contact with the Other in order to become satisfied, and therefore a conventional tourist trip may well satisfy a large amount of reach. This kind of reach can be directed towards deeper feelings of togetherness with friends, for example. Of course, there are people who desire a lot of reach towards things that may altogether have little to do with travel (e.g. economic success). In these cases the experiences that could be characterised as rites of passage are likely to be something else than travel.

This discussion should not be understood as *the* explanation of travel as a rite of passage. For example, recurring backpacking travel often has less to do with a rite of passage than cyclical tourism. Even a single trip may contain several different phases; rough treks off the beaten track one week may reflect the reach for identity, whereas socialising with fellow travellers on the pool-side in the next is primarily reaching for social interaction. Furthermore, a single trip may not necessarily reflect our intentions that draw from our life plan.

---

[1] Most of the backpackers that I interviewed were like this. The travels of the conventional tourists I interviewed were not associated with a changing life situation, but with a vacation that facilitated the travel.

Tourist Discourse and Personal Memories

In this work I have emphasised the role of the adoption of the tourist discourse as a central framework that organises travel experiences. Despite this emphasis, I do not intend to imply that the conventions of the tourist discourse would necessarily completely determine our experience of travel. Our existential freedom to define ourselves as we wish is also present in our travel experiences; we can experience what we want. But in 'real life' this existential freedom works only in theory. Our definition of ourselves is greatly affected by the socio-cultural and material environment in which we happen to make that definition. Similarly, our freedom to experience what we want on our travel is limited by our own capabilities and the structures of travel. By purchasing travel as a product, we usually surrender our freedom to do as we wish to those structures. It is easier than creating our travel experiences right from the beginning; after all, most of us are users rather than creators. However, despite the central role of the conventions of the tourist discourse in shaping our travel experiences, these experiences still have unique personal elements in them.

The memories of a trip are often easy to recognise as derivatives from the conventions of the tourist discourse. Even the most fragmented memories become easily attached to the meanings and structures of these conventions (compare MacCannell, 1976, p. 13). These memories are clearly narratives, at least when they are communicated. Ultimately, no narrative makes sense without a discourse of which the narrative is a part. Thus the narratives need a discourse, and in the context of travel the natural discourse to adopt for the purpose is the tourist discourse. Even the memories that are not communicated always appear in a particular context. They are, for example, representations of the quaintness of the Other. In the process in which memories (fragmented or not) are placed (consciously or unconsciously) in a larger framework, stereotyping is both natural and inevitable. Stereotyping as an element of the tourist discourse provides the necessary coherence and the expressions needed:

> My afterwards impression of Turkey is its exoticness, the strangeness and presence of the Islamic culture (Satu, 28).

The memories thus receive some common denominators and in the process easily become the domains of the stereotypes adopted from the tourist discourse. In the above case the shallow experience of the Other has not changed the constitution of the Other; it is still the domain of the exotic which can be invested with the characteristics of our dreams. This is possible because in this kind of shallow immediate experience we may just have lived the stereotypes, and the Other has had little chance to speak for itself. The memories then naturally speak the language of the stereotypes also. The memories deal with the public meanings of our experiences. These public meanings are inherent in the conventions of the tourist discourse, and as we internalise the conventions we also internalise those meanings. Thus fragmented memories are reconstructed into narratives of the trip that draw primarily from the public sphere of meanings.

However, even travel within a pronounced tourist space with very similar experiences to many others, still produces very personal memories. These can have such specific meanings that they do not necessarily need support from a framework that has primarily public origins. The meanings are specific in the sense that they only have personal significance that arises from our personality and interests. Other people could judge some of these memories as being quite unimportant from the perspective of the trip as a whole:

> I remember best when in one place we were refused entry to a disco even though we were sober. Raussi got a punch on his face instead (Kaapo, 27).

> It was the time for fasting [Ramadan], and I remember my amazement at what weird customs there are. There was that cannon they used to wake people up to eat in the middle of the night. Then there was that tin pipe in the toilet seat; did we wonder what on earth its purpose could have been? (Martti, 29).

In the latter quote there are memories with public and private components. These private components in memories are so common that they clearly demonstrate that the conventions of the tourist discourse do not exclusively determine every aspect of the meanings we give to things and events while travelling. This distinction between the public and private components of memories is conceptual; there is no real distinction in experience, as the categories of public and private are opposite ends of the same continuum rather than mutually exclusive categories. We have so completely internalised the public meanings that they are always to some extent present even in our most personal meanings and experiences. The fact that we ourselves distinguish between the memories we share with other people and the memories that are exclusively our own does not really reflect the distinction between public and private memories; our own memories can be filled by public meanings. But nevertheless, not all are, thus the conventions of the tourist discourse do not have exclusive power over our experiences.

It is telling that both of the above quotations are from the Finnish conventional tourists whom I knew well. It would be natural to suppose that the backpackers would have more experiences that relate primarily to personal meanings, as their travel relies much less on a structured programme. Here my different relationship to the respective groups of interviewed people caused me to receive more personal accounts from the Finnish conventional tourists. A short-term acquaintance with some of the backpackers was simply not enough to guarantee as much common ground. Backpackers often travel alone or in pairs, therefore their accounts of their experiences are usually accounts to people who have not been sharing their experience at that very moment. It is thus harder to express deeply personal experiences, since they have to be made intelligible in some public framework first. The conventional tourists could take it for granted that I was familiar with the framework (of the events and personalities) in which the experiences took place, and knew that I would therefore understand the personal elements in those experiences. Nevertheless, I believe that the scope for deeply personal experiences is greater in backpacking. The effort to reveal them is just hampered by difficulty of communicating those personal meanings.

The importance of personal experiences in travel may be emphasised by the travellers' conscious effort to rebel against the tourist discourse. Actively seeking to pay attention to the seemingly irrelevant, and enjoying its oddness in relation to the conventions can do this. I am just thinking about that pipe inside the toilet seat. We can also deliberately ignore the tourist discourse's presentation of the Other by concentrating on some other diversionary activities like drinking and wilfully offending other travellers and local people. The conventional tourists sometimes engage themselves into this kind of rebellion in reaction to their perception that the presentation of the tourist discourse is overly artificial. An example of this would be our deliberate drunkenness on a sightseeing tour of the city of Istanbul in order to find it (the tour) at all amusing. A strategy of backpackers to try to rebel against the influence of the conventions of the backpackers discourse is to visit places that are not mentioned in the guidebooks. These are individuals who feel that their need for personal reach and experience beyond too much external mediation is not met by visiting only the places 'sanctioned' by the guidebooks. All of the backpackers I interviewed had mostly been to these 'sanctioned' places, but

I also met people who said they had used their guidebook to deliberately avoid places that were mentioned there. This is easier to do in countries where the Other is not that different from the travellers' own society, but when this is not the case, the number of people doing so is likely to decrease. Whether we are backpackers or conventional tourists, trying to gain personal experiences that derive as little as possible from the conventions of the tourist discourse can appear as conscious rebellion against those conventions.

Travel as Geography of Dreams

The idea of travel away from home is often geography of dreams. Prior to travel our images and impressions of the Other places are characterised by our willingness to project our dreams on them. The eventual experience, however, may prove inhospitable to those dreams, especially if they are based on unreasonable grounds. The immediate experience has a twofold character: on the one hand it provides the immediacy which can create an exhilarating feeling of involvement with the world (or something desired) and on the other it can make what is experienced feel very ordinary. Experiencing something we have dreamt about may thus consummate and even surpass the dream, or shatter it. An example of the latter was Steinbeck's (1962, p. 122) experience of Fargo; his experience of the place in its mundaneity was in complete opposition to his dreams about it. In a similar manner, I contemplated the relationship between our dreams and the reality of their fulfilment after spending five days on a beautiful Pacific island:

> Dreams are weird. You want them to become fulfilled, but once they are, they do not feel as wonderful as you thought they would. All the good and beautiful you expected turn out to be just quite usual with all the worries of normal everyday life. In a way you get disappointed with the contrast between a dream and real life, the contrast that you realise when you live your dream. Thus, a dream to remain a dream must be beyond our grasp (Personal diary 1988, my translation from Finnish).

The island I had visited was exactly as I had always imagined a South Pacific paradise island to be. Despite being apparently a paradise, the days there felt like normal life without much paradise-like gloss, especially since the mosquitoes did not leave me alone in the evenings.

The presence-at-hand of even a paradise gives way to its readiness-to-hand because whatever is done or experienced eventually loses its character of being something new, and turns into a mere part of the normal flow of events. The appearance of readiness-to-hand may be delayed if the travel industry envelops the tourists with surroundings and spectacles, which sustain their euphoria. Nevertheless, these travel experiences take place as part of the conventions of the tourist discourse, which often inadvertently turns the presence-at-hand of the Other into the readiness-to-hand of the features in the tour programme and tourist space (despite the travel industry's efforts to actually emphasise the presence-at-hand of the Other). In the process, some of the elements, which would facilitate reach beyond our normal day-to-day existence to the domain of dreams disappear. In other words, we just witness events or spectacles on the stage of our lives, which themselves remain largely the same. Our mosquito bites are still itchy and we are not the heroes we were in our dreams. This does not mean that our travel would necessarily be boring and miserable, it can still be experienced as worthwhile and fun, it is just that the immediately lived moments are seldom as ideal as our dreams of them. In the midst of the experience it may not feel like the manifestation of the reach we have desired, but afterwards, in our memory, the experience can transform into that. For example, afterwards the memory of my experience of the Pacific island became again peculiarly coloured by the dreams stubbornly associated with the idea of Pacific islands as paradise. Steinbeck also reports how even his mundane experience of Fargo did not have a lasting effect on how he perceived the place:

> ...I (...) paused to lick my mythological wounds. And I found with joy that the fact of Fargo had in no way disturbed my mind's picture of it. I could still think of Fargo as I always had - blizzard driven, heat-blasted, dust-raddled. I am happy to report that in the war between reality and romance, reality is not the stronger (Steinbeck, 1962, p. 122).

When we recollect and reconstruct our past experiences, it is natural to be selective and imaginative. This is helped by the fact that we tend to better remember the facts, which support our stereotypes and prior images, and that we overestimate information that correlates with our impressions and ignore what does not. Through these processes we align our memories to correspond with the dreams that preceded the experiences and set the expectations. Thus the memories of our experiences do not represent only our experiences, but also our prior dreams of those experiences. This contributes to the fact that memories tend to become golden. This happens because an essential characteristic of a memory is that it occupies a common domain with dreams, namely the past. The process in which our experiences turn into dreamlike memories exemplifies the relation between dreams and reach. They both are directed towards anything beyond the immediacy of this moment; they imply something that is not here and now, like Other places and times. Dreams are thus mental representations of our desire to reach, and also a way of reaching.

Even the hardships experienced in travel, which were a source of great distress when they happened, transform into adventure in our memories. We can detach ourselves from the harshness of the immediate involvement and see the experience as if from outside. Thus a friend of mine recollects our devastatingly unsuccessful attempt to engage in profitable black-market currency exchange in Istanbul (we ended up being cheated and lost a considerable amount of money):

> It pissed us off then, but now when you think about it afterwards, you happily accept that it was an experience to pay for (Martti, 29).

This discussion may depict too gloomy a picture of travel. My emphasis on the mundane aspects of the immediate experience is intended to pay attention to the differences between our experiences as they are dreamt of or remembered and as they are immediately experienced. Of course, the actual experiences can also be exhilarating precisely because they are lived in their immediacy. They can correspond with or contradict our dreams about them, or even be something totally unexpected. In any case, the association of motives, prior impressions, and the experiences themselves largely generate the memories of the experiences. Even the unexpected experiences are *eventually* incorporated to this framework. Because the conventions of the tourist discourse are so important in forming the framework, also the memories are closely associated with those conventions. In fact, these memories are important contributors to and sustainers of the discourse, as can be seen from the following extract of a travelogue:

> Hawaii - the island of fairytales, which every Finn has sometimes dreamt about... The lushness of the tropics, cheerfulness of the people, the wonderful tastes of new exotic fruits, and the beauty of the island immediately beyond the skyscrapers of Honolulu made at least us to dream about returning to Hawaii some day (Cantell, 1990, p. 21; my translation from Finnish).

Often this kind of 'nostalgia for the future' takes place already in the midst of the experience. We incorporate some aspects of dreaming in our immediate experience. The dream of return - a common theme of daydreaming - gives the experience additional emotional depth. It is an unconscious way to narrow the gap between our dreams and immediate experiences. Although we have experienced the object of the nostalgia already, the nostalgia may still be based on equally distorted impressions as the dreams before the experience. This testifies to the power of the frameworks in which the experiences are incorporated. One of the most powerful of such frameworks is formed by dreams.

It thus seems that our life in relation to travel is characterised by a process in which our dreams initiate travel, the travel turns into memories, and the memories transform into dreams about travel again.

Home After Travel

Some degree of culture confusion can be experienced after returning home. In practice this means that it may take a while before everything experienced at home reverts to 'normal' after the return (Gullahorn and Gullahorn, 1963; Lundstedt, 1963; Argyle, 1982; Hottola, 1999, p. 117).

For the conventional tourists (who typically travel during their vacation) this period consists mainly of brief initial relief, or even euphoria at being back home, but soon after they may find it hard to face the regular routines of the everyday. In addition, a strong contrast may exist between the euphoria experienced on travel and the perceived mundaneity of home. This is apparent from the comments about how nice it is to come back home, but how hard it is to get used to those routines from which the trip temporarily liberated us. Much of this depends on whether the travel was experienced as release or detachment; those who have to return to dull routines they do not perceive meaningful find it hard to stomach the loss of temporary freedom the travel provided. Thus people who share a similar situation at home as the unemployed Martti, or the lady who had lost her baby, could easily despair on return, prompted by the instant drop back to the unpleasant realities of home after the oblivion or probably soothing release of travel.

On the other hand, those who are happy with their everyday existence are likely to experience a delightfully fresh look at things at home on return. For a moment, at least, some things at home appear as present-at-hand. Elements from the Other can be incorporated in interests at home. For example, Erkki (a carpenter) planned to try some of the styles he had seen on his travels, and Kaapo (a geography teacher) revived his interest in geology after his trips to the lava fields of Lanzarote. This presence-at-hand may thus trigger a short period of disillusionment or euphoria at being back home, depending on our situation there.

Because a conventional tourist's experience takes only a short time, the experience of presence-at-hand on return is soon likely to wear off and life becomes 'business as usual'. Thus to extend the term culture confusion to cover these relatively brief experiences of having a fresh look at home is an overstatement in the case of conventional tourists. The presence-at-hand felt has little to do with culture, but more with the break from the normal everyday life, the break the vacation trip has facilitated. Furthermore, the only 'shock' the return is likely to cause probably relates to the loss of freedom from everyday routines. Of course, even for some conventional tourists, the trip may have been associated with extensive reach, like a pilgrimage or a love affair. In these cases the return home may be characterised by more stirred emotions, comparable with those of the backpackers.

Return from a backpacking trip, which may have been long in duration and possibly been a rite of passage, provides potential for much more change than the return from a conventional tourist trip. I remember when I returned home from my first big trip around the world, my initial euphoria was great. However, I suddenly found that the aspirations and values of my own society felt wrong. The ideals I had adopted during my trip conflicted with the ones I found at home, and I felt some degree of alienation. In time I nevertheless learned to relate my experiences to the surrounding social environment and, as a result, became better able to define the aims of my life.

Because backpacking travel can bring forth great changes in our attitudes and perspectives towards home, the presence-at-hand felt on return can have strong effects. There can be great difficulties in adjusting to the life-style of home, which so drastically differs from the life-style while travelling. The experience of the presence-at-hand of home can vary from feelings of being a little stupefied to experiencing strong alienation from the surrounding values. The strength of this reaction depends on the duration of the trip, the extent of the experiential difference between lives at home and on the trip, and on the extent to which the trip has been a rite of passage. The difference of the culture between home and the Other is not necessarily a contributing factor, since even the backpackers' experience can be so separated from the culture of the Other. The difference lies between being on the way and being home. Switching from the discourse of freedom of travel to the one of responsibilities of home is not always easy. Therefore on return the confusion (as in culture confusion) is caused by the change in the way our day-to-day living is organised, not as much by the culture, unless the practices of travel and being at home are described as culture.

There are also other aspects that cause confusion. After a long trip there can be changes that have been taking place at home while we have been away. Usually the most significant of such changes is the change in the attitudes of the people towards the travellers. Experiences of new places are held to provide knowledge, maybe even wisdom, and thus the traveller may gain status (Helms, 1988, p. 4). Nevertheless, in most conventional tourism the time spent away from home is seldom long enough to allow much change at home. Based on my personal experience, I would say that by far the most important change takes place in the travellers themselves, if the nature and duration of the trip allow this. The change in ourselves makes us see our home as present-at-hand. The change consists of the new perspectives that follow from the detachment from home, and of the new social, or even existential, role that results from the trip being a rite of passage. Thus the adjustment problems at home have more to do with the changes in ourselves than with changes in our home. In fact, an important contributor to these problems is precisely that our home, which has remained relatively unchanged, tries to reassert itself on us who have changed. Thus the initial problems that may occur in our adjustment to the life at home are consequences of our inability to smoothly integrate the perspectives and new attitudes we have got while travelling with the actual daily life at home.

A partial reason for this may be the inability to share the travel experience. I remember the frustration arising from trying to convey to my friends and relatives the profound changes in the way I saw the world and life after my first big trip around the world. I found that most of them could not relate at all to my message, which itself was hard to express in words in a way that would have satisfied me. My efforts must have sounded pathetic and cliché-ridden; I could not express my experience. People at home may have not shared similar experiences, therefore it can be futile to try to convey the meaning of what we have experienced. On a trip with travel companions, or with other travellers, it is easier to get the message through. These people have similar experiences to ours, or at least share the underlying situation from which the experiences are evaluated. Thus the meanings of these more or less shared experiences make sense to the fellow travellers, but once at home, there may suddenly be few people who would deeply grasp our experiences and the changes they have brought about in us. The meanings of these changes have to be experienced before it is possible to have even the potential to fully understand them. Returning home to find that few people can understand our experiences in the way we would like may thus be a great source of disillusionment. Not to mention a situation when the others may not even be interested.

The experience of home from a new, present-at-hand perspective is also an element in the reversal of home and reach. Initially, prior to the trip, our desire to reach is projected onto the Other. While away and suffering from disillusionment, the *locality of our existence* makes itself acutely felt. Thus our home turns into an element of reach; we dream of returning with a new attitude. After the return, that dream turns into reality while the reality of the travel turns into a memory and a dream. The bias of memory, and the dreams it generates, tend to emphasise the positive aspects of what is remembered. On the trip this makes us perceive our home as something better than we experience when we actually live there. But after the return, we warmly remember the trip and contrast it with the acutely perceived negative aspects of home, which were so easy to forget when home was just dreamt about. Thus another remarkable contributor to the adjustment problems of the return home is the discrepancy between home as it is dreamt about while away and home as it is immediately lived (Figure 10.1). Thus there surely is confusion after the return. The confusion arises from trying to place the renewed self into the framework of home that has remained largely the same. The confusion has to do with identity, just as in culture confusion that takes place on travel.

This impact of travel wears out in time, and gradually we incorporate what we have learnt into the socio-cultural context of our home.[2] Partly this amounts to readjusting to the socio-cultural system, which we, after all, have largely internalised, and fading of the feelings evoked by the travel. The impact of the reversal of home and reach that happened while away and the new insights gained through detachment from home are overshadowed by the immediate involvement with the daily tasks. In the process however, the things learned on the trip become integrated into our socio-cultural heritage in an inconspicuous way. We integrate the old and new ideas about how our lives should be lived. In the end, the travel appears as an experience that helped to define our identity and find our role in society.

---

[2] A cynic could say that this just illustrates how our society has the ability to subdue high ideals that are not concordant with its cold values associated with competitiveness.

Two Elements of Travel Experience

On travel the essential elements are on the one hand the experience of the Other, and on the other the experience of new perspectives on home. These two experiences overlap. The experience of the Other prompts the new perspectives on home, while the whole basis for the experience of the Other is home: its socio-cultural heritage and our personality it has shaped.

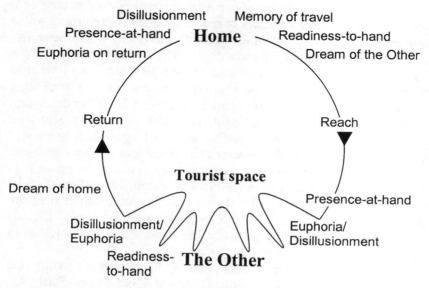

Figure 10.1 Travel as circle from home to the Other and back
The everyday life at home with its readiness-to-hand makes us dream about the Other. We think that travelling elsewhere can satisfy our reach. The presence-at-hand of the Other provides new things at which to marvel. In time those things turn more or less ready-to-hand, and prompt dreams in which the positive aspects of home are easily emphasised. On return a brief period of euphoria about the new presence-at-hand of home is experienced, but it can soon turn into some degree of disillusionment. After some time life becomes 'business as usual'. The memory of travel and the perceived readiness-to-hand of home start the cycle again. The figure illustrates and relates the psychological processes of travel that have arisen in this work.

In this light it seems that even the major search motives (search for presence-at-hand and novelty), which apparently reflect the desire to reach for the Other, are ultimately directed towards the renewal of our experience of home and the everyday life associated with it. In this pursuit the Other has thus primarily an instrumental role; the experience of the Other is sought in order to achieve improved quality of life at home. More or less consciously we perceive the experience of the Other as a vehicle which provides the necessary detachment to see our home from a new perspective.

The dialectic between home and reach provides a new perspective to travel studies. It helps us to understand not only the motivational basis of our encounter with the Other, but also the meaning of that encounter in the larger context of our lives. Indeed, this work has its emphasis on the experience of the Other, but it nevertheless gives rise to further conceptualisation of the dialectic of home and travel. The experiences of travel and home become a dialectic in which the experience of travel gives new aspects to the experience of home, which in turn creates new motives to travel. Thus the circle of travel (Figure 10.1) should really form spirals, in which each separate trip provides a new relationship between our home and us.

Framework for Tourist's Experience of the Other

I have used the distinction between conventional tourists and backpackers to highlight some differences in the experiences of different tourists. Differences were found in numerous contexts during the course of this work: compared to the conventional tourists, backpackers' motivations tend to be more self-development oriented, they travel mostly independent from any organised groups, they act within differing discourses, their experience of culture shock is more intensive, and their lives are likely to be more affected by travel.

However, the similarities between the experiences of the two groups are also numerous, and indeed significant: the motivations are largely based on the same markers, they experience the Other through a tourist space (albeit from a different one), they are similarly affected by their respective discourses, they see the same sights and take mainly similar pictures, and their experience of the Other people is largely limited to the narrow paths of institutionalised interaction. On these similarities I base my conceptual framework for tourist's experience of the Other, which incorporates the common factors affecting both of these two modes of travel. The framework evolves as follows:

When we encounter the Other, we have a certain experience of it (Figure 10.2).

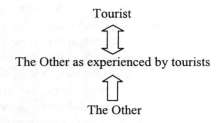

Figure 10.2 The Other as experienced by tourists

The Other is always experienced through the situation in which that experience takes place. The experience also affects ourselves (Figure 10.3).

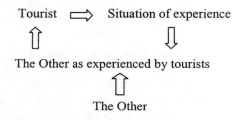

Figure 10.3 Situation of experience

The situation of experience, in turn, is affected by the process of culture confusion. At the same time the situation itself contributes to the process. Our situation, on the other hand, draws from our socio-cultural heritage and personality, through which we experience. These have impact on the culture confusion, and they are inseparable parts of what we are (Figure 10.4).

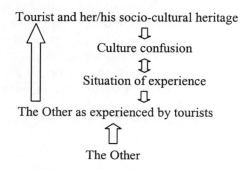

Figure 10.4 Culture confusion and the experience of the Other

The external influence by the travel industry further complicates the picture so that a result is the tourist discourse, in which the different impacts on tourist's experience interact. From this discourse emerge the myths that give meaning to the Other and the experience of it. Some of these myths are initiated, or at least sustained by the travel industry (Figure 10.5).

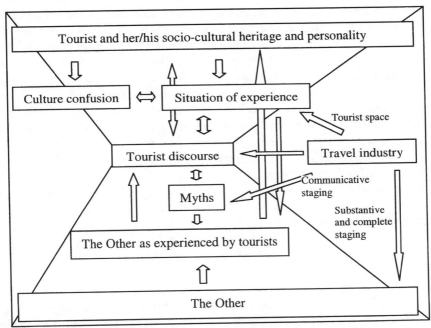

Figure 10.5 Framework for tourist's experience of the Other

We have here an illustration of the structures involved in tourist's experience of the Other. Here a short description: Our situation during travel largely derives from our *socio-cultural heritage* and *personality*, the structures created by the *travel industry* (like tourist space), and the process of *culture confusion*. Our *situation* in the experience affects the extent of our culture confusion in turn, and also on what kind of a *discourse* we operate within. That discourse provides the (Barthesian) *myths*, which largely give meanings to the *Other* and to our experience of it. Apart from the myths of the tourist discourse, the Other as experienced by tourists is also affected by the travel industry. This takes place through substantive and complete staging, which create and modify some of the features of the Other. From our situation we can also arrive at a very personal experience, which is not initially mediated through the tourist discourse. The tourist discourse is a blend of elements from the travel industry, our socio-cultural heritage, and the Other as experienced by individual tourists. Every individual experience, even if it was not mediated by the tourist discourse, eventually contributes to the tourist discourse when the experience is communicated to others. There is finally dialectic between the discourse and our socio-cultural heritage, as they both embrace each other. Outside of the scope of this work is the impact of tourist discourse on the Other itself.

Travel as circle of experience of home and the Other (Figure 10.1) illustrates the psychological processes that take place inside the minds of the travellers. In the framework for tourist's experience of the Other (Figure 10.5) those psychological processes take place in all of the input and feedback connections between our personality, culture confusion, situation of experience, the tourist discourse, myths, and the Other as experienced by tourists. The difference between the two frameworks is precisely, that the former is concerned with the *psychological processes within an individual*, whereas the latter illustrates the *structures that create the individual travel experiences*. In the following I shall conclude some of the themes of this work while I introduce the framework for tourist's experience of the Other piece by piece.

Experience – Discourse – Socio-Cultural Heritage

Every individual trip is done in relation to an existing discourse (if nothing else, the relation exists because of an intention to avoid any existing discourses). Therefore, although we may have not yet personally contributed to the discourse, we nevertheless adopt elements of the discourse created by others before us.

Our socio-cultural heritage and personality are bases from which our life situations at any given moment draw. They affect our decisions on whether or not to travel, where to travel, and how to carry it out and, mostly unconsciously: what to reach for through travel. All these decisions are made in relation to what we already know, which, in turn, is closely related to the place in which we live our daily lives. Thus, as we have seen, our experience of our own place is the catalyst to reach for other places. Whether we have a long-term dream of travel to experience the Other, or simply need to spend our vacation holiday somewhere Other, those dreams and needs seldom arise from the qualities of the Other as such. Rather, they derive from the structures and values of our own society, and from the resulting discourse in which the Other is represented to us. Thus, our ideas of what the Other is like have developed in our socio-cultural and personal contexts. This is why I have omitted the separate notion of motives from the Figure 10.5. As expressions of different kinds of reach, motives are fundamentally connected to these socio-cultural and personal contexts. After we have experienced the Other, that experience has an impact on our socio-cultural heritage and personal stock of knowledge. The impact is mediated by the tourist discourse, in which the narratives about the Other take shape. In other words, the individual experiences of the Other by visitors accumulate into a discourse, which becomes part of our socio-cultural heritage.

The formation of the tourist discourse is inevitable as soon as travellers share their experiences with others. As the exchange of ideas on any aspect of life is a significant element of human interaction, also travel as an important source of powerful experiences is naturally subjected to such an exchange. All the backpackers I interviewed emphasised the personal development they gained on their travel. Obviously the personal development is not necessarily dependent on whether the experience is communicated to others, but the communication still reflects the willingness, if not compulsion, to share a personally significant experience. It is a natural part of defining and establishing our identity in the eyes of others at home as well as of fellow travellers. Another important theme through which the backpackers contribute to the tourist discourse is sharing information with other travellers. I have already discussed how central the information passed from one traveller to another is in directing people to certain places and activities. It also demonstrates knowledge of places and things, and thus underlines the authority of those who can act as sources of such information in relation to those who do not yet possess it.

The conventional tourists also have the need to convey what they encountered on the trip to those who stayed behind. An element of this can be showing off the knowledge and experiences gained, by ostensibly just passing them on. Simply: to gain any status from the trip in the eyes of others, the others have to know about it. The main difference between my backpackers and conventional tourists arises from the fact that the latter were group tourists, who had largely shared the experience itself with familiar people. Thus for them, sharing experiences afterwards did not always have much to do with informing those who stayed behind, because many of the closest people in any case knew the experiences. Rather, mutual recollection of the shared experiences is an effective way to reinforce personal relationships. In this way, many travel experiences receive their full meaning only after they are passed on. The postcards from exotic locations, travel photographs that are shown to friends and relatives, and the enthusiastic accounts of returned travellers, all mark the consummation of travel as a quest for (new) experiences. They are our attempt to convey our consummated reach. This communication of individual experiences forms a discourse of what is worth seeing and doing, how travel changes travellers, what it is like to encounter the Other, and possibly, what the Other is like. However, this discourse mostly differs little from the discourse, which originally set the framework for the experiences.

As the collection of accounts of how and why to travel, the tourist discourse naturally contributes to, and is part of, our socio-cultural heritage. In fact, the whole concept of tourist discourse is just an expressional tool to give shape to this varied collection of ideas, which operate within our culture. It is therefore not justified to consider the tourist discourse as an independent totality that acts on individual travellers totally on its own. Of course, this should be clear right from the beginning, if the nature of the term discourse is understood correctly. Any framework which we use in making sense of the world, and in which we place our experiences, is part of some discourse. A discourse cannot determine our acts, although whatever we do as a social act, in any case is, or becomes, part of some discourse. But it is a different thing altogether to speak about the conventions of, for example, the tourist discourse. Any discourse has its core, which is more or less convention-ridden. Despite our existential freedom, we are often content to follow these conventions instead of acting from our own initiative. This is why the conventions of the tourist discourse feature so prominently in this thesis. Judging from the behaviour of all the travellers I have met, I am ready to say that these conventions largely direct the travel experience of most people. Even the people, who consciously rebel against them, are compelled to use them as the framework against which to rebel. The tourist discourse is not a cultural vacuum; it is part of our culture.

Situation of Experience

The actual purchase of the trip reflects our adaptation to our own culture. We purchase a trip that we expect to satisfy the specific need for reach we have. Depending on our personality and the aims we have for a particular trip, we may choose to become some kind of a conventional tourist, or more or less institutionalised backpackers, for example. This decision has far reaching implications on how much the infrastructure of the travel industry is going to surround us and structure our situation in our destination. But of course, our situation is not entirely dependent on the structures provided by the travel industry. There are personal elements in our experiences and the situations in which they take place. These often derive from our personality, and our willingness to experience things with as few distorting filters as possible. This is why there is the direct connection from our situation of experience to the Other as experienced by tourists in the Figure 10.5.

More often than not, however, most personal experiences take place within the conventions of the tourist discourse. Thus the distinction between private and public meanings is obscured because the former mainly operates from and within the tenets of the latter. Our willingness to incorporate the public meanings of places within our own personal experiences results in institutionalised travel. We end up in situations shared with a vast number of other visitors. If we want to emphasise the personal sphere of meanings by acquiring some distinctively personal experiences, the degree of our reliance on tourist space and explanations provided by the tourist discourse has to be smaller. Thus one of the distinguishing elements between different individual experiences of the Other is the degree of institutionalisation of those experiences. The more institutionalised the experience, the more the resulting private meanings resemble those of the public ones. Part of this institutionalisation is the fame of the attractions; places and attractions whose markers are in the stock of knowledge of a large number of people are typically experienced from an institutionalised, already well-established framework. Thus, an institutionalised experience contributes to the tourist discourse by strengthening and sustaining its already established conventions, instead of bringing new and possibly original elements into it.

The situation in which we experience the Other is greatly affected by our psychological reactions in the course of the culture confusion. Our personalities, socio-cultural heritage, and the situation of experience all, in turn, affect the extent to which the culture confusion process directs our experience. Everyone will experience the process, but at least within my interviewees it seems that in optimistic people fear and disillusionment are less severe, or even absent.[3] Optimism is likely to allow them to pay attention to the positive aspects of events, whereas the pessimists are

---

[3] Of course, the assessment of whether someone was an optimist or pessimist, was based on my own subjective judgement. Therefore I was much better equipped to make that assessment from the conventional tourists whom I knew well.

concerned about the negative and potentially negative. The optimists can better rely on and immerse themselves into their dreams, which then become an integral part of the experience. The pessimists cannot detach themselves as well from the possible insecurity, or from the mundaneity of the situations at hand.

Significant differences between our own culture and the culture of the Other also contribute to the extent of the culture confusion process, but only if we are immersed or immerse ourselves enough in the Other culture. In the most typical institutionalised travel there is insufficient time and intensity of contact to experience the whole process of culture confusion. Initially, the most inexperienced visitors may be fearful, but after a short period of time the fear is likely to change into euphoria of the presence-at-hand of the Other. Euphoria is what most visitors feel right from the beginning, and during a short stay it may well be the only emotion experienced. Many experiences during the travel and dreams entertained after the trip should be understood as results of the euphoric state of mind in which the experiences have usually taken place. Euphoria experienced on the trip can starkly contrast with our everyday experience at home, which seldom is characterised by such a feeling.

Travellers who stay longer in their destination start usually feel the disillusionment. They are largely unable to see their situation without the disillusionment caused by the limited ability to comprehend much of the surrounding events. However, conventional tourists seldom stay in their destinations long enough to become too much disillusioned.[4] Disillusionment is mostly felt by the backpackers, who travel for extended periods of time. Because they often change places in rapid succession in order to avoid boredom, their disillusionment is not necessarily based on features of a particular culture. Mostly the disillusionment arises from the exhaustion of continuously having to make an effort to conform or adjust their behaviour to the surroundings, which nevertheless differ from home. A drastic difference between the cultures of the Other and the travellers' own culture heightens this requirement. Furthermore, the routinisation of the everyday of travel gradually decreases the experience of positive presence-at-hand and the consequent euphoria. At some stage the effort of conforming and adjusting becomes strenuous and disillusionment follows.

The emotion of culture confusion at a given moment largely directs our experience of a situation at that moment. A euphoric traveller may

---

[4] On the other hand, persons with pessimistic and negative prevailing attitudes do not necessarily need a lot of time for it.

thoroughly enjoy the presence-at-hand of a situation, which a disillusioned one finds merely annoying. For example, the former may find an approach of a street vendor an exciting encounter with a local person, while the disillusioned one considers the vendor merely as another provocation.

Many Tourist Discourses

Although each different mode of travel has its own discourse, for the sake of convenience I have written about *the* touristic discourse in this work. The different varieties of travel (e.g. conventional tourism, backpacking, honeymooning, eco-tourism, adventure travel) are all expressions of differing, although strongly overlapping, tourist discourses. Despite our existential freedom to do what we want (within the limits of facticities), the conventions within the discourses of tourism are integral for the formation of the travel experience. Travellers' experiences draw primarily from these established conventions. However, our personality and socio-cultural heritage (and often economic limitations), i.e. our willingness to set out for a certain kind of travel, nevertheless has an effect on what kind of a discourse we will become part of on our travel. By choosing a mode of travel, we (mostly unconsciously) also choose the discourse within which we operate. This choice is strongly related to our life situation and to our consequent capacity to accept (and indeed, know of) different modes of travel. For the young interviewees of mine the choice of the mode of travel predominantly reflects either the search for personal development (backpacking), or search for a refreshing break from everyday routines, and especially in the case of group travel, reinforcement of the group ties (conventional tourism).

The tourist discourse in both backpacking and conventional tourism proposes that travel has a lot to do with personal development. However, there is a marked difference between this idea of the discourse and the reality of how the travel experiences are actually lived. The institutionalisation of travel has produced circumstances in which even a backpacker does not necessarily have to be much involved with the unmediated Other. But, according to the tourist discourse, it is precisely this contact with the Other that triggers the mechanisms through which the personal development should be acquired. In backpacker travel the search for personal development is nevertheless often achieved, because the critical factor in producing personal development is not the contact with the Other, but the experience of the presence-at-hand of travel.

In my material the conventional tourists were merely searching for a break from everyday life, and reinforcement of group ties with close friends. There is little concern with personal development, although it can naturally reside latently behind those more ostensible goals (as, in fact, it may do in any new experience that is sought in order to evoke presence-at-hand). Group travel has been used extensively as a means to reinforce group ties. First, travel keeps the group together and gives it common goals and experiences, which create and reinforce group identity. Second, the Other provides a background against which the significance of Us (the 'in-group') can be compared. The togetherness and high intersubjectivity within Us becomes emphasised, when it is compared to the distant and often incomprehensible Other. Thus the group tourists' experience of the Other easily serves to underscore the ties within the group, rather than educate about the Other. Of course, the extent of this unbalance depends much of the cohesion of the group prior the trip. People unfamiliar to each other and formed into a travel group, may seek the knowledge of the Other rather than ties within the group, especially if they do not get along with their travel companions. But even then, I'd suggest that the distance and separation from the Other turns the travel companionship into one of the most important travel experiences, *whether positive or negative*. On group travel, the Other has primarily an instrumental role; it facilitates the creation and reinforcement of ties within the group. It is also one of the excuses to get away from home and experience the presence-at-hand that the trip, not necessarily so much the Other, provides. This is also the most important aspect of the conventional tourism in general; to experience change, for which the exploration of the Other may sometimes be just an excuse.

Then, why do some people travel as backpackers and others as conventional tourists? Any one trip does not necessarily reflect the travellers' innermost needs and aspirations that guide their lives and the decisions they make. Rather, a single trip is an expression of the economic realities, as well as the needs and aspirations present in the very life situation that prompts that trip. Of course, those situations arise partly from the personality and from the long-term aspirations of the person. Because the first backpacking trip is essentially a rite of passage, the situation that prompts it is often associated with some kind of a change in the person's life. The mere fact that such travel takes a long time means that there must be a break from commitments that usually require presence at home (e.g. study, work). People become first-time backpackers, when their life situation calls for detachment from home in order to facilitate some kind of a quest for, or strengthening of identity. The recurring backpacking trips are then expressions of the life-style, in which the discourse of independence is prevalent.

For the conventional tourists, there does not need to be a life situation that would require this kind of identity quest.[5] Instead, their life situation allows them to use travel as a means of detaching themselves from home in order to experience change, i.e. presence-at-hand. That experience is often an end in itself, not necessarily an instrument for self-development and identity. The life situations that prompt this kind of travel are typically the yearly holidays; they allow and encourage the temporary detachment from home in order to recover and recreate. Most of the backpackers I interviewed had travelled before as conventional tourists. Also from my own experience I know, that even though as a young backpacker I had detested conventional tourists, just a few months later I found myself participating in such form of tourism. The life situations change, and the individual trips tend to reflect the situations from which the very trip arises.

Institutionalisation of the Discourses No discourse can exist without more than one participant. An important characteristic of discourses is that as they become commonly shared, they become institutionalised. In the case of different tourist discourses they become established ways to act out our desire for reach. As such they have evolved to cater for different kinds of reach. The clearest example of this tendency is the institutionalisation of the backpacker discourse. Initially it developed as an 'anti-discourse'; it was supposed to free the travellers from the dependence on the touristic infrastructure, which so forcefully separated the travellers from the locals by the means of the tourist space. But eventually backpacking became just another institutionalised discourse with its own public meanings which were eventually shared by millions of travellers journeying around the world. Now backpacking is an institutionalised brand of tourism that caters for those who (paradoxically) want to experience travel without discourses imposed on them. Nevertheless, its own discourse is the one of authentic personal experiences.

One of the initial criteria that were used to create the distinction between backpackers and conventional tourists here was the different degree of institutionalisation of these two types of tourism. In the course of the thesis it has appeared that this difference has not proved to be nearly as

---

[5] Although I am not trying to deny that possibility. Not all people want to, or perceive themselves as capable of travelling as backpackers.

significant as initially thought. Cohen's (1972) distinction between institutionalised and non-institutionalised travellers is clearly outdated, because the segment he distinguished as non-institutionalised (explorers, drifters, i.e. various types of backpackers) has since become substantially institutionalised. All the backpackers I interviewed were institutionalised travellers; they relied strongly on the infrastructure created specifically for backpackers, and avoided places where they would not have been able to find such facilities. This is the mainstream of backpacking. In my travels I have met only few individuals, who could still be characterised as genuine explorers (or drifters, which are not tourists at all), who would go where finding accommodation is not guaranteed by the reassuring mention in a guidebook or by other travellers. Furthermore, even these few genuine explorers are at some stage of their travel forced to use the services and facilities that are touristic institutions like airlines and hostels. Thus at least part of their travel is so similar to institutionalised travel, that it is often impossible to make the distinction without getting familiar with the explorers' trip as a whole. On these grounds I'd say that the discourses of conventional tourism and backpacking are both institutionalised. On the fringe of backpacking, there are some exploration-oriented travellers who sometimes explore places outside the effects of the institutionalisation of travel. But the mainstream of backpacking, represented in my interview material, is heavily institutionalised.

The travel industry benefits from the institutionalisation of discourses, and therefore it is closely attached to this institutionalisation. The travel industry is both an indication of, and a contributor to, the institutionalisation. The institutionalisation usually means that it becomes possible for the travel industry to carve out products, commodities that contain the elements from the discourses. The results are not only packaged holiday trips for relaxation and adventure, for example, but also specific infrastructure for the tourists, and all kinds of guidebooks and accessories designed for their consumption. The natural consequence is advertising which both creates and uses elements of those discourses in its attempt to sell products. For example, the fact that travel has become an institutionalised means of self-development is utilised by the travel industry. It has realised the importance of the prospect of self-development for the motivation of potential travellers and actively sustains the idea in travel advertising.

There are some forms of counter-reaction to this institutionalisation of most kinds of tourism. In the previous chapter I presented the ways in which this rebellion appears, like actively seeking to pay attention to the seemingly irrelevant, concentrating on an activity that has little to do with the presentation of the Other, and avoiding 'touristic' places. Here are three more strategies of this rebellion. First, a backpacking trip can be seen as an unnecessarily inconvenient ordeal, since it can be perceived to offer just another kind of set of institutionalised experiences. This was expressed by some conventional tourists as one of the reasons why they thought that a conventional tourist trip would deliver what they expected from travel at least as well as a backpacking trip, and with less effort. Conventional tourism is adopted and used as a playground, in which various roles are to be played and the play enjoyed with little or no concern about the Other as such. The Other remains just a pleasant backdrop, the only requirement for it is that it must be there, and that it presents itself as pleasant. The futility of the search for authenticity in the Other is readily recognised, but the social play accompanied by the travel experiences is nevertheless enjoyed.[6] This is what in tourism research literature has been called 'postmodern' tourism.

The second strategy to rebel and to search for something 'real' is to indulge in more and more adventurous experiences, as the popularity of white-water rafting, bungey-jumps, and abseiling suggest. These adrenalin-pumping experiences are pointedly authentic in the sense that they directly address our fears and the reach for our limits. We can feel the authenticity immediately; there is nothing inauthentic in our encounter with the force of gravity. Any concern with the Other has been replaced by the attempt to expand our psychological reach (i.e. conquering our fears, an important aspect of self-development). The problem is that these experiences require a considerable extent of preparation so that the presence of a suitably oriented industry and thus instant institutionalisation is inevitable. Also the expenses involved are a limiting factor for many.

The third strategy is the above-mentioned genuine exploration. This reflects the need to personally experience a genuine unmediated Other. The problem is that not many people have the persistence and capacity to withstand the inconveniences associated with travelling on rugged areas with few or no facilities for travellers.

I think that these three modes of travel are likely to gain popularity in the near future. As this happens, increasingly ingenious modes will develop

---

[6] This reflects the third strategy of distancing oneself from the routines of everyday life, as described by Cohen and Taylor (1976, p. 34). The three strategies for this distancing are: self-consciousness, consciousness of this self consciousness, and consciously reinvesting in the routine. The same strategies could easily be applied in managing a superficial experience of travel. The third strategy clearly applies to tourists just described in the text.

to counteract institutionalisation, while the travel industry strives ever harder to commodify and thus institutionalise them.

The Other as Experienced by Tourists

The features of a place that we experience as tourists are more or less representations of the ideas about the Other which operate within the tourist discourse. In other words, how the tourists experience the Other for most people arises less from the Other itself than from the ideas and dreams projected on it. This projection is done by the tourists themselves, and by the deliberate and creative staging by the travel industry. Thus the Other of our experience is not an objective entity that awaits clear definition, but a collection of images and experiences which takes shape according to the framework we have adopted.

The places and people of the Other, and even a good deal of our experiences of it, rarely remain unaffected by the travel industry. The industry builds hotels, stages performances, takes us to places that are worth seeing, and organises our program there. The substantive changes the travel industry generates are accompanied by communicative manipulation, which is part of the tourist discourse. Of course, there is no organised conspiracy that aims for the commercialisation of our experience of the Other, but nevertheless, any institutionalised tourist discourse is powerful in making this happen. The impact caused by the substantive intervention of the travel industry in what the Other is like for tourists is incorporated in the tourist discourse. This, together with the amount of 'discursional propaganda' the tourists are exposed to, makes it extremely hard for conventional tourists to experience the Other without the framework of the conventions of the tourist discourse. If this institutionalisation of the way in which the tourists encounter the Other decreases, and the number of mediating filters consequently diminishes, the possibilities for genuinely personal experiences increase. However, few tourists travel in a way that would facilitate this; even the backpackers I interviewed had adopted the institutionalised backpacker discourse. The genuinely personal experiences mostly happen by surprise, as a consequence of some unforeseen circumstances, that temporarily dissolve tourist space and the conventions of the tourist discourse. Also the power of a strong individual personality can sometimes attach meanings to things in a way that does not immediately find correspondence within the tourist discourse. Nevertheless, it may be hard to express this to others without recourse to the tourist discourse.

The tourist's experiences of the Other contribute back to the tourist discourse. Same kind of interaction happens between individuals and their society. The impact of one tourist's experience on the tourist discourse is not likely to be great, but as in the case of the impact of individuals on society, there are always a few individuals whose impact can have a significant effect. Such people could be writers, whose experiences become common markers through wide distribution of their accounts (e.g. novels, guidebooks).[7] Most of us contribute by sharing our experiences with others. Thus the tourist discourse encompasses and is formed by the sum of individual travel experiences. But not only this, the impact from the travel industry, both direct through implantation of myths in travellers' minds, and indirect through the containment of the tourists experiences, is very important in forming the discourse.

Because the individual experiences of travellers, the impact of the travel industry, and the Other itself are so inherently tied to one another, it is difficult to say which of these elements that form the tourist discourse is the most important. The Other itself is weaker than the travel industry and the individual experiences; although it contains the initial reason for the travellers and the industry to become involved, it is often overtaken by the processes initiated by the industry and travellers. Sometimes the travel industry even creates or seeks to create the Other, which then has little reference to anything but dreams. This is the case with various fantasylands; the Other does not necessarily refer to a particular place or people, but to a more or less imaginary narrative. Thus the Other itself is often merely instrumental from the perspective of operating tourism as an industry. There would not be many individual experiences without the travel industry, however. It creates the means to travel. On the other hand, the travel industry would be powerless, if its 'propaganda' would not be sustained in the individual accounts of travel experiences. Therefore these two are probably equally, and most significantly important in forming the tourist discourse. It is interesting to notice the paradox that, although the experience of the Other is a central aim of travel, the Other itself can be a surprisingly small contributor to the actual travel experience.

---

[7] Some guidebooks invite feedback from travellers; this is another way in which single experiences can greatly contribute to public knowledge and thus to the tourist discourse.

How to Experience Myths and the Geography of Dreams

In the 'Barthesian' meaning of the term myth used in this work, any discourses are complex sedimentations of myths because of the symbolism inherent in them. The discourses are where these myths originate, reside, and become meaningful. The myths tell us what to expect from our experiences and how to see the Other, they convey the public meanings that our experiences are expected to have. Examples of myths are the idea that the exotic Other is a survivor from a past era, and that our encounter with that Other is a certain means of self-development. A way in which the travel industry creates and reinforces myths is advertising. Advertising makes the myths it presents into integral parts of the tourist discourse. A peculiar characteristic of myths is that they are largely unconscious symbol systems. Their conscious disclosure requires a reflective and informed mind, and even then the task is not always easy.

This would, however, be useful, because the myths are statements about the prevailing 'realities'. They are statements, which usually express a viewpoint on the Other. If we as tourists take that viewpoint as granted without reflection, we merely consume the Other as it is presented to us, rather than create our own personal relationship to it. On the other hand, by recognising the myths and the discourses that create them, our awareness of the sense of place of the Other would be greatly increased. We would still be likely to have rather shallow knowledge of the Other and remain outsiders, but at least we would have personally deconstructed an institutionalised presentation of the Other. This would be a personal element in our experience and it would create some sort of a personal relationship with the Other, because of the feeling that we have been able to see through the communicative staging. Then again, in an ostensibly artificial destination, an essential element in enjoying it can be exactly the opposite; the enjoyment is more likely, if we adopt and participate in the myths that are supposed to give meaning to the place and the experience of it. But even this can be done in a reflective mode, by recognising the importance of the myths in providing the desired experience. In this way it becomes possible to consciously play the role that the myths designate to a happy visitor. The exposure of the myths involved in a travel experience is exactly what cynical travellers who feel contempt for the 'ordinary tourist' (who is always someone else) may do. It is their strategy to elevate themselves above the other tourists. But we should get beyond this disdain, to the enjoyment of solving a puzzle in which the myths, the Other, and our experience are the pieces.

These are the strategies to participate into the geography of dreams. They provide an answer to people who see famous sights and end up wondering 'so what?' Optimally, the experience of places and sights should teach us to recognise the structures, which make us experience something the way we do. If those places and sights do not live up to the expectations the narratives of the tourist discourse have aroused in us, we could still take delight in examining those narratives and discerning the processes in which they are created. Ultimately, this examination could be furthered to the examination of self. Our own reactions and experiences are also results of certain structures and circumstances that have contributed to what we have become. For me, the ultimate goal in phenomenology is to learn to be able to recognise the role of these structures and circumstances in our experience, and thus achieve better knowledge, and maybe even betterment, of ourselves.

11 Home, Reach and the Experience of the Other: Experience of Place

In this work the concern with tourist's experie... appeared as contact with the Other. In travel the experience of p... encompasses the experience of the Other, and *vice versa*. Thus the role of place in allowing us to develop the dialectic between home and the Other is central; we need a place away from home to accommodate the representation of the Other, our home place could not do it, because we associate it with familiar things. In travel we use the experience of the new place as a vehicle for reaching for the Other, whether this Other occupies spatial, or/and another dimension(s) of our existential space. Of course, the encounters with some elements of the Other do not necessarily require as much spatial reach as to demand travel away from home. However, without the change of place associated with travel it would not be easy to become sensitive to whatever Other there may be close to home. In the everyday life at home we tend to exclude the Other from our natural attitude; it is not normally noticed. The change of place in travel prompts us to 'tune' ourselves to become sensitive to the Other. Doing so is a part of the discourse of travel that we adopt; we are supposed to do so.

The tourist's experience of place is thus instrumental to the experience of the Other, but the experience of the Other is not an end in itself either. The Other is sought to arrive at situations in which we reach for new experiences, which are the ultimate goals of travel. The presence-at-hand of the Other provides these situations; things (physical, people, relations, ideas, etc.) that are encountered present themselves (or are presented to us) in a new, unaccustomed way. This is reach, which in travel is ostensibly directed to new places and the Other, but in the end drives for new experiences in various dimensions of our existential space. We reach for presence-at-hand, which is sought to provide change from and balance to the readiness-to-hand of home. Thus travel is a part of our attempt to define ourselves in the world and find our place in it. This can occur because travel forces us to construct new relations between the world and ourselves. Much of the discussion in this work has implied that the Other is defined through Our concepts and categories. This does not exclude the

273

the Other is used to define ourselves. The way we make sense of
...ld is based on this duality.

Our need to find a balance between home and reach, and the
...nsequent dynamics of readiness-to-hand and presence-at-hand, creates
the conceptual basis to express travel as dialectics between home and the
Other. These concepts of humanistic geography are thus a key in creating
the framework of travel as circle of experience of home and the Other
(Figure 10.1). This conceptualisation places a great deal of emphasis on the
processes that take place inside a tourist's mind. This clearly goes beyond
post-structural analysis on travel as consumption of commodities with
certain politics and power structures. To complement this personal
perspective, I have proposed a framework for tourist's experience of the
Other (Figure 10.5). The aspects that affect tourist's experience of the
Other and their interrelations are illustrated in it. This is to underline the
fact that even the most personal experiences and meanings do not appear
without larger contexts.

Thus the work largely follows the post-structural idea of tourism as
consumption of the commodified Other. But the notion of travel as
balancing between home and reach takes the analysis beyond this. The need
to reach for the Other arises from personal dreams and wishes. These, in
turn, are connected to the effort of making life as meaningful as possible.
Thus travel as reach for the Other involves the evaluation of personal
values. In this process the Other becomes woven into the web of personal
meanings; it is not a mere commodified product for tourist consumption.
We use the Other and the place it occupies for defining ourselves.

Bibliography

Abler, Ronald F., Marcus, Melvin G. and Olson, Judy M. (eds) (1992), *Geography's Inner Worlds: Pervasive Themes in Contemporary American Geography*, Rutgers University Press, New Brunswick.

Adler, Judith (1985), 'Youth on the Road: Reflections on the History of Tramping', *Annals of Tourism Research*, vol. 12, pp. 335-354.

Adler, Peter S. (1975), 'The Transitional Experience: An Alternative View of Culture Shock', *Journal of Humanistic Psychology*, vol. 15, pp. 13-23.

Agnew, John A. and Duncan, James S. (1989), 'Introduction', in Agnew, John A. and Duncan, James S. (eds), *The Power of Place: Bringing together geographical and sociological imagination*, Unwin Hyman, Boston, pp. 1-8.

Albers, Patricia C. and James, William R. (1983), 'Tourism and the Changing Photographic Image of the Great Lakes Indians', *Annals of Tourism Research*, vol. 10, pp. 123-148.

Albers, Patricia C. and James, William R. (1988), 'Travel Photography: A Methodological Approach', *Annals of Tourism Research*, vol. 15, pp. 134-158.

Anastasopoulos, Petros G. (1992), 'Tourism and Attitude Change: Greek Tourists Visiting Turkey', *Annals of Tourism Research*, vol. 19, pp. 629-642.

Anderson, K. (1991), *Vancouver's Chinatown: Radical Discourse in Canada 1875-1980*, McGill-Queen's University Press, Montreal.

Ap, John (1992), 'Residents Perceptions on Tourism Impacts', *Annals of Tourism Research*, vol. 19, pp. 665-690.

Argyle, Michael (1982), 'Inter-Cultural Communication', in Bochner, Stephen (ed), *Cultures in Contact: Studies in Cross-Cultural Interaction*, Pergamon Press, Oxford, pp. 61-79.

Ateljevic, Irena (2000), 'Circuits of tourism: Stepping Beyond the Production/Consumption Dichotomy', *Tourism Geographies*, vol. 27, pp. 369-388.

Baldwin, Jeff (2000), 'Tourism development, wetland degradation and beach erosion in Antigua, West Indies', *Tourism Geographies* vol. 27, pp. 193-218.

Barnes, Trevor J. and Duncan, James S. (eds) (1992), *Writing Worlds: Discourse, text and metaphor in the representation of landscape*, Routledge, London.

Barthes, Roland (1972), *Mythologies*, Jonathan Cape, London.

Barthes, Roland (1977), *Image, Music, Text*, Hill and Wang, New York.

Berghe, Pierre L. van den (1994), *Quest for the Other: Ethnic Tourism in San Cristobal, Mexico*, University of Washington Press, Seattle.

Bichel, Peter (1971), *Stories for Children*, Calder and Boyars, London.

Bochner, Stephen (ed) (1982), *Cultures in Contact: Studies in Cross-Cultural Interaction*, Pergamon Press, Oxford.

Bollnow, O. F. (1967), 'Lived-Space', in Lawrence, N. and O'Connor D. (eds), *Readings in Existential Phenomenology*, Prentice Hall, Englewood Cliffs, pp. 178-186.

Boorstin, Daniel (1972), *The Image: A Guide to Pseudo-Events in America*, Atheneum, New York.

Brett, David (1996), *The Construction of Heritage*, Cork University Press, Cork.

Brewer, Jeffrey D. (1984), 'Tourism and Ethnic Stereotypes: Variations in a Mexican Town', *Annals of Tourism Research*, vol. 11, pp. 487-501.

Britton, S. (1991), 'Tourism, capital, and place: towards a critical geography of tourism'. *Environment and Planning : Society and Space*, vol. 9, pp. 451-478.

Bruner, Edward M. and Kirschenblatt-Gimblett, Barbara (1994), 'Maasai on the Lawn: Tourist Realism in East Africa', *Cultural Anthropology*, vol. 9, pp. 435-470.

Bruner, Edward M. (1991), 'Transformation of Self in Tourism', *Annals of Tourism Research*, vol. 18, pp. 238-250.

Bullington, Jennifer and Karlsson, Gunnar (1984), 'Introduction to Phenomenological Psychological Research', in *Scandinavian Journal of Psychology*, vol. 25. pp. 51-63.

Burgess, Jaquelin and Wood, Peter (1988), 'Decoding Docklands: Place Advertising and Decision-Making Strategies of the Small Firm', in Eyles, John and Smith, David M. (eds), *Qualitative methods in Human Geography*, Polity Press, Padstow, pp. 94-117.

Butler, Richard W. (1980), 'The Concept of Tourist Area Cycle of Evolution: Implications for Management of Resources', in *Canadian Geographer*, vol. 24, pp. 5-12.

Butler, Richard W. (2000), 'Tourism and the environment: a geographical perspective', *Tourism Geographies*, vol. 27, pp. 337–358.

Buttimer, Anne (1976), 'Grasping the dynamism of lifeworld', in *Annals of the Association of American Geographers*, vol. 66, pp. 277-292.

Buttimer, Anne (1980), 'Home, Reach, and the Sense of Place', in Buttimer, Anne and Seamon, David (eds), *The Human Experience of Space and Place*, Croom Helm, London, pp. 166-187.

Buttimer, Anne and Seamon, David (eds) (1980), *The Human Experience of Space and Place*, Croom Helm, London.

Calvino, Italo (1974), *Invisible Cities*, Secker and Warburg, London.

Cater, E. (1993), 'Ecotourism in the third world: problems for sustainable tourism development,' in *Tourism Management*, vol. 14, pp. 85-90.

Chon, Kye-Sung (1991), 'Tourism Destination Image Modification Process: Marketing Implications', *Tourism Management*, vol. 12, pp. 68-72.

Clarke, Jackie (1992), 'A Marketing Spotlight on the Youth 'Four S's' Consumer', *Tourism Management*, vol. 13, pp. 321-327.

Clifford, James (1986), 'Introduction: Partial Truths', in Clifford, James and Marcus, George (eds), *Writing Culture: the Poetics and Politics of Ethnography*, University of California Press, Berkeley, pp. 1-26.

Clifford, James and Marcus, George (eds) (1986), *Writing Culture: the Poetics and Politics of Ethnography*, University of California Press, Berkeley.

Cohen, Eric (1972), 'Toward a Sociology of International Tourism', *Social Research*, vol. 39, pp. 164-182.

Cohen, Eric (1974), 'Who is a tourist? A conceptual clarification', *Sociological Review*, vol. 22, pp. 527-555.

Cohen, Eric (1979a), 'A Phenomenology of Tourist Experiences', *Sociology*, vol. 13, pp. 179-201.

Cohen, Eric (1979b), 'Rethinking the Sociology of Tourism', *Annals of Tourism Research*, vol. 6, pp. 18-35.

Cohen, Eric (1982), 'Mariginal Paradises: Bungalow Tourism on the Islands of Southern Thailand', *Annals of Tourism Research*, vol. 9, pp. 189-228.

Cohen, Eric (1985), 'The Tourist Guide: The Origins, Structure and Dynamics of a Role', *Annals of Tourism Research*, vol. 12, pp. 5-29.

Cohen, Eric (1988a), 'Traditions in the Qualitative Sociology of Tourism', *Annals of Tourism Research*, vol. 15, pp. 29-46.

Cohen, Eric (1988b), 'Authenticity and Commoditization in Tourism', *Annals of Tourism Research*, vol. 15, pp. 371-386.

Cohen, Eric (1989), '"Primitive and Remote": Hill Tribe Trekking in Thailand', *Annals of Tourism Research*, vol. 16, pp. 30-61.

Cohen, Eric (1992), 'Pilgrimage Centers: Concentric and Excentric', *Annals of Tourism Research*, vol. 19, pp. 33-50.

Cohen, Eric, Nir, Yeshayahu and Almagor, Uri (1992), 'Stranger-Local Interaction in Photography', *Annals of Tourism Research*, vol. 19, pp. 213-233.

Cohen, Stanley and Taylor, Laurie (1976), *Escape Attempts: The Theory and Practice of Resistance to Everyday Life*, Allen Lane, London.

Cook, Ian G. (1981), 'Consciousness and the Novel: Fact or Fiction in the Works of D.H. Lawrence', in Pocock, Douglas C. D. (ed), *Humanistic Geography and Literature: Essays of the Experience of Place*, Croom Helm, London, pp. 66-84

Cooper, C.P. and Ozdil, I. (1992), 'From Mass to "Responsible" Tourism: the Turkish Experience', in *Tourism Management*, vol. 13, pp. 377-386.

Cooper, Chris and Jackson, Stephen (1989), 'Destination Life Cycle: The Island of Man Case Study', in *Annals of Tourism Research*, vol. 16, pp. 377-398.

Couclelis, Helen (1992), 'Location, Place, Region, and Space', in Abler, Ronald F., Marcus, Melvin G. and Olson, Judy M. (eds), *Geography's Inner Worlds: Pervasive Themes in Contemporary American Geography*, Rutgers University Press, New Brunswick, pp. 215-233.

Craik, Jennifer (1991), *Resorting to Tourism: Cultural Policies for Tourist Development in Australia*, Allen and Unwin, Sydney.

Crompton, John L. (1979), 'Motivations for Leisure Vacation', *Annals of Tourism Research*, vol. 6, pp. 408-424.

Crystal, Eric (1977), 'Tourism in Toraja (Sulawesi, Indonesia)', in Smith, Valene L. (ed), *Hosts and Guests: The Anthropology of Tourism*, University of Pensylvania Press, pp. 109-125.

Culler, Jonathan (1981), 'Semiotics of Tourism', *American Journal of Semiotics* vol. 1, pp. 127-140.

D'Amore, Louis J. (1993), 'A code of ethics and guidelines for socially and environmentally responsible tourism', *Journal of Travel Research*, vol. 31, pp. 64-66.

Daniels, Stephen (1985), 'Arguments for a Humanistic Geography', in Johnston, R. J. (ed), *The Future of Geography*, Methuen, London, pp. 143-158.

Daniels, Stephen (1992), 'The Implications of Industry: Turner and Leeds', in Barnes, Trevor J. and Duncan, James S. (eds), *Writing Worlds: Discourse, text and metaphor in the representation of landscape*, Routledge, London, pp. 38-49.

Daniels, Stephen and Cosgrove, Denis (1993), 'Spectacle and Text: Landscape Metaphors in Cultural Geography', in Duncan, James and Ley, David (eds), *Place/Culture/Representation*, Routledge, London, pp. 57-77.

Dann, Graham M. S. (1977), 'Anomie, Ego-enhancement and Tourism', *Annals of Tourism Research*, vol. 4, pp. 184-194.

Dann, Graham M. S. (1981), 'Tourism Motivation: An Appraisal', *Annals of Tourism Research*, vol. 8, pp. 187-219.

Dann, Graham M. S. (1992), 'Travelogs and the Management of Unfamiliarity', in *Journal of Travel Research* vol. 30, pp. 59-63.

Dann, Graham M.S. (1996), 'The Language of Tourism: A Sociolinguistic Perspective', Cab International, Walkingford.

Dann, Graham and Nash, Dennison and Pearce, Philip (1988), 'Methodology in Tourism Research', *Annals of Tourism Research*, vol. 15, pp. 1-28.

Dear, Michael (1988), 'The postmodern challenge: reconstructing human geography', *Transactions, Institute of British Geographers*, vol. 13, pp. 262-274.

Deleuze, Gilles (1994) (orig. 1968), *Difference and Repetition*, Columbia University Press.

Demars, Stanford E. (1990), 'Romanticism and American National Parks', *Journal of Cultural Geography*, vol. 11, pp. 17-24.

Desmond, Jane C. (1999), *Staging Tourism: Bodies on Display from Waikiki to Sea World*, The University of Chicago Press, Chicago.

Dogan, Hasan Zafer (1989), 'Forms of Adjustment: Sociocultural Impacts of Tourism', *Annals of Tourism Research*, vol. 16, pp. 216-236.

Donovan, Jenny (1988), '"When you're ill, you gotta carry it": Health and Illness in the Lives of Black People in London', in Eyles, John and Smith, David M. (eds), *Qualitative methods in Human Geography*, Polity Press, Padstow, pp. 180-196.

Draper, Dianne and Kariel, Herbert G. (1990), Future of Tourist Environments, *Journal of Cultural Geography*, vol. 11, pp. 139-155.

Duncan, James (1993), 'Sites of Representation: Place, Time and the Discourse of the Other', in Duncan, James and Ley, David (eds), *Place/Culture/Representation*, Routledge, London, pp. 39-56.

Duncan, James S. (1978), 'The Social Construction of Unreality: An Interactionist Approach to the Tourist's Cognition of Environment', in Ley, David and Samuels, Marwyn (eds), *Humanistic Geography: Prospects and Problems*, Croom Helm, London, pp. 269-282.

Duncan, James and Ley, David (eds) (1993), *Place/Culture/Representation*, Routledge, London.

Durkheim, Emile (1976), *The Elementary Forms of Religious Life: A Study in Religious Sociology* (orig. 1915), Allen and Unwin, London.

Eade, John (1992), 'Pilgrimage and Tourism at Lourdes, France', *Annals of Tourism Research*, vol. 19, pp. 18-32.

Eagles, Paul F. J. (1992), 'The Travel Motivations of Canadian Ecotourists', *Journal of Travel Research*, vol. 31, pp. 3-7.

Echtner, C.M. and J.R. Brent Ritchie (1991), 'The meaning and measurement of destination image', in *Journal of Tourism Studies*, vol. 2, pp. 2-12.

Edensor, Tim (2000), 'Staging Tourism: Tourists as Performers', *Annals of Tourism Research*, vol. 27, pp. 322-344.

Entrikin, J. Nicholas (1976), 'Contemporary humanism in geography', in *Annals of the Association of American Geographers*, vol. 66, pp. 615-632.

Entrikin, J. Nicholas (1991), *The Betweeness of Place: Towards a Geography of Modernity*, Macmillan, Worcester.

Evans, Mel (1988), 'Participant Observation: The Researcher as Research Tool', in Eyles, John and Smith, David M. (eds), *Qualitative methods in Human Geography*, Polity Press, Padstow, pp. 197-218.

Evans-Pritchard, Deirdre (1989), 'How "They" See "Us": Native American Images of Tourists', *Annals of Tourism Research*, vol. 16, pp. 89-105.

Eyles, John (1988), 'Interpreting the Geographical World: Qualitative Approaches in Geographical Research', in Eyles, John and Smith, David M. (eds), *Qualitative methods in Human Geography*, Polity Press, Padstow, pp. 1-16.

Eyles, John and Smith, David M. (eds) (1988), *Qualitative methods in Human Geography*, Polity Press, Padstow.

Fabian, Johannes (1983), *Time and the Other: How Anthropology Makes Its Object*, Columbia University Press, New York.

Fakeye, Paul C. and Crompton, Jonh R. (1991), 'Image Differences Between Prospective, First-Time, and Repeat Visitors to the Lower Rio Grande Valley', *Journal of Travel Research*, vol. 30, pp. 10-16.

Farrell, Bryan H. (1979), 'Tourism's Human Conflicts: Cases from the Pacific', *Annals of Tourism Research*, vol. 6, pp. 122-136.

Farrell, Bryan H. (1982), *Hawaii, the Legend That Sells*, The University Press of Hawaii, Honolulu.

Farrell, Bryan H. and Runyan, Dean (1991), 'Ecology and Tourism', *Annals of Tourism Research*, vol. 18, pp. 26-40.

Fell, Joseph   (1979), *Heideigger and Sartre: an essay on being and place*, Columbia University Press, New York.

Fennell, David A. (1999), *Ecotourism: An Introduction*, Routledge, London.

Filmer, Paul, Phillipson, Michael, Silverman, David and Walsh, David (eds) (1972), *New Directions of Sociological Theory*, Collier and MacMillan Publishers Limited, London.

Folch-Serra, M. (1989), 'Geography and post-modernism: Linking humanism and development studies', *The Canadian Geographer*, vol. 33, pp. 66-75.

Fridgen, Joseph D. (1984), 'Environmental Psychology and Tourism', *Annals of Tourism Research*, vol. 11, pp. 19-39.

Furnham, Adrian (1984), 'Tourism and Culture Shock', *Annals of Tourism Research*, vol. 11, pp. 41-57.

Furnham, Adrian and Bochner, Stephen (1982), 'Social Difficulty in a Foreign Culture: an Empirical Analysis of Culture Shock', in Bochner, Stephen (ed), *Cultures in Contact: Studies in Cross-Cultural Interaction*, Pergamon Press, Oxford, pp. 161-198.

Gale, Stephen and Olsson, Gunnar (eds) (1979), *Philosophy in Geography*, D. Reidel Publishing Company, Dordrecht.

Gee, Chuck Y., Choy, Dexter J. L. and Makens, James C. (1989), *The Travel Industry*, Van Nostrand Reinhold, New York.

Gennep, Arnold van (1965) (Orig. 1908), *The Rites of Passage*, Routledge and Kegan Paul, London.

Gergen, Kenneth J. and Gergen, Mary M. (1986), *Social Psychology*, Springer Verlag, New York.

Gibson, Edward (1978), 'Understanding the Subjective Meanings of Places', in Ley, David and Samuels, Marwyn (eds), *Humanistic Geography: Prospects and Problems*, Croom Helm, London, pp. 138-154.

Godkin, Michael A. (1980), 'Identity and Place: Clinical Applications Based on Notions of Rootedness and Uprootedness', in Buttimer, Anne and Seamon, David (eds), *The Human Experience of Space and Place*, Croom Helm, London, pp. 73-85.

Goodall, Brian (1987), *The Penguin Dictionary of Human Geography*, Penguin Books, London.

Goossens, Cees (2000), 'Tourism information and pleasure motivation', *Annals of Tourism Research*, vol. 27, pp. 301-321.

Gordon, Ian and Goodall, Brian (2000), 'Localities and tourism', *Tourism Geographies*, vol. 27, pp. 290-311.

Gottlieb, Alma (1982), 'Americans' Vacations', *Annals of Tourism Research*, vol. 9, pp. 165-187.

Gould, Peter and Olsson, Gunnar (eds) (1982), *A Search for the Common Ground*, Pion Limited, London.

Graburn, Nelson (1977), 'Tourism: The Sacred Journey', in Smith, Valene L. (ed), *Hosts and Guests: The Anthropology of Tourism*, University of Pensylvania Press, pp. 17-31.

Graburn, Nelson (1983), 'The Anthropology of Tourism', *Annals of Tourism Research*, vol. 10 , pp. 9-33.

Greenwood, Davydd J. (1977), 'Culture by the Pound', in Smith, Valene L. (ed), *Hosts and Guests: The Anthropology of Tourism*, University of Pensylvania Press, pp. 129-138.

Gregory, Derek (1978), *Ideology, Science and Human Geography*, Hutchinson, London.

Guelke, Leonard (1981), 'Idealism', in Harvey, Milton E. and Holly, Brian P. (eds), *Themes in Geographic Thought*, Croom Helm, London, pp. 133-147.

Guelke, Leonard (ed.) (1986), *Geography and Humanistic Knowledge*, Waterloo Lectures in Geography, vol. 2, Department of Geography Publication Series No. 25, Department of Geography, University of Waterloo, Waterloo.

Gullahorn, John T. and Gullahorn, Jeanne E. (1963), 'An Extension of the U-Curve Hypothesis', in *Journal of Social Issues*, vol. 19, pp. 33-47.

Gunn, Clare (1988), *Vacationscape: Designing Tourist Regions*, Van Nostrand Reinhold Company, New York.

Gurwitch, Aron (1970), 'Problems of the Life-World', in Natanson, Maurice (ed), *Phenomenology and Social Reality: Essays in Memory of Alfred Schutz*, Martinus Nijhoff, Hague, pp. 35-61.

Guthrie, George M. (1966), 'Cultural Preparation for the Philippines', in Textor, R.B. (ed), *Cultural Frontiers of the Peace Corps*, The M.I.T. Press, Cambridge, Massachussetts, pp. 15-34.

Haarni, Tuukka and Karvinen, Marko and Koskela, Hille and Tani, Sirpa (1997), *Tila, paikka ja maisema – Tutkimusretkiä uuteen maantieteeseen*, Vastapaino, Tampere.

Haigh, Rowan (1995), *Backpackers in Australia*, Occasional Paper No. 20, Bureau of Tourism Research, Canberra.

Halewood, Chris and Hannam, Kevin (2001), 'Viking Heritage tourism Authenticity and Commodification', *Annals of Tourism Research*, vol. 28, pp. 565-580.

Hall, Derek (1992), 'Albania's Changing Tourism Environment', *Journal of Cultural Geography*, vol. 12, pp. 35-44.

Hanefors, Monica and Larsson, Lena (1993), 'Video Strategies Used by Tour Operators: What Is Really Communicated?', in *Tourism Management*, vol. 14, pp. 27-33.

Harkin, Michael (1995), 'Modernist Anthropology and Tourism of the Authentic', *Annals of Tourism Research*, vol. 22, pp. 650-670.

Harris, Marvin (1986), *Good to Eat: Riddles of Food and Culture*, Allen and Unwin, London.

Harvey, D. (1989), *The Condition of Postmodernity: An Enquiry into the Origins of Cultural Change*, Basil Blackwell, Oxford.

Harvey, Milton E. and Holly, Brian P. (eds) (1981), *Themes in Geographic Thought*, Croom Helm, London.

Heath, Ernie and Wall, Geoffrey (1992), *Marketing Tourism Destinations: a Strategic Planning Approach*, John Wiley and Sons, Inc., New York.

Heidegger, Martin (1985), *History of the Concept of Time*, Indiana University Press, Bloomington.

Heikkinen, Mervi (1993), 'Tie spatiaalisena metaforana', in *Alue ja ympäristö*, vol. 22, pp. 8-19.

Helms, Mary W. (1988), *Ulysses' Sail: an Ethnographic Odyssey of Power, Knowledge, and Geographical Distance*, Princeton University Press, Princeton.

Herberle, R. (1938), 'The causes of the rural-urban migration: a survey of German theories', *American Journal of Sociology*, vol. 43, pp. 932-950.

Hobbs, Joseph, J. (1992), 'Sacred Space and Tourist Development at Jebel Musa (Mt. Sinai), Egypt', *Journal of Cultural Geography*, vol. 12, pp. 99-113.

Hoffmann, Peter R. (1992), 'Tourism and Language in Mexico's Los Cabos', *Journal of Cultural Geography*, vol. 12, pp. 77-92.

Holloway, Christopher and Plant, R.V. (1992), *Marketing for Tourism*, Pitman, London.

Horne, Donald (1992), *The Intelligent Tourist*, Margaret Gee, Sydney.

Hottola, Petri (1999), *The Intercultural Body. Western Woman, Culture Confusion and Control of Space in the South Asian Travel Scene*, University of Joensuu, Department of Geography, Publications no. 7, Joensuu.

Hourani, Albert (1991), *Islam in European Thought*, Cambridge University Press, Cambridge.

Houston, James M. (1978), 'The Concepts of "Place" and "Land" in Judaeo-Christian Tradition', in Ley, David and Samuels, Marwyn (eds), *Humanistic Geography: Prospects and Problems*, Croom Helm, London, pp. 224-237.

Ihde, Don (1977), *Experimental Phenomenology: An Introduction*, Capricorn Books, New York.

Inskeep, Edward (1991), *Tourism Planning: An Integrated and Sustainable Development Approach*, Van Nostrand Reinhold, New York.

Johnson, Peter and Thomas, Barry (1992) (eds), *Choice and Demand in Tourism*, Mansell, Guildford.

Johnston, Charles Samuel (2001), 'Shoring the Foundations of the Destination Life Cycle Model, Part 1: Ontological and Epistemological Considerations', *Tourism Geographies*, vol. 3, pp. 2-28.

Johnston, Lynda (2001), '(Other) Bodies and Tourism Studies', *Annals of Tourism Research*, vol. 28, pp. 180-201.

Johnston, R. J. (1983), *Philosophy and Human Geography: An Introduction to Contemporary Approaches*, Edward Arnold, London.

Johnston, R. J. (ed) (1985), *The Future of Geography*, Methuen, London.

Johnston, R. J., Taylor, P.J. and Watts M.J. (eds) (1995), *Geographies of Global Change: Remapping the World in the Late Twentieth Century*, Blackwell, Oxford.

Jokinen, Eeva and Veijola, Soile (1990), *Oman elamansä turistit*, Alkoholipoliittinen tutkimuslaitos, Valtion painatuskeskus, Helsinki.

Kale, Sudhir H. and McIntyre, Roger P. and Weir, Katherine M. (1987), 'Marketing Overseas Tour Packages to the Youth Segment: An Empirical Analysis', *Journal of Travel Research*, vol. 25, pp. 20-24.

Kallio, Minka (1994), *Tutusta tuntemattomaan: Australiansuomalaisten paikkakokemukset*, An unpublished licenciate thesis, Department of Geography, University of Joensuu.

Kapferer, Bruce (1986), 'Performance and Structuring of Meaning and Experience', in Victor W. and Bruner, Edward M. (eds), *The Anthropology of Experience*, University of Illinois Press, Urbana, pp. 188-203.

Karjalainen, Pauli (1986a), *Geodiversity as a Lived World: on the Geography of Existence*, University of Joensuu, Publications in Social Sciences no. 7, University of Joensuu, Joensuu.

Karjalainen, Pauli (1986b), 'Paikka ja maisema elettynä ja esitettynä', *Kotiseutu* 3, pp. 113-117.

Karjalainen, Pauli Tapani (1987), *Ympäriston eletty mieli*, Tiedonantoja, Occasional Papers no. 2, University of Joensuu, Human Geography and Planning, Joensuu.

Karjalainen, Pauli Tapani (1991), 'Matters of Environmental Interest: Thoughts of Meaning and Place', in *The National Geographical Journal of India*, vol. 37, pp. 9-16.

Karjalainen, Pauli Tapani (ed) (1993), *Different Geographies*, University of Joensuu, Department of Geography and Regional Planning, Joensuu.

Karjalainen, Pauli Tapani (ed) (1993), *Maantieteen maisemissa: Aiheita kulttuurimaantieteen alalta*, Joensuun yliopisto, Kulttuuri- ja suunnittelumaantiede, tiedonantoja no. 25, Joensuu.

Karjalainen, Pauli Tapani (1993a), 'Geografioita, kieliä', in Karjalainen, Pauli Tapani (ed), *Maantieteen maisemissa: Aiheita kulttuurimaantieteen alalta*, Joensuun yliopisto, Kulttuuri- ja suunnittelumaantiede, tiedonantoja no. 25, Joensuu, pp. 9-18.

Karjalainen, Pauli Tapani (1993b), 'From this place forward: geodiversity revisited', in Karjalainen, Pauli Tapani (ed), *Different Geographies*, University of Joensuu, Department of Geography and Regional Planning, Joensuu, pp. 27-42.

Katajala, Kimmo (ed) (1995), *Manaajista maalaisaateliin: Tulkintoja toisesta historian, antropologian ja maantieteen välimaastossa*, Suomalaisen Kirjallisuuden Seura, Helsinki.

Keith, Michael (1988), 'Racial Conflict and the No-Go Areas of London', in Eyles, John and Smith, David M. (eds), *Qualitative methods in Human Geography*, Polity Press, Padstow, pp. 39-48.

Kelles, Anita (1984), *Antropologisen kenttätyön ongelmia: tutkijan persoonan, sukupuolen ja kulttuuritaustan vaikutuksesta antropologiseen tutkimukseen*, Suomen antropologinen seura, Helsinki.

284   *Tourist's Experience of Place*

Knuuttila, Seppo and Paasi, Anssi (1995), 'Tila, kulttuuri ja mentaliteetti, Maantieteen ja antropologian yhteyksiä etsimässä', in Katajala, Kimmo (ed), *Manaajista maalaisaateliin: Tulkintoja toisesta historian, antropologian ja maantieteen välimaastossa*, Suomalaisen Kirjallisuuden Seura, Helsinki, pp. 28-94.

Krippendorf, Jost (1987), *The Holiday Makers: Understanding the Impact of Leisure and Travel*, Heinemann, London.

Kvale, Steinar and Grenness, Carl Eric (1967), 'Skinner and Sartre: Towards a Radical Phenomenology of Behaviour?', *Review of Existential Psychology and Psychiatry* 1967, vol. 7, pp. 128-150.

Kylmänen, Marjo (ed) (1994), *Me ja muut: kulttuuri, identiteetti, toiseus*, Vastapaino, Tampere.

Lawrence, N. and O'Connor D. (eds) (1967), *Readings in Existential Phenomenology*, Prentice Hall, Englewood Cliffs.

Lee, E.S. (1966), 'A theory of migration', *Demography*, vol. 3, pp. 47-57.

Lee, Tae-Hee and Crompton, John (1992), 'Measuring Novelty Seeking in Tourism', *Annals of Tourism Research*, vol. 19, pp. 732-751.

Lehtinen, Ari Aukusti (1993), 'Kulttuuristuminen yhteiskuntatutkimuksessa: ihmisläheisyyttä vai todellisuuspakoa?', in Karjalainen, Pauli Tapani (ed), *Maantieteen maisemissa: Aiheita kulttuurimaantieteen alalta*, Joensuun yliopisto, Kulttuuri- ja suunnittelumaantiede, tiedonantoja no. 25, Joensuu, pp. 73-81.

Lewis, G.J. (1982), *Human Migration: A Geographical Perspective*, St. Martin Press, New York.

Ley, David (1979), 'Social Geography and the Taken for Granted World', in Gale, Stephen and Olsson, Gunnar (eds), *Philosophy in Geography*, D. Reidel Publishing Company, Dordrecht.

Ley, David and Samuels, Marwyn (eds) (1978), *Humanistic Geography: Prospects and Problems*, Croom Helm, London.

Ley, David and Samuels, Marwyn (1978), 'Introduction, Context of Modern Humanism in Geography', in Ley, David and Samuels, Marwyn (eds), *Humanistic Geography: Prospects and Problems*, Croom Helm, London, pp. 1-18.

Loker, Laurie [no date], *The Backpacker Phenomenon II: More Answers to Further Questions*, Department of Tourism, James Cook University, Townsville.

Loker-Murphy, Laurie and Pearce, Philip L. (1995), 'Young Budget Travelers, Backpackers in Australia', *Annals of Tourism Research*, vol. 22, pp. 819-843.

Lowyck, Els, Van Langenhove, Luk and Bollaert, Livin (1992), 'Typologies of Tourist Roles', in Johnson, Peter and Thomas, Barry (eds), *Chose and Demand in Tourism*, Mansell, Guildford, pp. 13-32.

Lundstedt, Sven (1963), 'An Introduction to Some Evolving Problems in Cross-Cultural Research', in *Journal of Social Issues*, vol. 19, pp. 1-9.

Lutwak, Leonard (1984), *The role of Place in Literature*, Syracuse University Press, New York.

Löytty, Olli (1994), 'Niilin lähteillä – tutkimusmatka länsimaiseen Afrikka-diskurssiin', in Kylmänen, Marjo (ed), *Me ja muut: kulttuuri, identiteetti, toiseus*, Vastapaino, Tampere, pp. 113-130.

MacCannell, Dean (1976), *The Tourist: a New Theory of the Leisure Class*, Schocken Books, New York.

MacCannell, Dean (1992), *Empty Meeting Grounds: the tourist paper*, Routledge, London and New York.

Mallory, William E. and Simpson-Housley, Paul (eds) (1987), *Geography and Literature: A Meeting of the Disciplines*, Syracuse University Press, New York.

Mansfeld, Yoel (1990), 'Spatial patterns of international tourist flows: towards a theoretical framework', *Progress in Human Geography*, vol. 14. pp. 372-390.

Mansfeld, Yoel (1992), 'From Motivation to Actual Travel', *Annals of Tourism Research*, vol. 19, pp. 399-419.

Marchand, B. (1979), 'Dialectics and Geography' in Gale, Stephen and Olsson, Gunnar (eds), *Philosophy in Geography*, D. Reidel Publishing Company, Dordrecht, pp. 237-267.

Mason, Peter (1990), *Deconstructing America: Representations of the Other*, Routledge, New York.

Matoré, Georges (1966), 'Existential Space', *Landscape*, Spring 1966, pp. 5-6.

McCarthy, John (1994), *Are Sweet Dreams Made of This?: Tourism in Bali and Eastern Indonesia'*, Indonesia Resources and Information Program, Northcote.

McDowell, Linda (1995), 'Understanding Diversity: the Problem of/for Theory', in Johnston, R. J., Taylor, P. J. and Watts M. J. (eds), *Geographies of Global Change: Remapping the World in the Late Twentieth Century*, Blackwell, Oxford, pp. 280-294.

McGreevy (1992), 'Reading the Texts of Niagara Falls: the Metaphor of Death' in Barnes, Trevor J. and Duncan, James S. (eds), *Writing Worlds: Discourse, text and metaphor in the representation of landscape*, Routledge, London, pp. 50-72.

Mead, Margaret (1963), *Coming of Age in Samoa: A Study of Adolescence and Sex in Primitive Societies* (orig. 1928), Penguin Books, London.

Meleisea, Malama and Meleisea, Penelope S. (1985), '"The Best Kept Secret": Tourism in Western Samoa' in Rajotte, Freda and Crocombe, Ron (eds), *Pacific Tourism: As Islanders see it*, South Pacific Social Sciences Association and The Institute of Pacific Studies, Suva, pp. 35-46.

Metelka, Charles J. (1990), *'The Dictionary of Hospitality, Travel, and Tourism'*, Delmar Publishers Inc.

Meyer-Arendt, Klaus J. (1990), Gulf of Mexico Seaside Resorts, *Journal of Cultural Geography*, vol. 11, pp. 39-55.

Milman, Ady, Reichel, Arie and Pizam, Abraham (1990), 'The Impact of Tourism on Ethnic Attitudes: The Israeli-Egyptian Case', *Journal of Travel Research*, vol. 29, pp. 45-49.

Milne, Simon (1992), 'Tourism and Development in South Pacific Microstates', *Annals of Tourism Research*, vol. 19, pp. 191-212.

Minca, Claudio (2000), "The Bali Syndrome': The Explosion and Implosion of 'exotic' Tourist Spaces', *Tourism Geographies*, vol. 27, pp. 389-403.

Mitchell, Katharyne (1993), 'Multiculturalism of the United Colors of Capitalism?', *Antipode*, vol. 25, pp. 263-294.

Mitchell, Lisle S. and Murphy, Peter E. (1991), 'Geography and Tourism', *Annals of Tourism Research*, vol. 18, pp. 57-70.

Moeran, Brian (1983), 'The Language of Japanese Tourism' *Annals of Tourism Research*, vol. 10, pp. 93-108.

Moore, Gary T. and Golledge, Reginald G. (eds) (1976), *Environmental Knowing: Theories, Research, and Method*, Dowden, Hutchinson and Ross Inc., Stroudsburg.

Morris, Desmond (1967), *The Naked Ape: A Zoologist's Study of the Human Animal*, Jonathan Cape, London.

Mudimbe, V.Y. (1988), *The Invention of Africa: Gnosis, Philosophy, and the Order of Knowledge*, Indiana University Press, Bloomington.

Murphy, Laurie (2001), 'Exploring social interactions of backpackers', *Annals of Tourism Research*, vol. 28, pp. 50-67.

Murray, Kevin D. (1990), *Life as fiction: the Making Sense of Personal Change*, Unpublished PhD-thesis, Department of Psychology, University of Melbourne.

Natanson, Maurice (ed) (1970), *Phenomenology and Social Reality: Essays in Memory of Alfred Schutz*, Martinus Nijhoff, Hague.

Nordberg-Shulz, C. (1971), *Existence, Space and Architecture*, Preger, New York.

Oakes, Penelope J., Haslam, S. Alexander and Turner, John C. (1994), *Stereotyping and Social Reality*, Blackwell, Oxford.

Oakes, Timothy S. (1992), Cultural Geography and Chinese Ethnic Tourism, *Journal of Cultural Geography*, vol. 12, pp. 3-17.

Oberg, Kalervo (1960), 'Cultural Shock: Adjustment to New Cultural Environments', *Practical Anthropology*, vol. 7.

Olsson, Gunnar (1982), '-/-', in Gould, Peter and Olsson, Gunnar (eds), *A Search for the Common Ground*, Pion Limited, London, pp. 223-231.

Olsson, Gunnar and Gale, Stephen (eds) (1979), *Philosophy in Geography*, D.Reidel Publishing Company, Dordrecht.

Osterrieth, Anne (1982), 'Lived Space and Liveability of Cities', in Gould, Peter and Olsson, Gunnar (eds), *A Search for the Common Ground*, Pion Limited, London, pp. 58-68.

Oxford Handy Dictionary, (1991), Chancellor Press, London .

Paasi, Anssi (1984), *Aluetietoisuus ja alueellinen identiteetti ihmisen spatiaalisen sidoksen osana*, Publications of the Society of Planning Geography 13, The Society of Planning Geography, Joensuu.

Paasi, Anssi (1986), 'The Institutionalization of Regions: a theoretical framework for understanding the emergence of regions and the constitution of regional identity', *Fennia* 164,1, pp. 105-146.

Paasi, Anssi (1993), 'Notes on the changing idea of geography and the revival of regional geography', in Karjalainen, Pauli Tapani (ed), *Different Geographies*, University of Joensuu, Department of Geography and Regional Planning, Joensuu, pp. 43-58.

Papson, Stephen (1981), 'Spuriousness and Tourism: Politics of Two Canadian Provincial Government' *Annals of Tourism Research*, vol. 8, pp. 220-235.

Paterson John H. and Paterson Evangeline (1981), 'Shropshire: Reality and Symbol in the Work of Mary Webb' in Pocock, Douglas C. D. (ed), *Humanistic Geography and Literature: Essays of the Experience of Place*, Croom Helm, London, pp. 209-220.

Pearce, Philip L. (1982), 'Tourists and Their Hosts: Some Social and Psychological Effects of Inter-Cultural Contact', in Bochner, Stephen (ed), *Cultures in Contact: Studies in Cross-Cultural Interaction*, Pergamon press, Oxford, pp. 199-221.

Pearce, Philip L. (1988), *The Ulysses Factor: Evaluating Visitors in Tourist Settings*, Springer-Verlag, New York.

Phillipson, Michael (1972), 'Phenomenological Philosophy and Sociology', in Filmer, Paul, Phillipson, Michael, Silverman, David and Walsh, David, *New Directions of Sociological Theory*, Collier and MacMillan Publishers Limited, London, pp. 119-131.

Pickles, John (1985), *Phenomenology, Science and Geography: Spatiality and the Human Science*, Cambridge University Press, New York.

Pickles, John (1988), 'From Fact-World to the Life-World: The Phenomenological Method and Social Science Research', in Eyles, John and Smith, David M. (eds), *Qualitative methods in Human Geography*, Polity Press, Padstow, pp. 233-254.

Pickles, John [no date], 'Geography and Humanism', *Concepts and Techniques in Modern Geography No. 44*, Geo Books, Norwich.

Pickles, John and Watts, Michael J. (1992), 'Paradigms for Inquiry?', in Abler, Ronald F., Marcus, Melvin G. and Olson, Judy M. (eds), *Geography's Inner Worlds: Pervasive Themes in Contemporary American Geography*, Rutgers University Press, New Brunswick, pp. 301-326.

Pi-Sunyer, Oriol (1977), 'Tourists and tourism in a Catalan Maritime Community', in Smith, Valene L. (ed), *Hosts and Guests: The Anthropology of Tourism*, University of Pensylvania Press, pp. 149-155.

Pizam, Abraham, Jafari, Jafar and Milman, Ady (1991), 'Influence of Tourism on Attitudes - US Students Visiting USSR', *Tourism Management*, vol. 12, pp. 47-54.

Pocock, Douglas (1992), 'Catherine Cookson Country: Tourist Expectation and Experience', *Geography*, vol. 77, pp. 236-243.

Pocock, Douglas C. D. (ed) (1981), *Humanistic Geography and Literature: Essays of the Experience of Place*, Croom Helm, London.

Pocock, Douglas C. D. (1981), 'Introduction: Imaginative Literature and the Geographer', in Pocock, Douglas C. D. (ed), *Humanistic Geography and Literature: Essays of the Experience of Place*, Croom Helm, London, pp. 9-19.

Porteous, J. Douglas (1988), 'Topocide: The annihilation of Place', in Eyles, John and Smith, David M. (eds), *Qualitative methods in Human Geography*, Polity Press, Padstow, pp. 75-93.

Pratt, Mary Louise (1985), 'Scratches on the Face of the Country: or, What Mr. Barrow Saw in the Land of the Bushmen', *Critical Inquiry* 12, Autumn 1985, pp. 119-143.

Pred, Allan (1986), *Place, Practice and Structure: Social and Spatial Transformation in Southern Sweden 1750-1850*, Barnes and Noble Books, Totowa.

Pretes, Michael (1995),' Postmodern Tourism: The Santa Claus Industry', *Annals of Tourism Research*, vol. 22, pp. 1-15.

Raivo, Petri (1993), 'Kulttuurimaiseman ikonografia: lähtökohtia tutkimuksen jäsentymiselle', in Karjalainen, Pauli Tapani (ed.), *Maantieteen maisemissa: Aiheita kulttuurimaantieteen alalta*, Joensuun yliopisto, Kulttuuri- ja suunnittelumaantiede, tiedonantoja no. 25, Joensuu, pp. 29-41.

Raivo, Petri (1997), 'Kulttuurimaisema; Alue, näkymä vai tapa nähdä', in Haarni, Tuukka and Karvinen, Marko and Koskela, Hille and Tani, Sirpa (eds), *Tila, paikka ja maisema; Tutkimusretkiä uuteen maantieteeseen*, Vastapaino, Tampere. pp. 193-209.

Rajotte, Freda and Crocombe, Ron (eds) (1985), *Pacific Tourism: As Islanders see it*, South Pacific Social Sciences Association and The Institute of Pacific Studies, Suva.

Rapeli, Toivo (1987), *Maailmanmatkaaja*, Kirjapaja, Helsinki.

Reimer, Gwen Diane (1990), 'Packaging Dreams: Canadian Tour Operators in Work', *Annals of Tourism Research*, vol. 17, pp. 501-512.

Relph, Edward (1976), *Place and Placelessnes*, Pion Limited, London.

Relph, Edward (1981a), *Rational Landscapes and Humanistic Geography*, Croom Helm, London.

Relph, Edward (1981b), 'Phenomenology', in Harvey, Milton E. and Holly, Brian P. (eds), *Themes in Geographic Thought*, Croom Helm, London, pp. 99-114.

Relph, Edward (1991), 'Post-modern geography', *The Canadian Geographer*, vol. 35, pp. 98-105.

Relph, Ted (2000), 'Author's response', *Progress in Human Geography*, vol. 24, pp. 617-619.

Richards, Greg (1996), 'Production and Consumption of European Cultural Tourism', *Annals of Tourism Research*, vol. 23, pp. 261-284.

Riley, Pamela J. (1988), 'Road Culture of International Long-Term Budget Travellers', *Annals of Tourism Research*, vol. 15, pp. 313-328.

Riley, Roger W. and van Doren, Carlton S. (1992), 'Movies as Tourist Promotion: a "Pull" Factor in a "Push" Location' *Tourism Management*, vol. 13, pp. 267-274.

Robinson, Brian (1987), 'The Geography of a Crossroads: Modernism, Surrealism, and Geography', in Mallory, William E. and Simpson-Housley, Paul (eds), *Geography and Literature: A Meeting of the Disciplines*, Syracuse University Press, New York, pp. 185-198.

Rose, Courtice (1988), 'The Concept of Research and the Anglophone Minority in Quebec', in Eyles, John and Smith, David M. (eds), *Qualitative methods in Human Geography*, Polity Press, Padstow, pp. 156-179.

Ross Glenn F. (1991), 'Tourist destination images of the wet tropical rainforests of North Queensland', *Australian Psychologist*, 26, pp. 147-153.

Ross, Glenn F. (1993), 'Destination Evaluation and Vacation Preferences', in *Annals of Tourism Research*, vol. 20, pp. 477-489.

Ross, Glenn F. (1994), *The Psychology of Tourism*, Hospitality Press, Melbourne.

Sack, Robert David (1980), *Conceptions of Space in Social Thought: A Geographic Perspective*, The MacMillan Press Ltd, Hong Kong.

Sack, Robert David (1986), *Human Territoriality: Its Theory and History*, Cambridge University Press, Cambridge.

Said, Edward (1979), *Orientalism*, Vintage Books, New York.

Salzman, Philip Carl (1992), 'Antipositivismin kääntöpuoli', *Suomen Antropologi*, no 1, pp. 27-36.

Samuels, Marvyn S. (1978), 'Existentialism and Human Geography', in Ley, David and Samuels, Marwyn (eds), *Humanistic Geography: Prospects and Problems*, Croom Helm, London, 22-40.

Samuels, Marvyn S. (1981), 'An Existential Geography', in Harvey, Milton E. and Holly, Brian P. (eds), *Themes in Geographic Thought*, Croom Helm, London, pp. 115-132.

Schutz, Alfred (1962-1996), *Collected Papers*, Martinus Nijhoff, Hague.

Schutz, Alfred and Luckmann, Thomas (1973), *The Structures of the Life-World*, Northwestern University Press, Evanston.

Scott, Jamie and Simpson-Housley, Paul (1989), 'Relativizing the relativizers: on the postmodern challenge to human geography', *Transactions, Institute of British Geographers*, vol. 14. pp. 231-236.

Seamon, David (1976), 'Phenomenological Investigation of Imaginative Literature: a Commentary', in Moore, Gary T. and Golledge, Reginald G. (eds), *Environmental Knowing: Theories, Research, and Methods*, Dowden, Hutchinson and Ross Inc, Stroudsburg, pp. 286-290.

Seamon, David (1979), *A Geography of the Lifeworld: movement, rest and encounter*, Croom Helm, London.

Seamon, David (1985), 'Reconciling old and new worlds: The dwelling-journey relationship as portrayed in Vilhelm Moberg's "Emigrant" novel', in Seamon, David and Mugerauer, Robert (eds), *Dwelling, Place, and Environment: Towards the Phenomenology of Person and World*, Nijhoff, Dordrecht, pp. 227-245.

Seamon, David and Mugerauer, Robert (eds) (1985), *Dwelling, Place, and Environment: Towards the Phenomenology of Person and World*, Nijhoff, Dordrecht.

Selänniemi, Tom (1994), 'Touristic Reflections on a Marine Venus: an Anthropological Interpretation of Finnish Tourism to Rhodes', *Ethnologia Fennica*, vol. 22, pp. 35-42.

Shapiro, Gary (ed.) (1990), *After the Future: Postmodern Times and Places*, State University of New York Press, New York.

Shapiro, Gary (1990), 'Introduction', in Shapiro, Gary (ed), *After the Future: Postmodern Times and Places*, State University of New York Press, New York, pp. xi-xviii.

Sipilä, Jorma (1979), *Sosiaalisten ongelmien synty ja lievittäminen*, Tammi, Helsinki.

Smalley, William A. (1963), 'Culture Shock, Language Shock, and the Shock of Self-Discovery', *Practical Anthropology*, vol. 10.

Smith, David M. (1988), 'Towards an Interpretative Human Geography', in Eyles, John and Smith, David M. (eds), *Qualitative methods in Human Geography*, Polity Press, Padstow, pp. 255-267.

Smith, Jonathan (1992), 'The Slightly Different Thing That Is Said: Writing the Aesthetic Experience', in Barnes, Trevor J. and Duncan, James S. (eds), *Writing Worlds: Discourse, text and metaphor in the representation of landscape*, Routledge, London, pp. 73-85.

Smith, Susan (1988), 'The Analysis of Self in Everyday Life', in Eyles, John and Smith, David M. (eds), *Qualitative methods in Human Geography*, Polity Press, Padstow, pp. 17-38.

Smith, Valene (1979), 'Women: The Taste Makers in Tourism', *Annals of Tourism Research*, vol. 6, pp. 49-60.

Smith, Valene L. (ed) (1977), *Hosts and Guests: The Anthropology of Tourism*, University of Pensylvania Press.

Smith, Valene L. (1977), 'Eskimo Tourism: Micro-Models and Mariginal Men', in Smith, Valene L. (ed), *Hosts and Guests: The Anthropology of Tourism*, University of Pensylvania Press, pp. 51-70.

Smith, Valene (1992), 'Introduction: The Quest in Guest', *Annals of Tourism Research*, vol. 19, pp. 1-17.

Soja, E. (1989), *Postmodern Geographies: The Reassertion of Space in Critical Social Theory*, Verso Press, London.

Sontag, Susan (1977), *On Photography*, Allen Lane, London.

Spivak, Gayatri Chakravorty (1988), *In Other Worlds: Essays in Cultural Politics*, Routledge, New York.

Squire, Shelagh J. (1994), 'Accounting for cultural meanings: the interface between geography and tourism studies re-examined', *Progress in Human Geography*, vol. 18, pp. 1-16.

Steinbeck, John (1962), *Travels with Charley in Search of America*, Heinemann, London.

Steward, Robert, A., Powell, Graham E. and Chetwynd, S. Jane (1979), *Person Perception and Stereotyping*, Saxon House, Surrey.

Suvantola, Jaakko (1999), 'Turismi unelmien maantieteenä', in ELORE, no. 1/1999, URL:http://cc.joensuu.fi/~loristi/1_99/sis199.html, Suomen Kansantietouden Tutkijain Seura ry., Joensuu.

Taylor, John (2001), 'Authenticity and Sincerity in Tourism', *Annals of Tourism Research*, vol. 28, pp.7-26.

Textor, R.B. (1966), *Cultural Frontiers of the Peace Corps*, The M.I.T. Press, Cambridge, Mass.

The Dictionary of Human Geography (1986) Johnston, R. J., Gregory, Derek and Smith, David M. (eds) (2nd edit.), Blackwell Reference, Oxford.

Tomaselli, Keyan G. (1988), 'The Geography of Popular Memory in Post-Colonial South Africa: A Study of Afrikaans Cinema', in Eyles, John and Smith, David M. (eds), *Qualitative methods in Human Geography*. Polity Press, Padstow, pp. 136-155.

Toops, Stanley (1992), 'Tourism in Xinjiang, China', *Journal of Cultural Geography*, vol. 12, pp. 19-34.

Tuan, Yi-Fu (1974), *Topophilia: A Study of Environmental Perception, Attitudes, and Values*, Prentice-Hall, Englewood Cliffs.

Tuan, Yi-Fu (1976), 'Literature, Experience, and Environmental Knowing', in Moore, Gary T. and Golledge, Reginald G. (eds), *Environmental Knowing: Theories, Research, and Method*, Dowden, Hutchinson and Ross Inc., Stroudsburg, pp. 260-272.

Tuan, Yi-Fu 1977, *Space and Place: The Perspective of Experience*, University of Minnesota Press, Minnesota.

Tuan, Yi-Fu (1978), 'Literature and Geography: Implications for Geographical Research', in Ley, David and Samuels, Marwyn (eds), *Humanistic Geography: Prospects and Problems*, Croom Helm, London, pp. 194-206.

Tuan Yi-Fu (1979), 'Space and Place: Humanistic perspective', in Gale, Stephen and Olsson, Gunnar (eds), *Philosophy in Geography*, D. Reidel Publishing Company, Dordrecht, pp. 384-427.

Tuan Yi-Fu (1982), *Segmented World and Self: Group Life and Individual Consciousness*, University of Minnesota Press, Minnesota.

Turner, Graeme (1990), *British Cultural Studies: An Introduction*, Unwin Hyman, London.

Turner, Louis and Ash, John (1975), *The Golden Hordes, International Tourism and the Pleasure Periphery*, Constable, London.

Turner, Victor (1973), 'The Center Out There: Pilgrim's Goal', in *History of Religions 12*, pp. 191-230.

Turner, Victor (1974), *The Ritual Process*, Penguin, Harmondsworth.

Turner, Victor (1978), 'Comments and Conclusions', in Babcock, B. A. (ed), *Reversible World*, Cornell University Press, Ithaca, pp. 276-296.

Turner, Victor and Turner, Edith (1978), *Image and Pilgrimage in Christian Culture*, Columbia University Press, New York.

UNESCO (1976), 'The Effects of Tourism on Socio-Cultural Values', *Annals of Tourism Research*, vol. 4, pp. 74-105.

Urbain, Jean-Didier (1989), 'The Tourist Adventure and His Images', *Annals of Tourism Research*, vol. 16, pp. 106-118.

Urry, John (1990), *The Tourist Gaze: Leisure and Travel in Contemporary Societies*, Sage Publications, London.

Uzzell, David (1984), 'An Alternative Structuralistic Approach to the Psychology of Tourism Marketing', *Annals of Tourism Research*, vol. 11, pp. 79-99.

Vehkavaara, Mikko (1994), 'Orientalismikritiikki - keidas vai kangastus?', in Kylmänen, Marjo (ed), *Me ja muut: kulttuuri, identiteetti, toiseus*, Vastapaino, Tampere, 155-176.

Veijola, Soile (1987), *Turismin näyttämöt ja kulissit: huomioita suomalaisesta seuramatkaetiketistä*, Alkoholipoliittisen tutkimuslaitoksen tutkimusseloste no 179, Alko.

Victor W. and Bruner, Edward M. (eds) (1986), *The Anthropology of Experience*, University of Illinois Press, Urbana.

Vittersø, Joar and Vorkinn, Marit and Vistad, Odd Inge and Vaagland, Jorid (2000), 'Tourist experiences and attractions', *Annals of Tourism Research*, vol. 27, pp. 432-450.

Waitt, Gordon and McGuirk, Pauline (1994), 'Step into history: assimilating Millers Point into the tourist production process', Non-published seminar paper (Draft only).

Walle, A.H. (1993), 'Tourism and Traditional People: Forging Equitable Strategies', *Journal of Travel Research*, vol. 31, pp. 14-19.

Walmsley, D. J. and Jenkins J. M. (1992), 'Tourism Cognitive Mapping of Unfamiliar Environments', *Annals of Tourism Research*, vol. 19, pp. 268-286.

Walpole, Matthew J. and Goodwin, Harold J. (2000), 'Local economic impacts of dragon tourism in Indonesia', *Annals of Tourism Research*, vol. 27, pp. 559-576.

Webster's New Collegiate Dictionary (1980), G. and C. Merriam Company, Springfield.

Wei, Lu and Crompton, John L. and Reid, Leslie M. (1989), 'Experiences of US Visitors to China', *Tourism Management*, vol. 10, pp. 322-332.

Weightman, Barbara A. (1987), 'Third World Tourist Landscapes', *Annals of Tourism Research*, vol. 14, pp. 227-239.

Yan, Sue and McDonald, Cary (1990), 'Motivational Determinates of International Pleasure Time', *Journal of Travel Research*, vol. 29, pp. 42-44.

Young, Robert (1990), *White Mythologies: Writing History and the West*, Routledge, London.

OTHER MATERIAL CITED

Advertiser, April 1, 1995.
Aurinkomatkojen lomaopas, talvikausi 1990/91.
Australian, 25-26 March 1995.
Cantell, Jorma (1990), 'Matka maailman Ympari', in *Pirkka*, no 11.
Club Med: New Caledonia, Tahiti 1992.
Creative Tours: Thailand Apr 95-Mar 96.
Dalton, Bill (1973), *A Traveler's Notes, Indonesia*. Unpublished.
Escape 2/1995. STA.
Exodus Discovery Holidays 1994-1995.
Explore Holidays 1994, Explore Europe.
Garuda Indonesia and Cathay Pacific 1992, Hong Kong with Bali.
Helsingin Sanomat, Jan 6, 1994.
Indonesia: a travel survival kit (1986) (1st ed), Lonely Planet, Melbourne.
Indonesia: a travel survival kit (1992) (3rd ed), Lonely Planet, Melbourne.
Indonesia Handbook (1985), Moon Publications, Chico.
Jarmusch, Jim (1989), Mystery Train, A film.
Jetset Bali 1994-1995.
Malmberg, Ilkka (1990), 'Interreilaajat pysyvät raiteissaan', *Helsingin Sanomat, Kuukausiliite*, no. 18.
Mononen, Unto (1962), *Satumaa*, Fazer Musiikki.
Qantas, France 1994.
Qantas Jetabout Holidays: Fiji 1993-1994.
Singapore Airlines, Insight 1994, Egypt, Israel, Greece, Turkey, Jordan, Kenya.
South Africa Travel Guide.
South-East Asia on a Shoestring (1977) (2nd ed), Lonely Planet, Melbourne.
South-East Asia on a Shoestring (1992) (7th ed), Lonely Planet, Melbourne.
South-East Asia on a Shoestring (1994) (8th ed), Lonely Planet, Melbourne.
Swingaway: Thailand 1993.
The Trans-Siberian Railway and The Silk Route by Rail 1996, Sundowners.
Time: August 7, 1995.
Time: August 21, 1995.
TNT for Backpackers Magazine, Jan 1996, Sydney.
Vanuatu - brochure.
Viva! Holidays Thailand 1993/94.
Wheeler, Tony and Wheeler, Maureen (1973), *Across Asia on the Cheap*. Unpublished.

Index